AF900015

Development, Capitalism, and Rent

Hannes Warnecke-Berger
Editor

Development, Capitalism, and Rent

The Political Economy of Hartmut Elsenhans

palgrave
macmillan

Editor
Hannes Warnecke-Berger
University of Kassel
Kassel, Germany

ISBN 978-3-030-62604-4 ISBN 978-3-030-62605-1 (eBook)
https://doi.org/10.1007/978-3-030-62605-1

© The Editor(s) (if applicable) and The Author(s), under exclusive license to Springer Nature Switzerland AG 2021
This work is subject to copyright. All rights are solely and exclusively licensed by the Publisher, whether the whole or part of the material is concerned, specifically the rights of translation, reprinting, reuse of illustrations, recitation, broadcasting, reproduction on microfilms or in any other physical way, and transmission or information storage and retrieval, electronic adaptation, computer software, or by similar or dissimilar methodology now known or hereafter developed.
The use of general descriptive names, registered names, trademarks, service marks, etc. in this publication does not imply, even in the absence of a specific statement, that such names are exempt from the relevant protective laws and regulations and therefore free for general use.
The publisher, the authors and the editors are safe to assume that the advice and information in this book are believed to be true and accurate at the date of publication. Neither the publisher nor the authors or the editors give a warranty, expressed or implied, with respect to the material contained herein or for any errors or omissions that may have been made. The publisher remains neutral with regard to jurisdictional claims in published maps and institutional affiliations.

This Palgrave Macmillan imprint is published by the registered company Springer Nature Switzerland AG
The registered company address is: Gewerbestrasse 11, 6330 Cham, Switzerland

Contents

List of Contributors

Hartmut Elsenhans University of Leipzig, Leipzig, Germany

Hannes Warnecke-Berger University of Kassel, Kassel, Germany

CHAPTER 1

Introduction: Rent, Capitalism and the Challenges of Global Uneven Development—Hartmut Elsenhans' Work in Context

Hannes Warnecke-Berger

Rent is a shining, multifaceted but also a complex concept in political economy. Usually, rents are linked to commodities and natural resources, and just as raw material prices on world markets rent theory experiences its ups and downs. In the absence of crises when the world economy seems to run smoothly, rent theory is heavily disputed. In times of crisis, however, the explanatory value of rent theory gains attraction. Recently, rent theory experienced a certain revival in different fields of inquiry. Currently, at least three different strands of discussion highlight the role of rents in shaping society. First, rents are a focal point within the discussion on the resource curse (see Auty 2001; Collier and Hoeffler 2004; Ross 2012). A group of authors link economic rents from

H. Warnecke-Berger (✉)
University of Kassel, Kassel, Germany
e-mail: hwarneckeberger@uni-kassel.de

© The Author(s), under exclusive license to Springer Nature Switzerland AG 2021

H. Warnecke-Berger (ed.), *Development, Capitalism, and Rent*,
https://doi.org/10.1007/978-3-030-62605-1_1

natural resources to the onset and the duration of civil wars and obstacles to development and usually associate rents with violence and economic backwardness. Second, as a reaction to the world financial crisis of 2008, rent theory gained a wider audience. The concept of rent was used as a theoretical lens to analyze the production and circulation of "fictive capital" on world financial markets. Several authors argued that in the period before 2008, big business was able to benefit from financialization and hence used new financial products to accumulate monetary wealth (Epstein 2005; Hein 2012; Stockhammer 2004). The production of extra revenue from financial interactions—rents—has been identified as one root cause of the financial crisis and therefore, rent theory regained relevance. Third, in the aftermath of the financial crisis of 2008, cheap money floated the world economy, and much of this money flowed directly into save havens instead of into the real economy. Ironically, money that was initially intended to stimulate investments, economic growth and employment finally ended up in real estate and the pockets of the super-rich. This cheap money let rental payment of houses and apartments for large parts of the population to increase, particularly in cities and urban areas. Rent theory again gained supporters criticizing dynamics of exclusion and gentrification, particularly within geography (Andreucci et al. 2017; Birch 2017; Haila 2016).

Only few, however, associate rent with a fundamental politico-economic concept that serves to analyze the dynamics of capitalism, internal societal processes within developing societies in the Global South and at the same time the dynamics of international relations and the international system. It is this concept of rent that is at the core of the theoretical work of Hartmut Elsenhans. Much like the concept of rent itself, the oeuvre of Hartmut Elsenhans is as multifaceted and complex as it is theoretically demanding, politically challenging and provoking. In more than 700 publications and over 30 monographs Elsenhans has developed a perspective on global history, the dynamics of capitalism and prospects for the development of today's Global South. Elsenhans is a truly interdisciplinary scholar. He began studying political science, history, sociology and romance studies at the University of Tübingen in 1962 and obtained his diploma in political science in Berlin in 1967. He witnessed the turmoil of 1968 in Berlin and in Paris, where he stayed until 1970 at the well-known *Cycle Supérieur d'Etudes Politiques*. He received his PhD in 1973 with a fulminant work on the Algerian War of Independence from the Free University of Berlin (Elsenhans 1974). Only three years later, he habilitated with his work on "History and Economy of the European Conquest of the World. From the Age of the Discoveries to the First World War" (the book was only published in 2007, see Elsenhans 2007). He held positions as professor in Frankfurt, Marburg, Konstanz, and after the German reunification in Leipzig. Since 2007, he is professor emeritus of the University of Leipzig (for a detailed CV, see for instance Ouaissa 2018).

Initially, he approached capitalism from the periphery, from the Global South. On the empirical grounds of his work on Algeria and India, he developed the theory of the state class (Elsenhans 1981, see the English translation: Elsenhans) scrutinizing non-capitalist rent-based modes of production. He then continued to model the articulation of underdevelopment and strategies for development (Elsenhans 1988, 1994a). Based on these results, he linked development to underdevelopment, as opposed to the ideas of Frank or Amin however, he stepped forward to analyze the threat of globalizing underdevelopment (Elsenhans 2000a, 2002).

He shares these research interest with prominent scholars as they are not only among the core interests of the Classics of political economy from Adam Smith, David Ricardo, John Stuart Mill to Karl Marx and John Maynard Keynes, but of social theory per se—represented by Max Weber, Karl Polanyi, and Ferdinand Tönnies, to name only few. Elsenhans grew into an academic world which today appears as a scientific epoque of great endeavors. It was a time in which scholars focused on grand narratives, huge processes and big theories (to paraphrase Charles Tilly 1984). Apart from the Classics, therefore, he was in company of scholars like Samir Amin (whom he translated into German), Immanuel Wallerstein or André Gunder Frank. Maintaining his position in this company not only affords a lot of diligence and hard work, but even more important perhaps, never ending curiosity. His joy of reading and excerpting as well as his thirst for knowledge remains unquenched.

At the same time however, this academic sophistication and self-demand results in certain challenges, as one commentator once wrote about a dilemma of Elsenhans academic career. "The complexity of his language reflects the complexity of his line of argument, even in English. To do justice to his argument, the reader must be as well-read as the author" (Wilcock and Scholz 2016: 2; see also Menzel 2013), which in the end seems almost impossible given the meticulousness through which Elsenhans excerpts almost everything he is reading (and indeed, his excerpt database is ever increasing and today combines around 120,000 excerpted books and articles). But it is not only this theoretical sophistication and self-demand why Elsenhans' work hardly fits into a single category and what it makes it so hard to access in the first place. Elsenhans always pursued his own way, and his work escapes from traditional categorizations and is caught between ordinary academic disciplines: First, it is interdisciplinary; although rooted in political science and economy, it touches on sociology, philosophy and anthropology. It is part of International Relations and North-South relations. Elsenhans however provokes through presenting an alternative approach to mainstream perspectives within IR and development studies, between modernization theory and dependency approaches or realism and idealism. In this regard, it is an eclecticist account, and it is this non-conformity that all too often irritates the reader. Finally, his position cannot be easily attributed to a political stream—too "left" for the conservatives and too "pro-capitalist" for others. Apart from the often-provoking articles and comments, which not only brought him applause and recognition, it is perhaps particularly the concept of rent that frames his academic writings. And it is this concept of rent that is at the core of his theoretical writings that this book wants to deepen and to clarify.

This book is a tribute to Hartmut Elsenhans for his 80th birthday. It comprises a collection of unpublished papers and articles as well as chapters previously published in German and French. Planned as a *Festschrift*, the objective of this book is to introduce into the work of Elsenhans as well as to present his oeuvre to an English-speaking audience. From his early career, he has been interested in various research topics, in all of which rent plays a role as an analytical concept. Through this perspective, Elsenhans analyzes the historical genesis of capitalism, the dynamics of capitalism, as well as the global impact of capitalism, development, and thus the possibilities, the challenges as well as the limits of capitalist sociation. This introduction first contextualizes the notion of rent and clarifies how Hartmut Elsenhans uses the term. It then situates Hartmut Elsenhans' theoretical writings in the broader discussion on the contradictions of capitalism, prospects for development in the Global South and the dynamics of global uneven development.

1.1 Euthanasia of the Rentier?

In the well-known chapter 24 of his *General Theory*, John Maynard Keynes (2018 [1936]) developed his hope for the disappearance of the rentier within the capitalist social order. Well in contrast to Hartmut Elsenhans, Keynes expected that capitalism is strong enough to defend its internal logic against the power of the rentier and against economic rent. In this regard, Keynes was a preliminary endpoint of a long-lasting line of argumentation within the reasoning of political economy. The Classics of political economy and foremost Adam Smith (1976 [1776]) were far less certain on this point, and Elsenhans shares much of their concerns. In the work of Adam Smith, the absolute land rent is rooted in property relations and the ownership of land. Rent is something that the peasant has to pay to the landlord to obtain the right to work the land. In this sense, rent belongs to the *ancient régime* of European feudalism. When Adam Smith wrote his book, he expected the new social and economic order of capitalism to overcome traditional property relations, emancipating from the sheer and stable possession and ownership of land toward the dynamic investment into innovation and productivity increases. At the same time, this was the cornerstone of a proper labor theory of value. Smith clearly stated that the evolving economic order cannot and should not be based on the possession of land but must be grounded on the productivity of labor. David Ricardo (1951 [1817]) complemented Smith's idea. He turned rent into a relational concept. From then on, the concept of rent was further refined into what later Marx (1959 [1894]) called (absolute) ground rent and differential rents in Volume III of Capital. Absolute rent can be appropriated only because of the possession of land, because of property rights and sufficient or excessive demand for land. Differential rent appears as a surplus in relation to other and less productive plots of land, again postulating sufficient demand for land and agricultural products that makes it necessary to cultivate less productive plots. Similarly, Elsenhans, like Adam Smith, acknowledges the internal conditions of rent based on landed property within his rent-cum-marginality model (see Chapter 5) and then, like David Ricardo, turns toward the relational character of rent as differential rent (see Chapter 2).

In their writings on land and capitalism, the Classics tried to discover the "laws of motion" of capitalism. Capitalism was (and still is) something "in the making", a specific socioeconomic order that emancipated from its premodern political bonds and extra-economic forces. The Classics studied this new order and, at the same time, they defended it against its adversaries, against the forces of the *ancient régime* (for a history of ideas on the concept of rent, see, e.g., Fried 1998). Their books can be read as economic theory. They can, however, also be read as a call against the traditional order of things, both of the feudal world in which God and kings ruled the world and against the logic of the mercantilist state advocated by John Locke or Francois Quesnay. The Classics put into discussion a new foundation of economic life: a foundation based on labor work, on productivity and effort instead of habit and heritage, and on investment in a risky future instead of the administration of the given. This is why the concept of rent, while it describes a form of economic surplus that is appropriated by political means and extra-economic force, from the very beginning it entails a moral claim that economic life *should* be based on labor and productivity rather than on political redistribution of the fruits produced by others. Rent then is to be criticized as a form of unearned income, and it is unearned because it *should* not be appropriated by those who actually do appropriate it because those who appropriate it did not have to invest the same kind and amount of work as others. The work of Elsenhans further underpins this double meaning of rent. As the Classics, Elsenhans wants to defend capitalism against rent as it becomes clear in almost every chapter of this book.

Within the writings of the Classics, rent is always both, an analytical term to analyze political and economic processes and a political-practical term used by political activists who criticize the factual distribution of income as unjust. Often, it is this twofold meaning that leads to confusion, particularly in the works of Marx. On the one hand, it is a form of surplus, that is distinct to profit or interest, because it is appropriated by political means and based on a right of disposal, particularly the property of land, which is ultimately based on violence. From this persepctive, rent is a macroeconomic concept. On other hand, rent is the income of lazy landlords and of those who are part of the old and feudal order rather than of the new and developing capitalism. Here, rent is a microeconomic concept. Elsenhans reconciles both positions and shows that rents appear on the macro-level as a genuine form of economic surplus but highlights that rents are appropriated on the micro-level. Elsenhans even radicalizes this distinction. For him, rent is always situated on the macro-level as a distinct form of economic surplus. In this regard, the individual entrepreneur, be it capitalist or feudal landlord, may gain a certain amount of money after subtracting advanced payments in microeconomic terms, but she or he is not able to qualify this gain either as profit or rent.

In the course of the neoclassic offensive, rents became increasingly associated with market imperfections. The concept of rent therefore was deprived of its roots as a concept linking economic processes with the surrounding power and class struggle (see for this general trend, Hodgson 2001). Lacking a genuine macro-perspective on the concept, it therefore becomes impossible in the framework of the neoclassic to distinguish between different forms of surplus. This imprecision draws heavily on Jean Baptiste Say, where rent is the income from a particular factor of production, from land. In contrast to Jean-Baptiste Say (1972 [1972]), Elsenhans follows Marx in accentuating the embeddedness of capitalism in a certain and very specific class configuration and in highlighting the political nature of rent.

These different understandings of rent within the works of the Classics laid the ground for Elsenhans to develop his own theory. Therefore, for the proper understanding of the work of Elsenhans, some crucial issues can be extracted from this short history of the concept of rent. First, rent is a concept that interlinks the economic with the political realm. Although economic rents are produced within economic life, they are appropriated by political means. Insofar, the distinction between a political and an economic realm is central for the understanding of Elsenhans work. Here, he is following the Marxists rather than the Smith'ians, and Robert Brenner (on the Brenner debate, see Philpin and Aston 1985), Elisabeth Wood (1981) and Ernesto Laclau (1971) rather than their counterparts such as Wallerstein (1974), Amin (1973) or Frank (1969). For Elsenhans, as for Brenner or Wood, the distinction between politics and economics only becomes possible in capitalism, because there is no need and no opportunity for the leading class, the bourgeoisie, to resort to political means to appropriate economic surplus. The inner fractioning of the bourgeoisie and the resulting competition hinders every single entrepreneur to use political power to extract surplus from labor. This is not the case with rent: rent is always deeply interwoven with politics and with an institutional setting that allows for accessing economic surplus and extracting and appropriating rent.

This is important, because second, the critique of rent in the writings of the Classics—and here Elsenhans is more following classic political economy than modern economics—is based on both the existence of capitalism and on something non-capitalist. Rent is rooted in the non-capitalist sphere in historical antecessors of capitalism, that are based on historical developments in non-capitalist modes of production and in Europe of a centuries-long experience of feudalism. Elsenhans is maintaining this claim and even radicalizes it with regard to today's Global

South, following Rosa Luxemburg (1951 [1913])[1] in this matter. In addressing the interactions between capitalist and non-capitalist societies, she warned that capitalism is expansive and one day will integrate the entire world. Against Lenin (1964 [1916]), she argued in her theory on imperialism that not the drive for maintaining profits at the core of capitalism but the lack of demand for capitalist products will eventually push capitalism into crisis. Elsenhans shows in detail, that capitalism is and has ever been far too weak and far too fragile to completely overcome social structures in non-capitalist societies (Chapters 5, 6, and 7). Capitalism penetrates non-capitalist societies; however, it does not necessarily transform them with the result of self-sustaining growth. Thus, capitalism is by no means universal but threatened by an external non-capitalist logic of rent.

1.2 Contradictions of Capitalism

For Elsenhans, capitalism is characterized by external (Chapter 2) and internal (Chapters 3 and 4) contradictions. Externally, capitalism is threatened by the strength of rent-based social orders that predominate in the Global South. Internally, capitalism is threatened on the supply side by excessive technological developments through which monopolies and technological rents eventually weaken competition and the market forces. On the demand side, private households' excessive savings weaken consumption which eventually results in decreasing investment spending and profits.

From this internal and external contradictions of capitalism, Elsenhans derives both his theory on rising mass incomes as a precondition of capitalist growth as well as development strategies for economies of the Global South. Having falsified the usual factors put forward in the transition debate for the historical development of capitalism, namely trade, imperialism and the exploitation of the non-capitalist world on the one hand and cultural backwardness of the Global South or European superiority because of Protestantism or certain resource endowments on the other hand, Elsenhans shows that capitalist development was and still is based on rising mass income (Chapter 2). Initially, this was an empirical argument drawn from his detailed study of social and economic history

[1] The same argument today is important for feminist political economy, see, e.g., Gibson and Graham (2006).

(Elsenhans 1979b). However, it was this argument that brought Elsenhans to the post-Keynesian profit theory of Kalecki (1942). In a variation of Kalecki's argument, Elsenhans (2015) maintains that capitalist profit as the genuine form of economic surplus in capitalism is a monetary phenomenon that only emerges on a macro level. Furthermore, he shows that, on the one hand, this surplus can only emerge in the case of sufficient aggregate demand, and in a dynamic model that capitalism, on the other hand, is only able to grow if aggregate demand and particularly the real income of the mass of the population increase.

For Marxists as well as for neoliberals, this is a heretical argument. Although Elsenhans adopts a Marxist framework and large parts of Marxist historical materialism, he places the Kaleckian growth and profit theory at the core of his argument. On logical grounds, he rejects both Marxist growth and crisis theory of capitalism (Elsenhans 1979a) as well as neoclassical and new economic growth theory (Elsenhans 2000b). For Elsenhans, capitalism historically evolved because the subaltern class was strong and powerful enough to wrench surplus from the rich. In this sense, capitalism becomes not only revolutionary, as Marx maintained, but also civilizatory, because particularly the strength of the poor secures basic democratic voice (Elsenhans 1994b), however both happened by incidence (see Chapter 10).

As opposed to orthodox and monetary post-Keynesian macroeconomics, therefore, Elsenhans opens up his theory to the role of class struggle, and particularly to the bargaining power of the poor. While Keynes once converted the Malthusian problem of poverty from demography into an economic problem of unemployment, Elsenhans goes further and situates the crisis tendency of capitalism in class dynamics that eventually threaten the entire system. He maintains that if capitalist profit depends on investment spending and investment spending depends on the expectation of future sales, people need to buy products in order to stabilize the system. However, if people are unable to get access to economic surplus via real wage increases or even save their money instead of spending it, capitalism slips into crisis because of structurally hierarchical class imbalance such that capitalist are able to extract economic rents due to their political power. In this view, capitalism is not only prone to crisis because of underconsumptionist threats, but also prone to turning into a rentier system pervaded by clientelism, personal dependencies and exploitation, in short: into a neo-feudal world order (Elsenhans 2006). This is the internal crisis tendency of capitalism and Elsenhans is in fact close to positions such as post-democracy (e.g., Crouch 2004), however he underpins his analysis with a proper politico-economic analysis as opposed to looking exclusively at either the political or economic realm.

1.3 Global Uneven Development

Elsenhans adds an external crisis tendency to the future of capitalism, however, which is his Luxemburgian moment and his link to development studies and development theory. Having stated that economic rents are essentially non-capitalist and that capitalism depends on rising mass income and real wage growth, Elsenhans argues that today's Global South is not or not yet and not completely capitalist. Some prerequisites of the capitalist social order exist such as private property, wage labor, or even capitalist entrepreneurs. In this specific setting, however, these elements do not unfold the same effect of emergence by which capitalist societies are characterized. Based on labor surplus theories in the fashion of Arthur Lewis (1954) or Gustav Ranis and John Fei (1964), Elsenhans illustrates that the usual course of history brings about agrarian tributarian empires rather than natural capitalist societies (see Chapters 5 and 6). For Elsenhans, capitalism developed only in Western Europe (and later in the United States) as a historical contingency (following Robert Brenner in this regard). Within today's Global South, in contrast, labor surplus even increased when non-capitalist societies opened up to the world market and were exposed to capitalism (see Chapter 8). This line of argumentation explicitly does not relativize the atrocities and cruelties of colonialism and imperialism, however scrutinizes the allegedly causal relationship of capitalism and the exploitation of the rest of the world. Again, capitalism penetrates non-capitalist societies, but capitalism is too weak to transform them into self-sustaining systems, particularly because commodification, monetization, and the expansion of production and trade do not necessarily transform the class configuration and increase the bargaining power of the poor (see Chapter 7).

Elsenhans therefore identifies the continuity of global surplus labor as the current threat to the liberal world order (Chapter 2). While the Global South gained access to world markets through the export of merchandise exports due to currency devaluation, employment rates increase too slow as does world real wages in order to stabilize world aggregate demand and world consumption. Increasing income inequality therefore is rather the rule than the exception. This is, however, not necessarily caused by capitalist development, but rather based on systemic contradictions and the prevalence of economic rents. Ultimately, capitalism faces an internal contradiction, namely that the system is unable to maintain its own basis, and the external contradiction that the contact of capitalism with non-capitalist societies affects the system's stability and even worsens the internal contradiction. As opposed to positions that understand the dynamics of capitalism as the root cause for global uneven development, such as regulationalist scholars David Harvey (2006 [1982]), Robert Boyer (2015), Neil Brenner (2009), and Wolfgang Streeck (2013) or others, Elsenhans shows that external crisis tendencies and particularly the intersection of capitalism with non-capitalism are responsible for global uneven development. Thus, even with this perspective on crisis, Elsenhans is in between Marxist and neoclassical accounts of economic crises.

How do these contradictions retroact on the international system and on international relations? Marxists usually cite the decline of the profit rate as a root cause of uneven development and derive out of this crisis the expansive dynamics of capitalism and ultimately imperialism. Liberals, in contrast, maintain that trade, the division of labor and comparative advantages are at the core of capitalism's expansion. Again, Elsenhans is in between both positions. In fact, he partly adopts both positions but draws different conclusions. For him, rents are stronger than capitalism and as soon as internal contradictions of capitalism allow for rent to materialize instead of profit and if surplus labor in the Global South persists, the capitalist social order will lose ground. Even though some nations within the international system will (re)gain power, as realism in IR predicts, and even though the international system will tend toward a multipolar order, the underlying processes of capitalist sociation are too weak to stabilize the liberal idea of democratic voice, checks and balances of political power, as well as economic and political citizenship. In this regard, Elsenhans not only adds an international perspective to the concept of rent, but he follows the Classics in their moral predictions: rent will distort and even overcome capitalism, particularly because Keynes' prediction of the euthanasia of the rentier seems to be unlikely to happen from this perspective. In his view, capitalism must be saved from capitalists because the capitalists are likely to turn into rentiers one day.

1.4 Structure of the Book

The following chapters comprise published and unpublished manuscripts that should be made accessible to the English-speaking audience and theoretical milestones in the course of Hartmut Elsenhans' academic career.

The first part of the book accentuates the internal and external contradictions of capitalism. It portrays capitalism as a system based on class struggle that is maintained by the bargaining power of the poor. The part illustrates Elsenhans' position as a major proponent of global Keynesianism. Chapter 2 focuses on the external contradictions of capitalism. This paper was originally presented 1982, yet never published. It served, however, as a blueprint for further publications. Until 1997, Elsenhans had always focused on this external contradiction of capitalism, which began to change with the following text in Chapter 3. This is the first text in which Elsenhans studies the internal contradictions of capitalism, anticipating much of what today again is heavily discussed in light of excessive market power of transnational corporations such as Google, Microsoft or Apple. Chapter 4 then turns toward the behavior of private households and their propensity to save. In the true fashion of a Keynesian scholar, Elsenhans here not only criticizes the privatization of pensions in Europe and elsewhere but further shows that capitalism entails a democratic dilemma: once private households become too rich and at the same time too anxious about their future, they pursue economic strategies that eventually threaten the entire economic system.

The second part of the book concentrates on internal processes within the Global South and on challenges, possibilities and limitations of development. It presents Elsenhans' development theory and derives various strategies for the Global South. In Chapter 5, Elsenhans develops his labor surplus theory which he calls marginality-cum-rent model and focuses on various measures to overcome underdevelopment. In Chapter 6, he concretizes these ideas and analyzes possibilities of the welfare state to overcome economic underdevelopment and discusses the challenges of channeling rent into development.

The third and final part of the book finally focuses on international relations and particularly on the interactions between capitalist and non-capitalist societies within the international system. It elaborates on international strategies to create a peaceful international environment. At the same time, it analyzes threats for international economic and political stability. Chapter 7 focuses on newly industrializing countries, the so-called East Asian miracle. It shows that South Korea and Taiwan have been relatively successful in channeling rent into development, thereby alternating their role in the international division of labor and the international system. Chapter 8 discusses the challenges of the claim for better raw material prices put forward in the discussion on the New International Economic Order. The book closes with a Postface by Hartmut Elsenhans.

References

Amin, Samir. 1973. *Le développement inégal. Essai sur les formations sociales du capitalisme périphérique*. Paris: Editions de Minuit.

Andreucci, Diego, Melissa García-Lamarca, Jonah Wedekind, and Erik Swyngedouw. 2017. "Value Grabbing". A Political Ecology of Rent. *Capitalism Nature Socialism* 28 (3): 8–47.

Auty, Richard M. 2001. The Political Economy of Resource-Driven Growth. *European Economic Review* 45 (4/6): 839–846.

Birch, Kean. 2017. Towards a Theory of Rentiership. *Dialogues in Human Geography* 7 (1): 109–111.

Boyer, Robert. 2015. *Économie politique des capitalismes: Théorie de la régulation et des crises*. Paris: La Découverte.

Brenner, Neil. 2009. A Thousand Leaves. Notes on the Geographies of Uneven Spatial Development. In *Leviathan Undone? Towards a Political Economy of Scale*, ed. Rianne Mahon and Roger Keil, 27–49. Vancouver: UBC Press.

Collier, Paul, and Anke Hoeffler. 2004. Greed and Grievance in Civil War. *Oxford Economic Papers* 56 (4): 563–595.

Crouch, Colin. 2004. *Post-Democracy*. Oxford: Oxford University Press.

Elsenhans, Hartmut. 1974. *Frankreichs Algerienkrieg 1954–1962. Entkolonialisierungsversuch einer kapitalistischen Metropole. Zum Zusammenbruch der Kolonialreiche*. Munich: Carl Hanser.

Elsenhans, Hartmut. 1979a. Das Gesetz des tendentiellen Falls der Profitrate. Einige Bemerkungen zu neoricardianischen und marxistischen Behauptungen. *Leviathan* 7 (4): 584–597.

Elsenhans, Hartmut 1979b. Grundlagen der Entwicklung der kapitalistischen Weltwirtschaft. In *Kapitalistische Weltökonomie. Kontroversen über ihren Ursprung und ihre Entwicklungsdynamik*, ed. Dieter Senghaas, 101–148. Frankfort on the Main: Suhrkamp.

Elsenhans, Hartmut. 1981. *Abhängiger Kapitalismus oder bürokratische Entwicklungsgesellschaft. Versuch über den Staat in der Dritten Welt*. Frankfort on the Main and New York: Campus.

Elsenhans, Hartmut. 1988. Probleme der politischen Ökonomie in unterentwickelten Gesellschaften. Von der begrenzten Aussagekraft rein wirtschaftswissenschaftlicher und rein politikwissenschaftlicher Modelle. In *Grenzen der Sozialwissenschaften*, ed. H. Mäding and R. Dahrendorf, 88–113. Konstanz: Universitätsverlag.

Elsenhans, Hartmut. 1994a. Rent, State and the Market: The Political Economy of the Transition to Self-Sustained Capitalism. In *Pakistan Development Review* 33 (4): 393–428.

Elsenhans, Hartmut. 1994b. Wirtschaftsliberalismus ohne bürgerliche Revolution: Wer stützt die liberale Weltwirtschaft im Süden. In *Umbruch in der Weltgesellschaft. Auf dem Wege zu einer „neuen Weltordnung"*, ed. Wolfgang Hein, 101–124. Hamburg: Deutsches Übersee-Institut.

Elsenhans, Hartmut. 1996 [1981]. *State, Class and Development*. New Delhi, London, Columbia, MO: Radiant; Sangam; South Asia Books.

Elsenhans, Hartmut. 2000a. Globalisation in a Labourist Keynesian Approach. *Journal of Social Studies* 89: 1–66.

Elsenhans, Hartmut. 2000b [1974]. *La guerre d'Algérie 1954–1962. La transition d'une France à une autre. Le passage de la IV à la Ve République*. Paris: Publisud.

Elsenhans, Hartmut. 2002. Macroeconomics in Globalization. Productivity, Wages, Profits, and Exchange Rates in an Era of Globalization. *Brazilian Journal of Political Economy* 22, 1 (85): 53–78.

Elsenhans, Hartmut. 2006. *Globalization between a Convoy Model and an Underconsumptionist Threat*. Münster: LIT Verlag.

Elsenhans, Hartmut. 2007. *Geschichte und Ökonomie der europäischen Welteroberung. Vom Zeitalter der Entdeckungen zum 1. Weltkrieg*. Herausgegeben mit einem Vorwort von Matthias Middell. Leipzig: Leipziger Universitätsverlag.

Elsenhans, Hartmut. 2015. *Saving Capitalism from the Capitalists. A Contribution to Global and Historical Keynesianism*. Beverly Hills, CA, London, New Delhi: Sage.

Epstein, Gerald A. (ed.). 2005. *Financialization and the World Economy*. Cheltenham: Edward Elgar.

Fei, John C.H., and Gustav Ranis. 1964. *Development of a Labor Surplus Economy. Theory and Policy*. Homewood, IL: Irwin.

Frank, André Gunder. 1969. *Latin America: Underdevelopment or Revolution. Essays on the Development of Underdevelopment and the Immediate Enemy*. New York: Monthly Review Press.

Fried, Barbara. 1998. *The Progressive Assault on Laissez Faire: Robert Hale and the First Law and Economics Movement*. Cambridge: Harvard University Press.

Gibson, Katherine, and Julie Graham. 2006. *The End of Capitalism (As We Knew It): A Feminist Critique of Political Economy*. Minneapolis: University of Minnesota Press.

Haila, Anne. 2016. *Urban Land Rent: Singapore as a Property State*. Chichester: Wiley.

Harvey, David. 2006. *The Limits to Capital* [1982]. London: Verso.

Hein, Eckhart. 2012. Financialization, Distribution, Capital Accumulation, and Productivity Growth in a Post-Kaleckian Model. *Journal of Post Keynesian Economics* 34 (3): 475–496.

Hodgson, Geoffrey M. 2001. *How Economics Forgot History: The Problem of Historical Specificity in Social Science*. London: Routledge.

Kalecki, Michal. 1942. A Theory of Profits. *Economic Journal* 52 (205–206): 258–267.

Keynes, John Maynard. 2018 [1936]. *The General Theory of Employment, Interest, and Money*. Cham: Palgrave Macmillan.

Laclau(h), Ernesto. 1971. Feudalism and Capitalism in Latin America. *New Left Review* 67 (1): 19–38.

Lenin, Vladimir Ilyich. 1964. *Imperialism, the Highest Stage of Capitalism. A Popular Outline* [1916]. Lenin Collected Works (22). Moscow: Progress Publishers.

Lewis, William Arthur. 1954. Economic Development with Unlimited Supply of Labour. *Manchester School of Economic and Social Studies* 22 (4) (May): 139–191.

Luxemburg, Rosa. 1951 [1913]. *The Accumulation of Capital*. London: Routledge & Kegan Paul.

Marx, Karl. 1959 [1894]. *Capital (3): The Process of Capital Production as a Whole* [1894]. New York: International Publishers.

Menzel, Ulrich. 2013. Aufstieg und Niedergang des kapitalistischen Weltsystems. Der Sechs-Bücher-Plan von Hartmut Elsenhans als Gegenentwurf zu Marx und Wallerstein. *Comparativ. Leipziger Beiträge zur Globalgeschichte und vergleichende Gesellschaftsforschung* 23 (4/5): 168–178.

Ouaissa, Rachid. 2018. Introduction. Hartmut Elsenhans et l'Algérie contemporaine. In *Naqd: Revue d'études et de critique sociale*, Hors-série 4 (2): 11–37.

Philpin, C.H.E., and Trevor H. Aston (eds.). 1985. *The Brenner Debate: Agrarian Class Structure and Economic Development in Pre-industrial Europe*. Cambridge: Cambridge University Press.

Ricardo, David. 1951. *On the Principles of Political Economy and Taxation* [1817]. The Works and Correspondence of David Ricardo (1). Cambridge et al.: Cambridge University Press.

Ross, Michael L. 2012. *The Oil Curse: How Petroleum Wealth Shapes the Development of Nations*. Princeton: Princeton University Press.

Say, Jean-Baptiste. 1972. *Traité d'économie politique* [1803]. Paris: Calmann-Lévy.

Smith, Adam. 1976. *An Inquiry into the Nature and Causes of the Wealth of Nations* [1776]. Oxford: Clarendon Press.

Stockhammer, Engelbert. 2004. Financialisation and the Slowdown of Accumulation. *Cambridge Journal of Economics* 28 (5): 719–741.

Streeck, Wolfgang. 2013. Gekaufte Zeit: Die vertagte Krise des demokratischen Kapitalismus. Berlin: Suhrkamp.

Wallerstein, Immanuel Maurice. 1974. *The Modern World-System (1). Capitalist Agriculture and the Origins of the European World-Economy in the Sixteenth Century*. New York, Orlando, FL: Academic Press.

Wilcock, Neil, and Corina Scholz. 2016. *Hartmut Elsenhans and a Critique of Capitalism: Conversations on Theory and Policy Implications*. Basingstoke, New York: Palgrave Macmillan.

Wood, Ellen Meiksins. 1981. The Separation of the Economic and the Political in Capitalism. *New Left Review* 127: 66–95.

PART I

Contradictions of Capitalism

CHAPTER 2

Contradictions of Self-Centered Development

Hartmut Elsenhans

2.1 Self-Centered Development and the Satisfaction of Basic Needs with Rising Mass Incomes in the Third World Is Important for the Maintenance of Political Equilibria and Growth in the Western Industrialized Countries

The problem of underdevelopment is getting a new dimension. Barnet and Müller (1974: 215) have stated that the American worker has been subject to Latin-Americanization because manufactured goods can be produced more cheaply in Latin America. This process of worldwide sourcing has grown larger and larger. Productivity in multinationals' plants in the newly industrializing countries is nearly equal to their plant

Paper for the 23rd Annual Convention of the International Studies Association, Cincinnati, 26th March, 1982, unpublished.

H. Elsenhans (✉)
University of Leipzig, Leipzig, Germany
e-mail: helsen@rz.uni-leipzig.de

© The Author(s), under exclusive license to Springer Nature Switzerland AG 2021

H. Warnecke-Berger (ed.), *Development, Capitalism, and Rent*,
https://doi.org/10.1007/978-3-030-62605-1_2

productivity in the industrial center, and wages are simultaneously much lower in the NICs. In the case of Volkswagen, the salary difference of the lowest wage groups between its German and its Brazilian plants is 6:1.

Multinational corporations, therefore, tend to replace high-cost labor in the industrial center with low-cost labor in the periphery. But this labor-replacement phenomenon is not due solely to the worldwide expansion of multinational companies, a point which has often been overemphasized. As Nayyar (1978: 71) and Hone (1974: 146–147) have already stated, and as Helleiner (1979: 73–75) originally rejected but now agrees to, the share of multinationals in manufacturing exports from the Third World is low and seems to be declining.

Vernon (1977: 257) rightly stresses the fact that the increasing efficiency of Third World countries in controlling foreign-owned affiliates—especially via the development of state-owned enterprises—will even pose a greater threat of low-labor-cost-induced intensive competition by Third World manufacturing industries on world markets. This is because state-owned enterprise, which ultimately relies on subsidies, will be able to continue production even in the case of dire market situations.

This paper will not discuss the appropriateness of analyzing the conditions for economic growth because this topic has been previously covered (Elsenhans 1976a, 1979b). In a Keynesian world, the replacement of high-cost labor by low-cost Third World labor means a reduction of the world's effective demand and even ultimately a threat to world growth.[1] The labor movements in the industrialized countries will not be able to meet this challenge. Wage restraint in the industrialized countries further diminishes effective demand. Limited wage increases to a level at which the difference in the world payroll—as created by the substitution of high wage by low wage labor—will be matched. This will further accelerate the process of delocalization of production. For the following reasons, there is no hope that wage increases in the Third World will counteract this process of a shrinking world consumption demand by economic mechanisms:

- Even if it is admitted that qualified labor is rare in the Third World, the enlargement of the process of delocalization will induce TNEs to develop technology which fits the relative factors costs in the Third

[1] I have treated this point in Elsenhans (1981c).

World and allows the use of unskilled labor.[2] This direction of investment policies, often called for by critics of TNEs, is already visible. In that case, TNEs can tap the nearly inexhaustible resources of the unemployed, the underemployed and the miserable potential rural workforce of the Third World.

- There is a simple quantity problem: In the industrialized countries of the West, there are 68 millions of jobs in manufacturing.[3] The ILO estimates the number of unemployed and underemployed in the Third World to be around 350 million.[4] Even the transfer of all jobs in manufacturing will not create full employment and therefore will lead to competition for labor by TNE affiliates in the Third World.
- The idea that new products which should be developed in the industrialized countries match the job crisis requires that for these new products markets are to be found, and therefore final demand is raised by rising wages.
- In the optimal scenario, industrialized countries would replace lost and shifted jobs with new employment by creating a new product. However, these new products would require new markets—which require rising mass incomes, a process undermined by the offshoring of manufacturing to the Third World. Furthermore, if technology becomes more and more mobile from the North to the South, these new products will not necessarily create a new monopolistically-detained productivity advantage in favor of industrialized countries' labor.
- Third World governments closely control labor and severely restrict labor's demands for wage increases, as all theorists about the corporatist or authoritarian bureaucratic state maintain.

The mechanism of growth in market economies—i.e., that rising real wages create new investment opportunities by capital deepening and market enlargement—is threatened by the new tendency of worldwide sourcing of the TNEs and the growing competitiveness of Third World countries. Some observers may welcome the tendency of equalization on a worldwide scale, but they should openly admit that this equalization tends

[2] Stewart (1974: 39), Barnet and Müller (1974: 170–171), and Salama (1978: 293).

[3] Calculated from data from the ILO (1980: 212–219).

[4] Numbers given by Bequele and Freedman (1979: 316) and Sabolo (1980: 484).

to align labor at the level of these cheap masses of potential workforce in the Third World.

Those who follow the briefly sketched scenario of these emerging new economic relations between the North and the South may argue that fair labor standards could be imposed in the Third World. The power of TNEs, however, makes the idea of fencing off a northern world market illusory. Additionally, export restraints imposed on Third World countries connected with the new protectionism will in the long run be ineffective and probably politically unfeasible. Even in small newly industrializing countries where real wages have gone up, as is the case in Singapore, industries are delocalized to cheaper regions. Mexico provides a potent example: Industries are leaving high-wage regions for low-wage regions in the same country. And even if wages in the formal sector of developing countries do rise, it is doubtful whether this is desirable, because it reinforces the tendencies of the constitution of labor aristocracies; widens the rural-urban divide; and increases the income gap between the formal and informal sectors.

The real problem, therefore, is that the supply price of unskilled labor in the Third World rises. This in turn creates mass markets there and establishes mechanisms of self-sustained and self-centered growth there. Promoting a policy of self-centered growth geared toward the increase of mass incomes in the Third World is no longer a problem of charity. Instead, this policy is the very condition of the long-term maintenance of a free world market.

2.2 Some Hints on the Nature of Development Processes in General

Some critics will object that the availability of cheap labor raises the rate of profit and therefore allows the acceleration of growth. Theoretical and historical experience, however, disprove this position.

- On a theoretical level, it can be demonstrated that, with constant real wages, the only investments which are viable are those which diminish incomes paid for labor, for intermediate products, and for capital goods per unit produced.[5]

- Whether such investment is capital-deepening or capital-saving is irrelevant. The lack of demand could be matched if the rate of growth of investment goes up. Why should investors create more and more productive plants if final and intermediate demand is diminishing? Harrod-Domar models demonstrate the exhaustion of multiplying and accelerating effects of autonomous investment and demand-induced investments.
- Historically, the process of economic growth took place only in countries with rising mass incomes. The Great Britain of the Industrial Revolution was a relatively egalitarian society compared to the rest of Europe.[6] The so-called regions of recent settlement became high-wage economies when access to land was free. The difference in historical achievement of these regions of recent settlement—such as Argentina, Australia, the United States or Brazil—can ultimately be explained only by their historical differences of income distribution.[7] Exemplary of this is Japan's history, which is full of effective peasant movements for higher incomes (Borton 1938: 7–8, 18–67). The Meiji land settlement transformed feudal rights into a land tax. Its impact on resource extraction from agriculture was diminished by price increases of agricultural products following intensive government spending for modernization.[8]
- Practically speaking, accumulation of capital means investment in machinery and building. Machinery, especially at low levels of

[5] Elsenhans (1981a: 155–157). In his rejoinder, Emmanuel (1981) does account for the devalorization of capital with rising productivity. He also mixes the quantity and the value system. Otherwise my thesis is right, as I have shown in Elsenhans (1981d: 3–7; 1996 [1981]: 363–369).

[6] The point with literature is made in English in Elsenhans (1983b).

[7] There is the so-called Argentina-Australia paradox, Leff (1972: 499), Saul (1960: 84–85), Strassmann (1956: 436), and Habakkuk (1962: 35–38); stress all the different income distribution, which was a consequence of the access to land. Moran (1970: 74–79), considers tariff policy as more important.

[8] The declining real burden on agriculture after 1868 is shown by Nakamura (1966: 429, 437) and Yamamura (1971: 402). The importance of the internal market in Japan is stressed by Nurkse (1953: 16), Craig et al. (1965: 494–495), and Ranis (1957: 597), demonstrates rising real wages in the last part of the nineteenth century in Japan, and (p. 594) much rural by-employment; cf. also Kelley and Williamson (1974: 23).

economic development, can only be used in the production of standardized and often low-quality products. One can use tools for building temples or pyramids, but one cannot expand the application of machinery for that purpose if one does not expand the production of temples or pyramids. The fewer types of products consumed, the more economies of scale can be attained by expanding the use of machinery. Additionally, the more homogeneous final demand is, the more homogeneous the demand for machinery and intermediate goods will be.

These observations apply to an even greater extent with regard to underdeveloped economies compared to developed economies.

- In developed economies, high-income classes consume luxury products, both domestically- and Third World-sourced. Luxury products sourced domestically are home-produced, which creates domestic employment possibilities. However, imported Third World-produced luxury products—which either have artistic value or are available from Third World countries for natural reasons—do not create impulses for the accumulation of machinery.
- In these underdeveloped countries, manufactured luxury products for high-income classes are either imported from the industrial countries or produced by local plants in small quantities. Due to their limited production quantities, these locally-produced luxury goods are economically inefficient. Therefore, most are incapable of competing on world markets and are dependent on investment-goods imports from the industrialized world. The direct and indirect import content of products for high-income receivers is high (Furtado 1971: 58).
- To catch up with the industrialized countries, underdeveloped economies must import technology. However, this requires large markets—indeed larger markets than in the leading countries of the industrial revolution. This is because technology has become increasingly geared to larger series.
- Low-income receivers normally consume a larger share of the incomes for home-produced products of low quality (Currie 1971). Lower-quality requirements allow the application of lower quality

and often of labor-intensive machines in the so-called informal sector.

If the "world market" of the industrialized world is not large enough to allow the absorption of surplus labor in the Third World via export-led growth, underdeveloped countries must rely on internal mass markets. These internal mass markets allow: The growth of so-called informal sectors, which are labor-intensive; the local construction of investment and intermediate goods (because of a more uniform demand and larger series); and the efficient use of imported technologies by profiting from economies of scale.

The objection that the implied redistribution of incomes causes the saving propensity to decrease is empirically unfounded. Furthermore, the objection that, in the case of rising incomes, low-income groups do not consume "traditional" products is not important[9] if these modern products can be produced by local enterprises using locally-produced investment goods.

2.3 An Outline of the Perspective of Overcoming Underdevelopment

The mass of the poor in the Third World live in rural areas. The mass of the new demand created by income redistribution goes to agriculture. Successful and egalitarian agrarian reform is the central aspect of overcoming underdevelopment (Elsenhans 1979a). These reforms create an enlargement of the internal market through rising mass incomes. These reforms create a rise of rural mass incomes by limiting transfers to mostly absentee landlords. Simultaneously, the reformed agrarian sector experiences a rise of agricultural production. It is known in Third World agrarian economics that small farms use more labor and produce more crops per unit of land.[10] This premise is not invalidated by the fact that large farms using modern inputs can surpass yields of small farms.[11] If agrarian reform

[9] Argument put forward by James (1976: 149). Counterproposition: Morawetz (1974: 18).

[10] This approach is elaborated on in Elsenhans (1982b).

[11] There is ample evidence, for literature see: Elsenhans (1979a: 512–513). Under the threat of agrarian reforms, landlords may modernize, as is shown by Kay (1976: 81) and Petras (1978: 138).

is accompanied by appropriate credit and industrial policies, these inputs are also used by small farmers, especially if risk problems are solved by such measures. A reformed smallholder agriculture may even be more efficient in modernizing because much of the necessary investment can be produced through unskilled labor, such as terracing to combat erosion or small hydraulic works. Owner-operators grouped in small cooperatives will be prepared to furnish that labor if the ultimate advantages accrue to themselves and their children. Agrarian reform therefore enables the mobilization of (now idle) work time into accumulation in the form of investive labor.

Two points must be made. On the one hand, raising agricultural production requires new inputs which are produced in a modern industrial sector (tube-wells, fertilizers, tubes, and even small tractors). However, rising agricultural production does not inherently correlate to rising labor productivity in agriculture. Indeed, compared to the productivity of employed labor—and not to the potentially active workforce—labor productivity may go down for a while.[12] The owner-operators' collective use of such equipment is necessary in case of indivisibilities. Under such conditions, a reformed agricultural sector is less intensive in the use of modern resources than an agriculture of big landlords for the following reasons:

- Modern inputs are only introduced if they raise production, not if they cut costs by displacing labor. For owner-operators, their "incomes," i.e., their subsistence, are not costs. Wherever labor can be used for the same purpose, equipment is not bought.
- Due to the rather identical land/labor ratio, relatively uniform equipment can be bought by the owner-operator cooperatives. Subsequently, economies of scale in production can be achieved in the long run.
- Economies of scale in transport are achieved because of the greater share of cultivable surfaces and the exchangeability of similar equipment and inputs.

[12] Cf. with Chinese data: Rawski (1976: 777). That consequence is clearly desired, cf. Elsenhans (1979a: 552).

I deduce, therefore, that overcoming underdevelopment requires the parallel build-up of an industrial sector to deliver the inputs required to modernize agriculture.

That agrarian reform may diminish the marketable surplus is normal: Agrarian reform is introduced in order to raise mass incomes.[13]

Owner-operators will be prepared to use additional labor in investive activities and in intensified use of land if material incentives are given. Any price policy that favors the urban population by keeping agricultural prices down via state-owned trading organizations with monopoly buying power must be abandoned. The Algerian and Chinese examples are telling. Agrarian reform led to production increases in Algeria, as long as the bureaucracy was too feeble to interfere in the market of the reformed sector.[14]

In China, peasants must produce a fixed quota of crops; however, they are free to sell the rest on markets. Therefore, surplus accrues to themselves.

If price policies leave marketable surplus to the peasants, products of nonagricultural sectors have to be offered for exchange of agricultural surplus. Industrial sectors producing simple consumption goods for the peasants will be necessary.

The studies on the so-called informal sector have shown that its expansion depends on the expansion of demand (cf. Lachaud 1980: 444). It uses low-skilled labor and little capital. However, if the final consumption demand is geared toward services and "artistic" handicraft, this sector will simply not be able to modernize its equipment and expand.

If low-income groups spend relatively more of their incomes on products from this sector, it can quantitatively grow by expanding employment of unskilled labor. If the modernization of the production of these goods requires only simpler technology, labor productivity and the skill of the mass of "industrial" workers will gradually rise.

However, there are products, especially intermediate goods, but even mass consumption goods that can only be produced efficiently with modern technology at any reasonable exchange rate of the national currency that is at any price relation between labor and "capital."

[13] To be clear about this point: That consequence may be quite desired, Elsenhans (1979a: 540).

[14] Elsenhans (1977a: 75–78); cf. already in 1974 the opposing view of *Terre et progrès*, March 1974: 15.

Therefore, investing in modern factories is necessary. The eventual capital intensity is no real objection against the building-up of this sector. This sector derives its eventual function from its product mix and not from the number of jobs created. If the products manufactured in the modern sector raise the productivity in the modernizing informal sector and the modernizing agriculture, this modern sector contributes to rising mass incomes.

The import of capital goods for this sector requires foreign exchange. Overcoming underdevelopment by self-centered growth does not preclude international cooperation and foreign trade. Export sectors are a valuable economic basis for financing domestic growth. This is especially true if appropriation of rent is possible—as in the case with raw materials.

The problems of an efficient self-centered growth strategy are then simply stated: How should a reformed agriculture and a modernizing informal sector be linked to a modern industrial sector? And how should this be financed by the foreign exchange earnings of an already competitive export sector? To solve this problem, the following operations are necessary.

By empirical investigation the profile of final demand, the mix of products consumed in case of rising mass incomes should be evaluated; the structure of consumption in different socio-cultural environments of those slightly better-off than the poorest 40% should give hints on the probable demand of those poorest ones, if they are brought to the level of consumption of the former ones. This will allow a projection of the structure of final demand in case of redistribution of income and rising mass incomes.

The possibilities of production of these goods—whose availability is necessary to meet the new profile of demand—is analyzed by the path of production back from final demand to intermediate demand and to technological requirements. The analysis of the path of production for final products required for mass consumption allows one to determine which of these products can be produced:

- by the informal sector with existing technology;
- by the informal sector if simple new inputs or products manufactured in the modern industry are made available for this sector;
- only by a modern sector.

If a good can be produced by both the informal sector and the modern sector, the modern sector should concentrate on producing products in which it has the greatest cost advantage. When forced to choose between importing a product or producing it in the local modern sector, local production should be concentrated upon the sectors with the highest foreign exchange saving. If the growth rate of mass consumption is too high, it is possible that total demand for imports from all sectors exceeds import capacity. In that case, temporary austerity may be reasonable until local modern plants enter production and provide formerly imported goods for agriculture and the "informal" sector.[15]

The problem, that redistribution requires planning and that "structural heterogeneity" continues to exist between a modern industrial sector, an informal industrial sector and a reformed agriculture, as well as an already competitive export sector gives insight in the fundamental contradictions of such a process of restructuring the economy.

- Planning requires bureaucracy and an increase in state economic activity, creating a class of bureaucrats who will not necessarily stick to the program of overcoming underdevelopment.
- The possible appropriation of funds into the export sectors increases the tendency of enlarged bureaucratic domination.
- A rapid industrialization process increases the urban-rural gap because qualified labor is scarce.
- Mobilizing the peasantry is made more difficult by an enlarged urban-rural income gap even if industrialization is originally intended to meet the needs of a reformed agricultural sector.
- State-imposed control of foreign trade may serve the interests of bureaucrats by avoiding market-based efficiency controls and by enlarging the possibilities of corruption.
- The necessity of planning and the privileged social position for the members of the administrative apparatus creates an ideology of planning. This ideology of planning may crush the dynamism of the informal sector—even if the product mix of the modern industrial sector serves the needs of the informal sector and of the reformed agricultural sector.

[15] Further details Elsenhans (1983a).

2.4 The Contradiction Between Planning and Equality

The paper does not intend to examine the global economic problems of the efficiency of planning. Rather, this paper merely acknowledges a conundrum: on the one hand, price signals do not orient investment to the sectors relevant for mass consumption. On the other hand, simple redistribution of income without previous restructuring of the productive apparatus leads to either inflation or balance of payment problems.[16] Private enterprises cannot invest in the perspective of future markets because these future markets' existence depends on political decisions.

Both planning and restructuring the economy require the appropriation of funds by an administrative apparatus. Hence, there is a necessity of increasing the capabilities of bureaucratic apparatuses. This necessity converges with other tendencies of increasing bureaucracies in the Third World. In the literature, the colonial past in general is mentioned, and sometimes the corporativist tradition of Ibero-America more specifically is referenced.

The social stratification present in the underdeveloped world today was characterized by the establishment of state classes, which some call agrarian bureaucracies or managerial classes.[17] But historical precedents are not sufficient. The crises of development, coupled with an increased demonstration effect, leads to social unrest. The ruling elites can respond with either repression or reforms. In both cases, political-bureaucratic apparatuses of a rather centralized type are expanding. The more rapidly that development-by-planning is tried, the larger these planning statal and parastatal agencies will become.[18]

We can observe that regardless of ideology or foreign policy orientation, in most of the underdeveloped countries the bulk of investible surplus is controlled by the state, even if the government share in GNP may be low. If there is little to appropriate, even a high government share

[16] Cf. Müller-Plantenberg and Hinkelammert (1973). For further literature: Elsenhans (1996 [1981]: 179–182).

[17] From the extensive literature I want to quote only Wittfogel (1969: 361–363), Chesneaux (1964: 41), and Tökei (1966: 61).

[18] The following developments are a summary of Elsenhans (1996 [1981]). For a French summary, Elsenhans (1982a).

of the total economic surplus may lead to a low share in GNP. Other indicators are more significant, such as the share of government in modern industry. Similarly indicative is the share of government in either nonagricultural employment or in sectors of production, where state enterprises operate as the means of intervention to "guide" private enterprise. If a class of civil "servants" controls the bulk of economic surplus and allocates said surplus, we must consider this class as a ruling class. I therefore call it a state class.[19]

The state class appropriates surplus collectively. Members of state classes are not dependent for their incomes nor for their continual membership in the ruling class from competitive efficiency on markets, as are capitalists.

The notion of state capitalism is therefore misleading. Via political decision-making processes, appropriated surplus is allocated to either consumption by the state class or to investment. If the surplus is allocated to investment, the branch and the technology to be applied are determined through political processes. The economic basis does determine the social and economic dynamics but only in a most mediated process, in which predominantly political instances intervene.

As a dominant class, the state class is not a bureaucracy of a Weberian type.[20] It is fragmented into rivaling segments, clans and cliques, the members of which are competing for income, prestige and influence in changing coalitions with other segments and with social groupings outside the state class. These state classes are different from the state classes of traditional empires, agrarian bureaucracies, etc., which are found in societies labeled oriental despotism, or Asiatic mode of production, by the fact, that they are ideologically committed to industrialization and development and not to the maintenance of an existing sanctified order.

They are different from the bureaucracies of so-called real socialism in Eastern Europe, because the working class is not numerically the most important exploited class and because the countries of the Third World are not members of one of the two great ideological camps of the North. There is not a predominance of the social struggle of bureaucracy versus

[19] I have elaborated the main lines of the argument in Elsenhans (1976c: 257–259; 1977b).

[20] Cf. already Eisenstadt (1963: 163).

working class. There is also no necessity of investing in modern military technology in order to keep up with the western industrial countries.

If we define a society by the way labor is organized and distributed between different occupations, by the method of extraction of surplus by the privileged class and by the way surplus is allocated, then in case of predominantly bureaucratic means of appropriation and allocation of surplus, the political dynamics of the ruling class are an element of the characterization of the respective mode of production. Therefore, I distinguish between the bureaucratic development society from the "Asiatic mode of production" and from the "real socialism" of Soviet type.

The existence of such a state class, which behaves between the pole of creating bases of legitimacy by reform or patronage and the pole of increasing its privileges, especially its consumption, may constitute a chance for overcoming underdevelopment as well as a danger for such a process.

The eventual chance is to be seen in the capability of such a state class, to invest funds in projects which in the light of actual effective demand are unprofitable, but which are reasonable if demand is restructured.

Nevertheless, there is no economic constraint which would force the state to do so. As workers are rather privileged and peasants rather powerless, there is little political control. Private enterprise, if existing, is reliant on government markets. TNE affiliates prefer calculable conditions and therefore the maintenance of the existing order. Political mobilization is normally conducive to repression and not reform. The rivalries between segments of the state class normally lead to increased consumption: It is easier to share the booty by increasing the numbers of your own segment in a deal with a rivaling one than to limit the increase of other segments. It is easier to create one's own clientele than to limit the growth of the clienteles of others.

Corruption in this process and the effort to have powerful allies outside the state-class and therefore the tendency to protect and to serve established interests should be mentioned.

The interesting problem, therefore, is by what mechanisms state classes tend to nevertheless make reforms. One should note that the state class is segmented and that an orientation of development to mass needs is costly. These understandings are key to understanding the tendency to reform: The more segments compete, the less the possibility for new segments to find a clientele among the already powerful established interests. Such new segments can promote their interests only if they try to represent mass interests in the political and economic project. These new segments then try to use this mass support in their attempt to achieve higher incomes, more influence and increased prestige.[21]

However, any such project will have difficulties if the productive apparatus does not respond to a new final demand. It is difficult to force the state class to admit that all previous investment was useless. The less the costs of restructuring the productive apparatus to mass needs, the more an egalitarian strategy of overcoming development may seem plausible to "neutrals" in the state class—and the easier the coalition-building for the new segment becomes.

Ideology and social origin may play an important role in a new segment's coming-to-power phase. This is because investment decisions may be implemented in that moment which ultimately requires certain social reforms—especially agrarian reform. The role of the Algerian agricultural input industry for the initiation of agrarian reform in that country may be mentioned.[22] "Planners" simply had to accept the falseness of their previous investment decision and hence lose face, or they transformed agriculture and motivated peasants to use the new inputs. But in the long run, any second generation reduces ideology or origin from the status of a "revolutionary heritage" to a venerable but verbal radicalism.[23]

2.5 State-Class and Rent

The observations we can make about the developments within the OPEC countries show that the availability of foreign exchange does not necessarily promote development for mass needs.[24] More generally, Kindleberger (1961: 290) has shown that an amelioration of the terms-of-trade may lead to a blockage of development. Benachenhou (1971: 920) has similarly insisted on the fact that rent is not a "progressive" income because it is not automatically invested in order to maintain competitiveness as is done with profit. These observations are important for

[21] Sklar (1967: 8), therefore speaks about the "regulary overthrow of one section of the ruling class by a somewhat younger, more efficient and more idealistically minded one."

[22] Cf. Elsenhans (1977a: 174) and Mekidèche (1980: 521).

[23] For discussions of revolutionary heritage and its dwindling, see: Meister (1977: 46). Further literature Elsenhans (1996 [1981]: 283–285).

[24] Especially Sid Ahmed (1980: XVI–XVIII, 422–449).

analyzing the contradictions of self-centered development in its external aspects. The export sector of underdeveloped countries may provide additional foreign exchange income for the state. The tradition of export taxes in developing countries—which dates back far longer than the oil price increases—shows that Third World countries' export sectors are competitive even if they are taxed (Goode et al. 1966: 455).

The financing of a strategy of overcoming underdevelopment, as well as the financing of an increased state class or a more efficient repressive apparatus, can be costly. If this is the case, the state class may proceed with the appropriation of rents by organizing cartels between underdeveloped countries. Applying such a strategy mobilizes national support with an anti-imperialist attitude, using the argument of unequal exchange and exploitation of the underdeveloped by the industrialized countries.

For three economic reasons, I consider the extension of rent appropriation as probable future strategies which would increase the financial resources of the state in the Third World.

- Raw material rents can be appropriated in the mineral sector if the costs of production or substitution in the industrialized world are great. For historic reasons, the low-cost deposits in the North are exhausted, whereas Third World deposits are often even untapped. Examples about differences in metal content of copper ore and iron ore can be given. The case of oil is obvious.
- Products of agricultural origin such as coffee, tea or cocoa may be considered as non-essential. However, this is not an economic category. The concept of consumer rent and the observable low elasticity of demand for those products in relation to income and price in the industrialized countries allow the calculation of minimum price rise—which means foreign exchange earnings are maximal for a cartel of countries producing such commodities (Elsenhans 1976b: 122–129). A price rise of 50% of coffee for the consumer in the Federal Republic of Germany 1974–1977 (with a price rise for raw coffee in DM of 150% and in US $ of 290%), has not diminished the coffee consumption of the normal German household. Possible price rises in Germany have been calculated at 600% for coffee and 1,300% for tea. (This is calculated as raw product, not consumer price, which contains manufacturing and selling costs, factors that would not be substantially changed.) Rent appropriation is also possible in the export of "unnecessary products".

- In case of increased manufactured exports, I do not necessarily see a safeguard against rent appropriation. The argument which proponents of export-led often put forward—that a realistically low exchange rate may promote manufactured exports—may serve as a point of departure. The observation that total factor productivities in the Third World are very different from sector to sector[25] must be restated: In reality, relative factor productivity differences compared to factor productivity in the industrialized countries are very different (Clague 1967: 492). At a given foreign exchange rate, some manufacturing production may be competitive with a higher exchange rate, others not. If the exchange rate is lowered, more manufacturing may be competitive. But in that case, under condition of perfect competition between plants in the Third World, the price of the products, already competitive with a higher exchange rate, will go down by the amount of the diminution of the international price of the value added by local labor. If the exchange rate goes down 50%, and if the local content is 50%, the product can profitably be sold at 75% of its original price.[26] Shirts become low-cost products just as bananas.

The product cycle theory postulates that Third World countries will first become competitive in "old products," especially in manufacturing.[27] If the elasticity of demand in relation to price is lower than 1, a devaluation may lead to a loss of foreign exchange. If shirt producers tax these products (and restrictive policies in the industrial countries against the exports of that type may show them the way), they can increase their foreign exchange incomes, even in manufacturing. The larger the scale of difference in factor productivity between different production lines, the greater the tendency of using this mechanism. Those who believe it is possible to absorb 350 million jobless people in the Third World must take into account that production lines must be transferred. This is complicated further by the fact that we don't even know the relative efficiency of Third World countries compared to industrialized countries. Singapore's

[25] Among others Aydalot (1968: 42) and Amin (1973).

[26] For a more detailed discussion, cf. Elsenhans (1981b: 6–8).

[27] Vernon (1966: 204). In that case, demand is elastic in relation to price only for a firm but not for the branch.

upgrading of its product mix by more state intervention (financed from the now traditional manufactured exports) seems to be based on this economic mechanism.

I conclude from this that the financial resources of the state classes will grow and that rent appropriation will become still more common. If financial resources open up **economic** possibilities for the building-up of a modern sector, they also can be used as **political** money for buying clients. Even if additional foreign exchange is used for investment, the specific nature of the decision-making process in a state class may lead to ineffective investment. In Algeria, the oil price boom has made all administrations covetous for sharing in the new money. Any available project was put forward in order to strengthen each planning agency's own respective economic sector. The weekly of the official party concluded that the oil price boom has destroyed the coherence of the Algerian planning.[28] Nevertheless, the spending of money by the administration has strengthened an adaptive private sector. The private sector is now officially recognized and—against the original intentions of the planners—may play the role of being the bridge between a modern sector of large plants and the satisfaction of mass needs. More generally, an enlargement of the financial resources diminishes the constraints under which a state class is operating. Instead of mobilizing the mass of workforce available, the state class may distribute money, which dampens social unrest. I always remember a young OPEC economist who told me that every dollar of additional income per barrel would equal a diminution of people ready to work in his country.

2.6 Rapid Industrialization and the Rural-Urban Gap

The idea that industrialization processes lead to increasing income differentials is commonplace in the literature. Researchers posited that this industrialization process was induced by the demand of existing high-income groups or by world market demand, especially if executed by

[28] Cf. *Révolution africaine*, 28 March 1980: 22: "En supprimant artificiellement les difficultes, la revalorisation du prix du pétrole en 1974 relèguera la planification à un rang très secondaire tout en annihilant les effets de la décentralisation très timide esquissée lors de la préparation du 2e plan quadriennal."

TNE affiliates. Therefore, for a long time, the U-curve theorem dominated discussions. This theorem made discussions of rising inequality in the development process taboo, because they asserted that after a period of more inequal income distribution, more equality would be obtained. The highly dubious assumption on which this reasoning is based shall not be discussed in this paper, nor shall the historical analogizing often linked to assertions of this type be explained (Adelman et al. 1976: 562; Lee 1977: 288).

What is to be examined is the following contradiction: The more efficient a state class is in appropriating surplus for investment, the more probable the "over-development" of the modern industrial sector and the more probable the emergence of labor aristocracies. There are six arguments for supporting this hypothesis, and I take the empirical evidence mainly from the case of Algeria in the period 1967–1980.

1. Basic industries, such as steel-making, fertilizer production, building materials, and chemicals—which produce inputs required for modernizing agriculture and the informal sector—are capital-intensive and especially technology-intensive. In the case of Algerian steel (Thierry 1982: 481–482), although these industries did not buy the highest technology, even the generally-known technology they introduced requires skilled labor. The Algerian case demonstrates that the rarefication of skilled labor leads to high wages in these sectors.[29] This tendency is strengthened by both the necessity of keeping labor turnover low and by the dominance of the aim of assimilating technology. Indeed, state enterprises in Algeria normally have a "better skilled" workforce than private enterprises (at least on paper). This is because they often tend to use the argument that a great mass of skilled personnel must be trained on the job—which leads to an overstaffing in skilled personnel.
2. If a new industry is launched, the managers of the plants give priority to reaching production (and not profit) targets. In order to conform to time limits, the manager will try to hire qualified labor at any cost. In Algeria, this process had led to restriction in labor mobility, which the new plants have effectively by-passed. Sectoral wage data show

[29] *Révolution africaine*, 25 April 1980: 26.

that newly launched sectors were wage leaders for any skill category of labor.[30]

3. The tendency to use economies of scale will lead to the construction of a restricted number of plants. The state-dominated building of industries will tend to monopolistic structures. In Algeria, branches are organized by one single "firm" (better: industry administration) which until recently had a monopoly of imports of the products involved in the production process.[31] In such a situation, industries have a price-fixing power. One can speak of exploitation of one branch by another one. If prices can be raised, management allows wage increases.
4. In the cases where rents in exports are possible, a nationalized firm (such as the national oil firm SONATRACH in Algeria) will be prepared to smooth labor relations by paying higher wages from these rents. More generally, in monopoly or rent-appropriating sectors, the decentralizing of decisions down to the firm level will increase the tendency of inefficient management of the economy, the overstaffing of the administrative personal by nepotisms, and the "corporatist" integration of the employed workforce into the firm.
5. If employed workers tend to constitute a labor aristocracy, workers' control of the enterprises is a very ambivalent method of checking the tendency of self-privileging shown by the management. The "gestion socialistes des entreprises" (Socialist firm management), even if considered as instrument of democratization of the economy, has had great difficulties in Algeria. Labor leaders are instructed to keep wages at a reasonable level and to mobilize workers for productivity increases—thus they are rather isolated form the rest of the workers. Complaints about non-democratic elections of labor representatives are made often. The control exercised by the state party-controlled trade union UGTA has proved inefficient, as is shown by the 1980 decision that party organizations should be established in the production plants. The government was prudent enough to delay and ultimately restrict workers' control in the richest one of the Algerian enterprises, the oil-producing

[30] Cf. Elsenhans (1977a: 149–150).

[31] *Révolution africaine*, 28 March 1980: 16, 25 April 1980: 164.

SONATRACH. This strategy was certainly in order to the limit the redistribution of the oil rent to the in-house workers.

6. If workers, especially skilled workers, are scarce, a process of overcoming underdevelopment (if it is to be successful) must limit workers' influence and eliminate one element of mass participation. Workers normally are the more politically conscious part of the underprivileged part of the population, for even if workers constitute a labor aristocracy, they are underprivileged in relation to the state class. In the workers versus state relation, class struggle as a means of control of the state class is perverted. It becomes a fight for sectional interests over the distribution of surplus where jobless people—especially the rural masses—are excluded. In order to obtain the necessary inputs for the development of agricultural and industrial sectors, one must build a modern sector of industry. Unfortunately, the economic requirements to build a modern sector of industry produce social consequences which are contradictory to the social and distributional requirements needed to overcome underdevelopment.

2.7 The Demobilization of the Peasantry

Self-centered development depends on an agrarian reform and the building-up of industries which provide new inputs and simple consumption goods to the rural population. By these means, it is hoped that peasants engage in increased efforts for raising yields and for investing work time in the restoration of soils, in the fight against erosion, in reforestation, and in the construction of hydraulic systems. Nevertheless, the aim of doing so is counteracted by political and social developments originating from the state class and the urban population.

Agrarian reform is decided and implemented only if the state class is dominated by segments who try to represent the interests of the masses. Normally these segments adhere to planist ideologies. Agrarian reform is then coupled with well-intended programs for providing inputs at low prices. Simultaneously, there should be a building-up of state-marketing organization. Referring to the necessity of austerity, prices for agricultural products are kept down. Peasants without material incentives refuse to deliver the extra-work time required for the modernization of agriculture. The number of peasants refusing plots in the course of the Algerian agrarian reform was important (Elsenhans 1977a: 164). Additionally, the superannuation of the workforce in agriculture cooperatives is notorious, and the peasants' complaints about their exploitation are consistently voiced in the Algerian press.

Chinese peasants seem to have viewed the cultural revolution especially as a desirable disorganization of the administrative apparatus, which hindered the city's ability to collect taxes.

The demonstration effect of the standard living achieved by urban workers adds to the discouragement of the peasants.

Modernizing agriculture by using new inputs is normally accompanied by agricultural extension work. But for members of the state class, the time spent posted in provincial towns and rural areas normally keeps them aloof from opportunities to get higher incomes, more influence, and more prestige. The golden rule for members of the state class is to rapidly return to the capital after some rural/provincial success. Easy success is needed; therefore, an alliance between the peripheral strata of the state class and powerful interests is normal. The Boumediene government has tried to counteract these tendencies through various measures. Students were sent as volunteers to the villages. Their reports have shown the disinterest of state and party officials in peasant needs. The extension of the rights of village councils has ultimately favored middle-class peasants and not poor peasants. In regional and national elections, peasants did not elect peasant candidates but rather more "honorable" persons who belong to the state class.

If demotivation of the peasants is not avoided, the tendency of bureaucratically commanding the rural workforce is reinforced. In post-agrarian reform Algeria, plans were extensively put forward to transform cooperatives into state farms with de facto wage labor.

2.8 The Foreign Economic Relations Contradictions

Ideologically speaking, state classes who promote processes of self-centered development do not propose autarchy. The rent element in exports and the necessity of building up a modern industrial sector with imported technology favor cooperation with foreign enterprise.

The difficulties of establishing new industries, however, preclude complete liberalization of foreign trade. The "infant industry" protection argument justifies protective measures.

The managers of the state-owned sector are the main advisors and decision makers on foreign trade policy, and they oppose liberalization not only for "infant industry" protection. As protection allows the continued inefficiency of the plant, it gives shelter against efficiency control. In Algeria, orientation of production to world market standards of cost and quality has often been called for, but export statistics do not show much success in this regard.

Behind a vision of the exploitive character of international capital, restrictions in the opening of the economy, which may have to be admitted, are deliberately turned by the state class into protection not of the process of restructuring of the economy, but into protection of the state class against efficiency criteria, the nonfulfillment of which would undermine its legitimacy. Unfortunately, the result is that the economy is not effectively restructured toward world market standards of efficiency.

Another consequence of the ambivalent foreign trade relation in a state class-directed process of self-centered development should be mentioned.

The rent dimension of foreign trade endangers not just coherence of economic planning but also increases fragmentation within the state class—and with the number of potential allies which dispose of resources. Consequently, the possibility of corruption increases. Winston (1979: 840) has shown that this will lead to a tendency of a technical choice in favor of capital-intensive package solutions, instead of the implementation of the economically rational strategies of depackaging and the import of more appropriate technology.

2.9 The Ideological Contradiction

Overcoming underdevelopment requires some planning. The more intensively the restructuring of the productive apparatus, the more planning and building up of state enterprises is necessary. But the positive effects of this restructuring depend on the preparedness of a small-scale "industrial" sector and of agriculture to use inputs. Planning of those sectors is impossible.

The following problem must be recognized: Even if a state-class is committed to overcoming underdevelopment, there are many hurdles to overcome. First, and especially if it takes corresponding investment decisions in the early phase of a still "revolutionary" state class (which, e.g., may be formed by cadres of national liberation movements), extensive planning with effective measures against foreign capital will take place. Goals of egalitarian distribution are officially espoused. Austerity is imposed. Agrarian reform is introduced. The state planning becomes legitimate in the eyes of the population. But increasing economic efficiency will enlarge the state sector. Paternalistic social policies and corporatist "guided" democracy do not provide economic or political controls against the state class and its tendency to enlarge its own privileges. An eventually growing private sector is kept within strict limits, and its potential for diversification remains unused. The Algerian discussion on the role of the private sector since 1981 is interesting in that respect.

If the state-class is less radically oriented, its achievements in restructuring the productive apparatus are less important and state intervention may be less. The legitimacy of planning and of the planning state class are especially less inculcated in the attitudes of underprivileged classes. Social conflicts may be more intensive, and the private sector may be more important. If such an economy may run into the amply described contradictions of import-substituting industrialization, the growth processes may nevertheless contribute to a more flexible productive apparatus. As the renewal of the discussion about agrarian reform in Brazil and the limited opening of the Brazilian political system in 1978–1980 show, restructuring may be possible with less state control and potentially higher linkage effects.

In the first case, an "egalitarian bureaucratic development society," which is a subtype of the bureaucratic development society, will achieve rather rapid success in first phases. However, it will be blocked by the unquestionable position of a state class clinging to socialist verbalism. The state class will use this rhetoric to prevent the promotion of decentralized economic decision making via market regulation through rising mass incomes. In the second case of an "inegalitarian bureaucratic development society", at first, the achievements for the satisfaction of basic needs will be unimportant. Ultimately, however, class conflict will be more open and the adaption of a private sector to rising mass incomes will be more dynamic.

Thus, in self-centered development, the very weight of a socialist ideology of the planning type, which is functional for restructuring the product mix of the economy, will ultimately become a threat to self-centered development.

2.10 Concluding Remark

The propositions that planning is necessary in underdeveloped economies, and that planning necessarily contributes to the creation of a state class with ambivalent consequences for the further process of self-centered development, has practical implications for governments in the North, which consider satisfaction of mass needs and rising mass incomes in the Third World as necessary for the maintenance of a free world economy. The more easily the productive apparatus can be geared toward mass needs and to the expected profile of demand, the less planning is required and the less incentives there are from that area of problems for the state class to grow. The more easily the productive apparatus can be geared to mass needs, the more probable it is that coalitions in the state-class emerge which are dominated by "more idealistically minded" segments of the state-class.

If restructuring is eased by existing productive capacities, then the two principal negative tendencies of the state classes—their orientation to self-privileging while neglecting mass needs, and their orientation to sanctification of state dominance in the economy with centralized planning—should at least be counteracted by the following procedures.

Industrialized countries should select development projects based on the project's potential utilization in a sequence of production processes that are geared to the profile of demand which will emerge in case of a future rise of mass incomes. At first, such a project may even benefit the interests of the privileged classes. However, the potential for reorientation is important.

Concessions in the North-South dialogue, especially on the problems of aid, access to markets and raw material prices, should be linked to structural reform in the Third World. The American government has excluded countries which do not fulfill conditions about raw material price formation or the respect of American property.

But if self-centered development in the Third World is a condition for the maintenance of political equilibria in the North because otherwise labor loses its bargaining power, why not inscribe in trade acts, aid commitments and charters of raw material organizations to be formed under the auspices of the United Nations requirements about the satisfaction of mass needs, the redistribution of incomes and criteria for the selection of projects? Today, concessions in the North-South dialogue could be an effective instrument in winning Third World partners for such a strategy. And labor in the industrialized countries could be an ally promoting that idea in the North.

References

Adelman, Irma, Taft Morris Cynthia, and Sherman Robinson. 1976. Policies for Equitable Growth. *World Development* 4 (7): 561–582.

Amin, Samir. 1973. *Le développement inégal. Essai sur les formations sociales du capitalisme périphérique*. Paris: Editions de Minuit.

Aydalot, Philippe. 1968. Essai sur les problèmes de la stratégie de l'industrialisation en économie sous-développée. L'exemple tunisien. In *Cahiers du CERES*, 1–175.

Barnet, Richard J., and Ronald E. Müller. 1974. *Global Reach. The Power of the Multinational Corporations*. New York: Simon & Schuster.

Benachenhou, Abdellatif. 1971. Le renversement de la problématique ricardienne des coûts comparés dans la théorie économique contemporaine. *Revue algérienne des sciences juridiques, économiques et politiques* 8 (4): 913–934.

Bequele, Assefa, and David H. Freedman. 1979. Employment and Basic Needs. An Overview. *International Labour Review* 118 (3): 315–329.

Borton, Hugh. 1938. Peasant Uprisings in Japan of the Tokugawa Period. *Transactions of the Asiatic Society of Japan* 26: 1–220.

Chesneaux, Jean. 1964. Le mode de production asiatique, quelques perspectives de recherche. *La Pensée* 114: 33–55.

Clague, Christopher K. 1967. An International Comparison of Industrial Efficiency. Peru and the United States. *Review of Economics and Statistics* 49 (4): 487–493.

Craig, Albert M., John K. Fairbank, and Edwin O. Reischauer. 1965. *East Asia. The Modern Transformation*. Boston, MA: Houghton Mifflin.

Currie, Lauchlin. 1971. The Exchange Constraint on Development. A Partial Solution to the Problem. *Economic Journal* 81 (324): 886–903.

Eisenstadt, Shmuel Noah. 1963. Problems of Emerging Bureaucracies in Developing Areas and New States. In *Industrialization and Society*, ed. Bert F. Hoselitz and Wilbert E. Moore, 159–174. The Hague, Paris: UNESCO; Mouton.

Elsenhans, Hartmut. 1976a. Lohnerhöhungen. Wachstumschance für den Kapitalismus. Eine Kritik am Gesetz vom tendenziellen Fall der Profitrate. *Forum DS. Zeitschrift für Theorie und Praxis des demokratischen Sozialismus* 1 (2): 78–133.

Elsenhans, Hartmut. 1976b. Ökonomie der Rohstoffproduktion am Beispiel Tee und Kaffee. Welche Preissteigerungen erlaubt ihr Markt in der BRD. *Leviathan* 4 (1): 122–129.

Elsenhans, Hartmut. 1976c. Zur Rolle der Staatsklasse bei der Überwindung von Unterentwicklung. In *Strategien gegen Unterentwicklung. Zwischen Weltmarkt und Eigenständigkeit*, ed. Alfred Schmidt, 250–265. Frankfort on Main, New York: Campus.

Elsenhans, Hartmut. 1977a. *Algerien. Koloniale und postkoloniale Reformpolitik.* Hamburg: Institut für Afrikakunde im Verbund der Stiftung Deutsches Übersee-Institut.

Elsenhans, Hartmut. 1977b. Die Staatsklasse/Staatsbourgeoisie in den unterentwickelten Ländern zwischen Privilegierung und Legitimationszwang. *Verfassung und Recht in Übersee* 10 (1): 29–42.

Elsenhans, Hartmut. 1979a. Agrarverfassung, Akkumulationsprozeß, Demokratisierung. In *Agrarreform in der Dritten Welt*, ed. Hartmut Elsenhans, 505–652. Frankfort on the Main, New York: Campus.

Elsenhans, Hartmut. 1979b. Gesellschaftsreform und Wirtschaftswachstum. Akkumulationsprobleme in der Bundesrepublik. *Forum DS. Zeitschrift für Theorie und Praxis des demokratischen Sozialismus* 4 (8): 135–170.

Elsenhans, Hartmut. 1981a. Commentaires. In *Technologie appropriée ou technologie sous-développée? Suivi d'une discussion avec Celso Furtado et Hartmut Elsenhans*, ed. Arghiri Emmanuel, 151–166. Paris: Presses Universitaires de France.

Elsenhans, Hartmut. 1981b. *Le rôle des multinationales dans une stratégie des besoins de base.* Quelques notes. European Association of Development Research and Training Institutes. General Conference 1981. Budapest: European Association of Development and Training Institutes.

Elsenhans, Hartmut. 1981c. Social Consequences of the NIEO. No Change for Continued Reformist Strategies in the Centre without Structural Change in the Periphery. In *Elements of World Instability: Armaments, Communication, Food, International Division of Labour*, ed. Egbert Jahn and Yoshikazu Sakamoto, 86–95. Proceedings of the Eighth International Peace Research Association Conference. Frankfort on Main, New York: Campus.

Elsenhans, Hartmut. 1981d. *Sur le bon emploi des schémas de reproduction. Contribution au Symposium de Paris sur l'ouvrage d'Arghiri Emmanuel 'Technologie Appropriée, Mirage ou Réalité'.* Working Group—Multinationales et Développement. European Association of Development Research and Training Institutes. General Conference 1981, Budapest, 11–14 November. Budapest: European Association of Development Research and Training Institutes.

Elsenhans, Hartmut. 1982a. Capitalisme d'Etat ou société bureaucratique de développement. *Etudes internationales* 13 (1): 3–22.

Elsenhans, Hartmut. 1982b. Die Überwindung von Unterentwicklung durch Massenproduktion für den Massenbedarf – Weiterentwicklung eines Ansatzes.

In *Handbuch der Dritten Welt (1). Unterentwicklung und Entwicklung – Theorien, Strategien, Indikatoren*, ed. Dieter Nohlen and Franz Nuscheler, 152–182. Hamburg: Hoffmann & Campe.

Elsenhans, Hartmut. 1983a. Politische Ökonomie und wirtschaftliche Entwicklung in der Dritten Welt. In *Gesamtwirtschaftliche Planung und Beratung*, ed. Gesellschaft für Technische Zusammenarbeit, 49–90. Materialien der GTZ-Fachtagung "Methodik und Organisation der Entwicklungsplanung" vom 15.11.1981 bis 27.11.1981 in Wachtenberg-Niederbachem. Eschborn: Gesellschaft für Technische Zusammenarbeit (GTZ).

Elsenhans, Hartmut. 1983b. Rising Mass Incomes as a Condition of Capitalist Growth. Implications for the World Economy. *International Organization* 37 (1): 1–38.

Elsenhans, Hartmut. 1996 [1981]. *State, Class and Development*. New Delhi, London, Columbia, MO: Radiant; Sangam; South Asia Books.

Emmanuel, Arghiri. 1981. Réponse à Hartmut Elsenhans. In *Technologie appropriée ou technologie sous-développée? Suivi d'une discussion avec Celso Furtado et Hartmut Elsenhans*, ed. Arghiri Emmanuel, 168–189. Paris: Presses Universitaires de France.

Furtado, Celso. 1971. Dépendance externe et la théorie économique. *Homme et la société* 22: 53–65.

Goode, Richard, George E. Lent, and P.D. Ohja. 1966. The Role of Export Taxes in Developing Countries. *IMF Staff Papers* 13 (3): 453–502.

Habakkuk, Hrothgar John. 1962. *American and British Technology in the Nineteenth Century. The Search for Labour-Saving Inventions*. Cambridge: Cambridge University Press.

Helleiner, Gerald K. 1979. Structural Trends of Third World Trade. Some Trends and Some Prospects. *Journal of Development Studies* 15 (3): 70–88.

Hone, Angus. 1974. Multinational Corporations and Multinational Buying Groups. Their Impact on the Growth of Asia's Exports of Manufactures. Myths and Realities. *World Development* 2 (2): 145–149.

ILO. 1980. *Yearbook of International Labour Statistics*. Geneva: International Labour Office.

James, Jeffrey. 1976. Products, Processes, and Incomes. *World Development* 4 (2): 143–149.

Kay, Cristóbal. 1976. Agrarian Reform and the Transition to Socialism. In *Allende's Chile*, ed. Philip O'Brien, 79–105. New York: Praeger.

Kelley, Allen C., and Jeffrey Gale Williamson. 1974. *Lessons from Japanese Development. An Analytical Economic History*. Chicago, IL, London: The University of Chicago Press.

Kindleberger, Charles P. 1961. Foreign Trade and Economic Growth. Lessons from Britain and France 1850–1913. *Economic History Review* 14 (3): 289–305.

Lachaud, Jean-Pierre. 1980. Les lois de fonctionnement du secteur informel 'traditionnel'. Présentation d'un modèle. *Tiers Monde* 21 (82): 435–444.

Lee, Eddy. 1977. Development and Income Distribution. A Case Study of Sri Lanka and Malaysia. *World Development* 5 (4): 279–289.

Leff, Nathaniel H. 1972. Economic Retardation in Nineteenth-Century Brazil. *Economic History Review* 25 (3): 489–507.

Meister, Albert. 1977. *La participation pour le développement*. Paris: Editions ouvrières.

Mekidèche, Mustapha. 1980. Le secteur des hydrocarbures. Quelle contribution au développement économique et social de l'Algérie? *Tiers Monde* 21 (83): 509–530.

Moran, Theodore H. 1970. The 'Development' of Argentina and Australia. The Radical Party of Argentina and the Labour Party of Australia in the Process of Economic and Political Development. *Comparative Politics* 3 (1): 71–92.

Morawetz, David. 1974. Employment Implications of Industrialisation in Developing Countries. *Economic Journal* 84 (335): 491–542.

Müller-Plantenberg, Urs, and Franz Hinkelammert. 1973. Condiciones y consecuencias de una política de redistribución de ingresos. *Cuadernos de La Realidad Nacional* 16 (2): 203–228.

Nakamura, James I. 1966. Meiji Land Reform, Redistribution of Income and Saving from Agriculture. *Economic Development and Cultural Change* 14 (4): 428–439.

Nayyar, Deepak. 1978. Transnational Corporations and Manufactured Exports from Poor Countries. *Economic Journal* 88 (349): 59–84.

Nurkse, Ragnar. 1953. *Problems of Capital Formation in Underdeveloped Countries*. New York: Oxford University Press.

Petras, James F. (ed.). 1978. *Critical Perspective on Imperialism and Social Class in the Third World*. New York, London: Monthly Review Press.

Ranis, Gustav. 1957. Factor Proportions in Japanese Economic Development. *American Economic Review* 47 (4): 594–608.

Rawski, Thomas G. 1976. Economic Growth and Employment in China. *World Development* 4 (8/9): 767–782.

Sabolo, Ives. 1980. Industrialisation, Exports and Employment. *International Labour Review* 119 (4): 481–493.

Salama, Pierre. 1978. Spécificités de l'internationalisation du capital en Amérique latine. *Tiers Monde* 19 (74): 260–267.

Saul, Samuel Berrick. 1960. *Studies in British Overseas Trade 1870–1914*. Liverpool: Liverpool University Press.

Sid Ahmed, Abdelkader. 1980. *L'OPEP. Passé, présent et avenir*. Alger: Office des Publications Universitaires.

Sklar, Richard L. 1967. Political Science and National Integration—A Radical Approach. *Journal of Modern African Studies* 5 (1): 1–11.

Stewart, Frances. 1974. Technology and Employment in LDC's. *World Development* 2 (3): 17–46.

Strassmann, W. Paul. 1956. Economic Growth and Income Distribution. *Quarterly Journal of Economics* 70 (3): 425–440.

Thierry, Simon-Pierre. 1982. La crise du système productif algérien. Productivité, mutations institutionnelles et formes de régulation d'une économie nationale. Grenoble: Dissertation.

Tökei, Ferenc. 1966. *Sur le mode de production asiatique*. Budapest: Akadémiai Kiadó.

Vernon, Raymond. 1966. International Investment and International Trade in the Product Cycle. *Quarterly Journal of Economics* 80 (2): 190–207.

Vernon, Raymond. 1977. Storm Over the Multinationals. Problems and Prospects. *Foreign Affairs* 55 (2): 243–262.

Winston, Gordon C. 1979. The Appeal of Inappropriate Technologies. Self-Inflicted Wages, Ethnic Pride and Corruption. *World Development* 7 (8/9): 835–845.

Wittfogel, Karl August. 1969. Results and Problems of the Study of Oriental Despotism. *Journal of Asian Studies* 28 (2): 357–365.

Yamamura, Kozo. 1971. The Increasing Poverty of the Samurai in Tokugawa Japan, 1660–1868. *Journal of Economic History* 31 (2): 378–406.

CHAPTER 3

Markets and Morals

Hartmut Elsenhans

A market economy is a-moral. It is, however, not anti-moral. Its a-moral character does not indicate moral decay. The market economy replaces the relatively low level of obedience to moral principles with obedience to new rules. The old moral principles are largely influenced by the powerful. The new rules are imposed on the powerful by labor.

A market economy is characterized by the pursuance of profit.[1] Neglecting the profit rate leads to bankruptcy and exclusion from the class of entrepreneurs. Profit is appropriated under the conditions of perfect competition. Therefore, entrepreneurs do not strive for profit. They only want to become richer and prefer more safe access to surplus.

Originally published as: Elsenhans, Hartmut. 1997. Markt und Moral. In *Die Eine Welt der vielen Wirklichkeiten. Pädagogische Orientierungen. Festschrift für Asit Datta*, ed. Harry Noormann and Gregor Lang-Wojtasik, 21–38. Frankfort on the Main: IKO-Verlag für Interkulturelle Kommunikation.

H. Elsenhans (✉)
University of Leipzig, Leipzig, Germany
e-mail: helsen@rz.uni-leipzig.de

[1] The argument is developed in Elsenhans (1996a).

© The Author(s), under exclusive license to Springer Nature Switzerland AG 2021

H. Warnecke-Berger (ed.), *Development, Capitalism, and Rent*,
https://doi.org/10.1007/978-3-030-62605-1_3

If a monopoly position is useful for becoming richer, they will not abolish it.

3.1 The Invisible Limits for Capitalists

Profit depends on spending on net investments. Suppose that there is perfect competition in a capitalist market economy, that there are only workers and entrepreneurs. As long as there is competition, entrepreneurs cannot raise their consumption substantially above the incomes of labor with comparable skills and workload. The privilege of entrepreneurs does not consist of their high consumption incomes but in the right of disposing of the social surplus. We do not consider the government sector because we assume in this demonstration that government does not spend more than it receives as taxes. All labor incomes are expected to be spent on consumption—meaning that workers do not save.

If there is no spending on net investment—i.e., no gross investment higher than productive consumption of inputs and equipment—then enterprises which produce consumption goods will not realize more sales than their own costs. Profits for particular enterprises are possible because of the quality and consumer orientation of their products. They are compensated by losses of other entrepreneurs in consumption goods production. This happens because the total amount of wages directly paid in the production of final consumption goods and indirectly paid in the production of different inputs and consumed equipment (amortization) all constitute the total demand for the consumption goods industry. Net profit for the collectivity of all consumption goods producers can emerge only if there are (labor) incomes from employment in enterprises which do not produce consumption goods, hence investment goods production that is higher than investment goods for replacement of worn-out equipment. Such new investment goods are produced only if investment goods producers can expect the deployment of capital to produce a similar rate of profit as they would receive in enterprises which produce consumption goods. If the profit rate in consumption goods is positive, the prices of investment goods must rise to a level wherein each investment goods producers receives a comparable rate of profit.

The usefulness in relation to costs of new products must be superior in comparison with old products in order for the new products to sell. Productivity must increase. Entrepreneurs perceive increases in productivity as decreasing unit cost of known products or increasing prices in case of new products for the factors engaged in production. For similar needs, already known products are replaced by new products produced with new technologies only in the case of the prices of new products decreasing. New products may satisfy new needs without making older ones superfluous. Then new products can be consumed only if purchasing power increases. Full employment, therefore, requires expanding demand: If the economy is characterized by permanent innovation, then either older products are produced with less cost or additional new needs are satisfied with new products. Capitalist market economies require rising incomes per hour worked—either by increasing real wages per hour worked or decreasing work hours. Only if this condition is met is continuously positive net investment spending possible.

Mainstream economists argue that wage increases depend on productivity increases. The realization of wage increases in line with productivity increases; however, this requires the empowerment of labor and its capacity to wage the class struggle. If this mechanism works, entrepreneurs will increase the demand for labor following the increase in labor productivity. The profit rate initially rises, the demand for labor increases, and after some time the increasing wages reach the level of marginal product of labor. Entrepreneurs will never increase labor's share of incomes because productivity alone increases. Such increases are necessary in order to attract additional workers only if labor is short in supply. Such scarcity can emerge only if all available labor produces a higher marginal product than is necessary for ensuring full employment. If productivity is lower, as must be assumed for the period of transition to capitalist market economies, this mechanism can come into operation only after some growth, when marginal product of labor is higher than the cost of reproduction of labor. Otherwise, there are other (jobless) workers: Entrepreneurs can draw on a principally unlimited reserve of labor.

Precapitalist societies are different from capitalist societies in this very aspect (Elsenhans 1994: 394–399). In precapitalist class societies, two classes are prevalent: classes of lords—who as oligarchies are more or less centralized—and state classes, who are more centralized. These two groups take surplus from the economy. They can maintain their political power if they are able to manage the problems of that part of the population which produces less than necessary for its reproduction. Compared to the adjustment of the size of the population to the possibilities of each active worker producing a marginal product higher than the reproduction costs, the option of providing some social security to the "superfluous" population is politically more appropriate, even for the ruling class of lords. Those who produce less than they must consume have to accept the existing order and have to avoid becoming rebels. The great majority of those, who produce less than they have to consume, will prefer dependency on the rulers to revolt. They offer services to the rulers which are possible at that low level of productivity, especially the readiness to engage in clientelist dependency.

The "moral" character of precapitalist societies is an expression of the social contract between average-skilled labor and the class of ruling lords. In case of marginality, labor with average skills can survive only, if it accepts dependency. The conditions of such dependency are negotiated within the framework provided by the principles of "moral economy." They are an expression of power relations, where the lower strata have high costs of transaction for imposing their demands. As long as the precapitalist lords are ready to grant a minimum level of opportunities for survival, the option of rebellion is not very attractive.

Capitalist economies do not need only a surplus but rather a surplus of each single worker, hence a marginal product of labor of each worker which is higher than his cost of reproduction. As long as the share of food in consumption (in case of poor people 50–60%) and hence the share of agriculture in employment are high, technical progress in manufacturing for mass consumption cannot substantially increase the marginal product of agricultural labor. In case of falling prices for manufactured products in relation to prices for food, the cost of reproduction of labor decreases in agriculture so that the level of marginality is raised and with it employment in agriculture. Such a process, however, has a limit: If prices for manufactured product should fall to 0, employment cannot increase beyond the level where additional food consumption of a worker and his family equals his marginal product in agriculture. In the closed economy, the marginal product of agricultural labor is decisive for the transition to capitalism. Therefore, the transition to capitalism never depended on high concentration of capital, as possessed for example by the long-distance monopoly trade companies; rather it depended on the increase of mass incomes in the wake of increasing productivity in agriculture (Elsenhans 1979b, 1983a, b).

There is a second precondition. In case the expected marginal product of labor must be realized on the market, its monetary value will depend on overall demand conditions. Only the case of high levels of employment increasing physical productivity will lead to scarcity of labor and rising nominal wages. Only with rising nominal wages will rising costs press for higher prices and hence for higher monetary values of production. In case of scarcity of labor and conditions of demand where rising prices can be imposed, marginal product increases, not only for goods where physical productivity has increased but for all goods in the production of which labor is scarce and nominal wages increase. Wages are at the same time a demand element and a cost element and marginal product cannot be explained by physical productivity increases without referring the demand element (Irsch 1979: 70–74). Marginal product can be low despite high productivity and productivity increases in physical terms, if there is a glut on the market.

Full employment is achieved in a capitalist economy only during times of high activity. Capitalist production is characterized by investment pushes, the so-called herding behavior of entrepreneurs. Enterprises proceed to investment if there are innovations which may render obsolete existing plant and equipment or if there is the perception of new markets—indeed both conditions often occur at the same time. In capitalist economies, there is a permanent danger of temporary overheating and subsequent cyclical unemployment during the business cycle. In the downswing prices and salaries tend to fall. A downswing can only be overcome if wages fall less than prices; this allows a new investment push based on innovations which once more lead to full employment. If prices fall less than wages during the downswing and labor loses its capacity to resist nominal wage decreases forcefully, there is the possibility of structural unemployment—which results in further disempowerment of labor.

Until the crisis of the 1930s, labor could substantially limit nominal wage decreases during downswings. Regularly prices fell more rapidly than wages. Despite unemployment, consumption demand increased in relation to employment. Profits fell rapidly owing to the absence of net investment. Often net profit became negative because of the low level of investment which was financed from amortization. Real wages increased despite unemployment and falling nominal wages. This supported final demand, so that newly emerging technical progress and the resulting pushes of investment could easily lead to new full employment.[2]

[2] Tucker (1936), Keynes (1939: 35–36), Richardson (1967: 108–112), Rosenberg (1934: 185), Montgomery (1938: 119–125), Woytinsky (1936: 61), and Habakkuk (1972: 275).

The crisis of the 1930s is the first phase of capitalist development, where in technically advanced economies this mechanism no longer operated so that even one of the leading neoliberals, Roepke (1936: 9), introduced a new type of crisis in the theoretical discussion, the so-called secondary crisis, where the process of accumulation was blocked by deficient demand, not so different from the analysis of Keynes. Countervailing political power became even more important—as shown by the rise of labor during this crisis and the subsequent defeat of fascism.

The power of labor can never endanger investment activities of enterprises, as labor cannot impose a level of consumption which threatens investment. Too high demands for mass consumption can only be satisfied by increasing capacities of production through investment and trigger investment with the result of an increase of the price level, so-called forced savings. Whatever the monetary incomes, any economy cannot increase supply beyond full capacity utilization in the short run. If entrepreneurs assume that a durable expansion of demand is indicated by increasing monetary incomes of labor, they react with investment in enlarging capacities of production. For this they do not use previously saved income, but labor and equipment for the production of investment goods. A normally functioning banking system can provide enough money through credit. Any credit an investor takes from a bank becomes a payment on a sight deposit of a supplier in a bank. The bank is eager to relend this money. The central bank applies the instruments of monetary policy, like minimum reserves or discounts rate policies, in order to limit credit expansion to the productive capacity of the economy. This is done in order to avoid inflation.

Labor cannot shift capacities in investment goods production to consumption goods production by its demand for consumption goods. When capacities of production are run at about 80%, any new plant in consumption goods production requires new investment goods. The production of such new investment goods requires new capacities of production if there is full capacity utilization. Enterprises do not produce investment goods or plants for investment goods production in order to have stocks of them in reserve; rather enterprises follow their estimation of the development of markets.

If mass incomes increase according to productivity increases, no one of the two classes of the pure capitalist market economy is interested in wide-ranging state interventionism. Both classes acquire bargaining power by their most selfish pursuit of their own interest. By rising real incomes labor creates new opportunities for profitable investment, and through new investment enterprises increase their demand for labor, increase wages by employment increases following the marginal product argument and create bargaining power of labor. This constitutes the politico-economic basis of the autonomy of civil society (Elsenhans 1991, 1997a, b). Both main classes of capitalist society push back against the patrimonial pre-capitalist state. The doubly free worker, described by Marx as proletarian, can exist only if there is sufficient effective demand and if the marginal product is higher than the cost of reproduction. If these conditions are not met, all workers have only the alternative either to revolt or to accept clientelist dependency from the lords. The lords can finance people with a lower marginal product than their costs of reproduction and which do not contribute to their economic resources if they remove economic competition among themselves, i.e., reintroduce the political mechanisms for appropriation of surplus.

Capitalist market economy is an event which was imposed by labor. It is a-moral because under the condition of sufficient effective demand for full employment, workers have no interest in a social contract with the lords where they would have to make concessions. Moreover, moral norms in any society are an arrangement where the poor have to make concessions to the powerful in the name of common values invented under the political and cultural hegemony of the lords. Tönnies (1935 [1887]: 40–51) has shown that the bourgeois society, as the form of social integration in capitalism, depends on exchange. Precapitalist "society" is characterized as community and needs common values (Kazancigil 1992: 42). The basic difference is between moral economy as compared to the capitalist market economy with its autonomous bourgeois society. Here, individuals are free to live according their own moral criteria, because competition among the rich and solidarity between the weak are imposed by the dull compulsion of economic relations.

3.2 Threats to the Operation of the Capitalist System by Its Own Development

Labor imposes discipline on the rich by its rising mass incomes. Only the resources necessary for investment financing can be appropriated as profit on the market. This system is endangered when labor is weakened in the wake of the availability of new reserves of cheap labor and decreasing competition between enterprises. Weakened competition between enterprises implies that expanding demand will not always—but only under certain conditions—be met with employment-creating net investment.

The first threat is linked to the impact of so-called globalization (Elsenhans 1996a). The impact of globalization cannot be averted through cautious wage increases alone or even wage decreases. Labor from the "low-wage countries" is not competitive because its product wages (i.e., real wages as measured in their consumption basket which can be purchased with these wages) are low in relation to real wages in the advanced capitalist industrial countries. Such a configuration would imply that the advanced capitalist countries have massive balance of trade deficits because they would sell on the world market less than they would buy from there. In reality, however, the technically backward countries experience great difficulties in achieving balance of trade surpluses—even though they would need such balance of trade surpluses because of their high indebtedness. Such surpluses would be helpful for their reducing the debt. Despite their higher wages in comparison with the technically backward countries, most of the advanced capitalist industrial countries achieve balance of trade surpluses. Because of their relatively high levels of competitiveness in a small segment of their production, advanced capitalist industrial countries achieve high earnings on the market, which results in high external value of their currencies. Suppose that they do not achieve such balance of trade surpluses: In that case, the external value of their currency would be lower. The international price of their labor costs would decrease, as the national costs of this labor is lower in international currencies than at a higher exchange rate. Even those among their workers who are not in the small highly productive segment would continue to be competitive. The lower external value of their currency would reduce their international labor cost.

Vice versa, it can be argued that the new competitiveness of the technically backward countries is first of all the result of their exchange rates, i.e., their capacity to keep the international price of their labor low. This is possible only because they are capable of supplying the basics for their labor in the export sector from local production. This labor remains cheap despite increasing exports as long that there is no tendency to full employment. Such a tendency could be triggered by wages paid in export employment. They would have to be high enough to impose the creation of demand for the internal market sector activities which would absorb additional labor so that eventually tensions on the labor market emerge. The marginal product of unskilled labor—and therefore average real wages as well as the propensity to import from consumption incomes—remains low. Devaluation therefore is not counteracted by price increases of labor in local currency.

In technically backward countries, productivity increases are mostly limited to some sectors, without increases in the marginal product of average labor. As some of these countries produce a surplus of food, salaries do not increase in national currency and can be kept at low levels relative to international prices through the instrument of devaluation.

Globalization is not the problem, per se. Rather, the problem is the intensification of the international division of labor, which extends to manufacturing items in economies where the social conditions for capitalism as described above have not yet emerged. Any cheapening of products by such a new division of labor has the same results as an increase in productivity at the world level. This productivity increase manifests itself, however, only in terms-of-trade improvements for the industrially more advanced countries. It is only here that there are the social conditions for a contribution to an increased worldwide consumptive capacity following the increasing worldwide capacity of production. Such structures are absent in the underdeveloped world; consequently, there is a danger of hollowing out the politico-economic mechanisms which operate in industrially advanced countries.[3] The low international price of labor in the technically backward countries also blocks the mechanism of redistribution of productivity increases in the technically advanced countries as well.

Advances in productivity in technically advanced countries are lower in many branches of production than in the export branches, which determine the exchange rates. As a result, workers in the advanced industrial countries with productivity advances that are lower than in the export branches therefore lose competitiveness. They become too expensive in relation to labor from the technical backward countries not because of low productivity, but because of the exchange rate. As a result, labor in the industrially advanced countries is segmented. The solidarity of the working class may also be destroyed (Elsenhans 1996b: 18–19).

The threat posed by globalization can be averted only if workers in the advanced countries understand globalization as a historically unique

[3] I have early on insisted on this aspect, without any response in relevant academia: Elsenhans (1976: 23–24; 1980: 484; 1981; 1987).

opportunity for creating the conditions for (mass-consumption-based) welfare capitalism at a global scale. If deepening globalization would lead to full employment also in the "low-wage countries" (with initially still low international labor cost), then the worldwide extension of capitalism would succeed (Elsenhans 1997c). Development policies which combine various measures in an eclectic manner can shorten this process. Agrarian reform, subsidies to the poor, and employment increases via government programs and projects of non-governmental organizations[4] channel rent to the poor in order to compensate for a too low marginal product of labor or increase this marginal product.

In opposition to this deepening of globalization, the business sector demands limitation of consumption and wage restraint, whereas part of the political left proposes national isolation of the markets in the name of socialism (Afheldt 1995, 1996).

The new opportunities of transforming new comparative cost advantage into low international labor costs by devaluation cannot be met by wage restraint in the advanced industrial countries. New balance of trade surpluses will just lead to new appreciation of the currencies and hence to rising international prices of their labor. In order to cope with this new competitiveness, advanced industrial countries would have to increase their real wages at the national level in order to maintain a significant and expanding internal demand. Due to the additional internal demand, they would have to increase imports from the less advanced countries. Both will mitigate the pressure for appreciation of their currencies. By favoring deepening globalization, they will contribute to increasing productivity in the wage goods sectors of the technically backward countries—resulting in rising wages there. The success of the less advanced countries in raising productivity in the export sectors ultimately proves the absence of technical obstacles for productivity increases. The only blockage to productivity increases in the internal-market-oriented sectors consists of social conditions, especially a too low demand for wage goods.

A second threat to maintaining capitalism—decreasing competition between enterprises—is a necessary consequence of capitalist development. This is not linked to Lenin's tendency to monopoly capitalism

[4] Kothari (1986) therefore considers that the NGOs are the vehicle of the extension of capitalism, however invoking other lines of causation.

because of the internal contradictions of capitalism. In fact, the transaction costs for starting production by new competitors increase if knowledge and experience become more important. Initially, the bargaining power of labor is based on the principally equal opportunity for each economically active citizen to avail themselves of the opportunities for making profit in the wake of expanding demand on the market. When barriers to entry emerge, enterprises invest in increasing capacities of production only if they achieve a profit rate which they consider sufficient. This profit rate must be higher than the market interest rate, for otherwise new competitors will leave their money in their saving accounts. Old established enterprises which have already acquired experience and knowledge can be supposed to be able to sell at prices much lower than the new entrants. This reduces the entrants' possible profit rate. The higher the short-term productivity advances of already-established enterprises, the higher the cost disadvantage for new competitors.

As long as an economy is characterized by perfect competition, the average profit rate cannot substantially differ from the rate of growth of the capital stock. This is no longer the case if any new competitor must finance high initial learning costs. The profit rate for old established enterprises tends to increase. The end of perfect competition is demonstrated by the widespread expectation of profit rates for net investment of 13–15%, which is far above the growth rate of the capital stock.

With such profit rate s, enterprises do not expect strong price competition in case of new investment. Whether a new car from one car manufacturer costs three percent more than a comparable car from another manufacturer rarely matters. During a crisis, the previous fall of prices of products in relation to nominal wages does not occur. Enterprises operating under the conditions of limited ("oligopolistic") competition react by reducing production instead of diminishing prices during crises. This had been demonstrated by Sohn-Rethel (1973: 47–48) for 1930s Germany during the world economy crisis.

The limitation of competition by learning costs of new competitors is an inevitable result of capitalist growth. Diversification of consumption results from rising mass incomes. Demand no longer is limited to a small range of different products. The costs of development of a particular product increase. Any production has a twofold result: There is a cheapening of the product to be sold, and the knowledge about this product and the methods of its manufacturing through which the development of new products is also cheapened. This holds true even outside the respective line of production. This knowledge is not freely available. New competitors can acquire it only by incurring additional costs and therefore cannot offer the same low prices as already-established enterprises. When the share of cost for this knowledge increases, already-established enterprises can impose prices which reflect these costs which they no longer have to incur. New competitors can finance the acquisition of this knowledge if the banks will provide the necessary finance but must accept additional costs in the form of paying bank interests. These barriers to entry increase because of economies of scale, which result from being able to supply large quantities to rapidly expanding markets and to enjoy decreasing unit costs.

The increasing importance of learning costs suffices to explain why the shift to more complex progress allows enterprises price-fixing which leads to profits which do not have their counterpart in net investment spending and the necessary finance for it. Under free competition, the enterprises as a whole suffer from a lack of demand and therefore reduced mass of profit in case of insufficient spending on investment. The resulting price fall leads to increasing purchasing power for the incomes of the consumers. New entrants produce at higher cost and enjoy lower profits than their established competitors because the new entrants must factor in their initially higher costs. Because of this, new competitors cannot undercut their established competitors' prices. Established enterprises earn rents based on an already acquired know-how. Knowledge embodied in the established enterprises blocks the process of "devalorization" of capital, which, following Marx, has been described by Sinn (1975: 688–689) as an important mechanism for disciplining capital.

Similar observations apply to the labor markets. Perfect competition implies that each worker in each enterprise can be employed at the average wage rate and contributes at this wage rate to net profits of the enterprise, provided appropriate development of demand. If there are no more such homogeneous labor markets, enterprises may employ much more productive, highly experienced in-house workers. Enterprises prefer them to the newly employed ones which they will employ only at lower wage rates. An average wage rate following formally demonstrated skills will induce enterprises to limit production because the optimal profit rate is achieved at lower levels of production (Göcke 1996). A level of profit emerges which exceeds the demand created through enterprise spending on labor in investment goods production, because net investment is low. Profits exceed the total financial requirements of the enterprise sector as a whole. Such productivity differences may lead to higher wages for the permanent staff compared to the lower wages for newly employed staff. Everyone tries to become permanent staff. The more skilled workers become immobile and can be attracted by new competitors only at high cost.

There are new inflexibilities and new monetary profits which do not lead automatically to investment, beyond the rigidities already analyzed by Keynes. This is because interest rates cannot become negative in monetary terms (except through inflation). Real consumption demand diminishes without compensation in the form of additional net investment. The microelectronics revolution intensifies this tendency: Production and productivity increases become saving on capital spending. In the upswing of the new long-term cycle due to the new wave of investment in the cyber economy, the usually lower wage increases (in comparison with production increases) are no longer compensated by the herding of investment spending. In the phase of herding of investment, there are capital savings instead of rising costs of additional plant and equipment. In previous cycles of increased investment spending, the economy saw rapid increases of employment via the increased demand for investment goods, as had been the case during the rise of the railways or the rise of cars and the respective infrastructures. Therefore, this new wave of innovation has other characteristics than the previous "Kondratievs" (Elsenhans 1979a: 145–147).

The relations of substitution between markets for different products are further weakened. J. B. Say (1972 [1803]: 140–141) had argued that sale proceeds which are in excess of costs of production (labor, inputs including amortization) will lead to demand for other products; these other products hence can also be sold at prices higher than the cost of production. Such a relation may exist between demands for different consumption goods. They are absent between the class of consumption goods and the class of investment goods. If the demand for investment goods rises, the supply for consumption goods may decline in real terms in case of high capacity utilization because of limits in productive capacity still available after investment goods demand is satisfied. But in case of a too low demand for consumption goods, there will regularly be no increased investment spending (Bhaduri 1986: 57–58).

At the same time, increasing welfare of labor reduces the growth rate of demand for material goods and disproportionately increases the demand for non-material goods such as security in the future, which is attempted through savings. Higher savings of labor are basically a lack of demand for the business sector. The creation of additional credit becomes easier because of such saving, and this may raise the threshold at which credit-financed investment leads to inflation. But lack of demand reduces the link between consumption expenditure and profit, as implied in the equation between net investment spending and profit. The higher the savings of households in relation to financial requirements for investment of business, the lower the possibilities of self-financing by business in the form of passing the additional costs of investment to the consumers by price rises. This applies as long as the central bank follows a restrictive monetary policy. At the level of macroeconomic equilibria, increasing household saving creates household demand for property in productive assets—which business reacts to by restricting investment due to lack of demand (Meade 1963: 673).

Labor is increasingly divided between the alternatives of saving and price stability on the one hand, and employment-creating monetary expansion on the other. Those who are threatened by unemployment favor job-creating expansive monetary policy. The regular staff, especially skilled workers, saves at an increased rate and therefore prioritizes price stability, which is also because here jobs are relatively safe.[5]

Already-established enterprises can impose profit-levels which cannot be reduced by new competitors. They do not benefit from demand-fostering expansionary monetary policies because of the dangers of inflation. Learning costs of possible new entrants require higher prices, which would come with an expansionary monetary policy. Imperfect competition and growing mass welfare lead to tensions. The central bank invokes these threats and counteracts these tensions by imposing restrictive monetary policies. They imply the threat of unemployment. The underconsumptionist crisis which may result does not lead to falling prices nor the devalorization of fixed capital as in the case of perfect competition. Unemployment therefore becomes structural.

The two classes of a capitalist market economy must cooperate in order to manage the situations of parallel inflationary and deflationary tendencies—they cannot do it without the other class. Labor must avoid exploiting all possibilities of wage increases in case of full employment. They must do so in order to make full employment economically and

[5] Helmut Schmidt's witticism of preferring 5% inflation to 5% unemployment no longer seems to be politically applicable.

politically possible during periods of high growth rates, which guarantee long-term high profit rates to business. This requires opting for a high growth path that is sufficient for attracting the surpluses based on market imperfections to be invested back into the economy. These are rents masquerading as business profits. Neo-corporatism, as that which exists in West Germany, requires the successful concentration with a high growth path and a strong working-class organization. If such a high growth path is missed as a result of the bargaining of the two sides—labor and business—then labor further becomes weakened. This is because business is not able to accelerate growth through capacity increasing investment spending.

3.3 Obstacles for Moralization of Capitalism in Case of Imperfect Competition

In a capitalist market economy with perfect competition, its two classes do not need an understanding of what is happening above them on the macroeconomic level that allows them to reach full employment and positive profit rates. They must merely want to enrich themselves. They reach macroeconomic equilibrium despite this not being their explicit intention. By raising real wages, labor does not want to contribute to more profitability of business. In a similar way, business does not want to increase the bargaining power of labor by spending on investment.

Capitalism and autonomous civil (bourgeois) society became possible because the economy could be managed in "anonymous" ways without an identifiable regulator. Precapitalist or "noncapitalist" economies with their "moral economy" require a consensus of the major social forces as to the aims of society. Not so for capitalism. It is this absence of the necessity of consensus around such aims that eliminates the threat of civil war or enslavement of the minority by the majority. This implies that in a capitalist market economy, the two classes can be mobilized only for relatively simple goals like increasing material well-being of any worker or any enterprise.

The implied low adjustment costs are no longer given: With increasing diversification of production, business becomes capable of imposing profits beyond necessary spending on investment—whereas labor no longer transfers incomes as demand for consumption goods when welfare increases. The system no longer operates according to textbook assumptions. Over a large range of underemployment, high transaction costs and increasing mass welfare allow the appropriation of monetary incomes, which no longer are going back into the production process. Businesses use additional monetary resources—for which there are no investment opportunities in the real economy—to purchase financial assets. Stock exchange speculation is one form of this. Because of high living standards and fear of unemployment due to deficient demand, labor, in a similarly way, uses important shares of its income for savings for a more secure future. Declining intensity of competition and rising mass welfare lead to the emergence of incomes which by the forms of their spending no longer create demand for the real economy without causing inflation against the saving workers or deflation against investment shy entrepreneurs.

The growing complexity of products and improving mass welfare pushes the system to a monetary illusion of its participants. Increasing stocks prices rarely increase the capacity of business for productivity increases (exception: access to cheap money for financing investment by issuing additional stock). Stock exchange speculation provides profit only if new speculators are ready to buy stock in the hope that the rates will further rise. If expectations about the expectation-based future behavior of fellow speculators deteriorate, then the market topples, loans given to the speculators are withdrawn, and the monetary mass invested in shares turns out to be a mere bubble.

But labor is also subject to monetary illusion. Labor considers saving as guarantee for the future. However, income not used for consumption is rarely actually stored for the future. At a macroeconomic level, non-consumption leads to lower production. Even if it is a durable consumer good, it is normally not stored for the future. If households in the Federal Republic of Germany transformed their savings into purchases—for example because they really do not do well—they could acquire additional products only to the limit of full capacity utilization of the productive apparatus. Even the attempt to buy from abroad would lead to a rapid deterioration of the external value of the German currency if the increasingly negative balance of trade would be not compensated by capital imports or liquidation of capital assets held abroad.

The contemporary discussion about old-age pensions demonstrates that the two classes of a capitalist market economy do not admit their own monetary illusion, even though they must face it in important but limited areas. Old-age pensions paid by the active generation of workers as contribution for the elderly may create legal entitlements to similar financing of the young generation's own old-age pensions in the future. Such payments are, however, narrowly linked to the future productive potential. Actual savings of private households do not increase the capacity of the economy to satisfy the promises for the future. Therefore, the actual restraint in consumption does not influence the future capacity of the economy to supply a surplus for old-age pensions. Today's contributions from actually active workers to today's pension payments for the elderly do not increase productive capacities of the future without entrepreneurs increasing investment (which can be financed by paper money through bank credit). Therefore, it is suggested to opt for private provision in the form of contributing to capital-based pension funds. Such savings, however, can be spent in the future only if in the future there are productive capacities to satisfy demand articulated on the basis of these private holdings. This means that the generation which is active in the future may not accept to pay for the elderly to the promised extent. This generation of the future may not accept to reduce its own consumption demand in favor of a level of demand articulated out of savings of the elderly and accept inflation. If the old-age pensioners want to consume one-third of the future production, then the active population must remain satisfied with two-thirds of the production they themselves have produced. In both cases, this mechanism applies totally independently from the form of financing of old-age pensions.

The a-moral character of capitalism depends on two conditions: low living standards of workers with correspondingly low propensity to save, and perfect competition with correspondingly low differentiation of production and therefore low shares of knowledge creation in productivity increases. Only if these two conditions are met will the simple struggles for enrichment of business and labor lead to macroeconomic equilibria with full employment. With more complex productive operators, there are barriers to entry based on knowledge, whereas welfare of labor raises the savings of households. Thus, both classes striving for more money no longer lead to economic growth but instead to lack of demand.

The decision to invest—the most vulnerable articulation of the different social structures in capitalism—is exposed to further strains (Elsenhans 1989: 18). The decision to invest is left to private business in capitalism. This is because with perfect competition, the assumption is justified that private business as a whole cannot realize "money"—i.e., earn profit on the market—if they do not spend on investment at the same time. The decision to invest is so important that it can be left to capitalist entrepreneurs only in case there is perfect competition. This renders formally private decision-making on investment exposed to real social control by competition. Article 15 of the German Basic Law and the Law on Stability of 1967 reflect this social embeddedness of property in means of production. Within capitalism, property is bound by social obligations and is not truly private. Therefore, the only place where property in means of production can be unbound from social obligations (and be truly private) is outside of capitalist structures—i.e., in rent-based structures where surpluses can be appropriated directly in their material forms, like a product or a labor rent. Whenever one of these two classes exit from this logic—either business by finding imperfect competition or labor by rejecting consumption—they would have to agree on macroeconomic mechanisms and prioritize macroeconomic equilibria, full employment, and growth instead of monetary enrichment. Labor would have to develop sufficient trust in the future in order to dispense with a rising propensity to save. Business as a class would have to accept a lowering of its demand for financial profits to the level of the requirements for financing net investment.

Both conditions seem to be difficult to realize. Each individual worker's household can increase its future security by saving more than average workers' households. Under perfect competition, total amount of profits depends on net investment, but the more successful enterprise can improve their growth possibilities by improving their profit rate in comparison with other enterprises because of higher competitiveness. Each enterprise will continue to strive for as high profits as possible. It will do this even in case these incomes in reality constitute rents which the respective enterprise can use immediately for a demand of goods and services. The anonymity of the market allows each particular agent to better achieve its goals by "non-cooperation." Also, under the new conditions of rising mass welfare and restricted competition, non-cooperation allows the individual enterprise the opportunity to gain more in relation to competing enterprises. Furthermore, non-cooperation between business and labor allows more economic gains for most individual enterprises than concentration on macroeconomic equilibria with full employment and high growth.

The two classes of a capitalist market economy can overcome this type of prisoner's dilemma by engaging in agreements on norms of behavior. They will have to remove the a-moral character of capitalism. They would have to admit the truly instrumental character of enrichment for the maintaining of the conditions of operation for capitalism.

Additionally, they would have to develop norms on how to limit the aspiration to enrichment without at the same time removing the mechanism of competition.

Both parties would have to agree on a moral pact which fixes norms of behavior. They would have to reach an agreement although the mechanisms of forcing them to do so have lost in efficiency. The disciplining function of competition is already restrained by knowledge-based, at-least-temporarily monopolistic situations. The utilization of income paid to labor for demand-creating purchases of produced products is weakened. Such a pattern can only further limit competition. Such a break may be compatible with further technical progress, because technical progress also existed in precapitalist societies. However, it excludes automatic sanctions against non-efficient producers of the type common for capitalist market economies. In that case, economic agents like enterprises (e.g., special segments of the working class, local governments, etc.) can engage in negotiations with other agents through which the anonymity of the market is removed. These negotiated rules structure exchanges between the agents.

The logic of such processes has been described in my analysis of state classes in the Third World (Elsenhans 1996c [1981]). If the anonymity of the market is removed, the emergence of rents follows shortly after (Elsenhans 1992). Rents were repressed under capitalism because the poor were capable to impose higher consumption standards for themselves.

The only surplus which could be appropriated was that which was proven necessary for investment spending. It was proved necessary by past really realized investment spending and in that case in the form of profit on an anonymous market. When masses no longer strive only for material improvement and the range of products is differentiated so that knowledge-based monopolies emerge, the possibilities for a-moral capitalism dwindle. Capitalism becomes immoral because of too low pressure from the side of mass demand. It becomes determined by political conflicts between all agents which no longer are subject to market competition. In this conflict, business is better placed than labor.

Comparing this immoral situation to the a-moral model of the market, it becomes clear that this a-moral character had a liberating effect for the humans. If the restricting impact of perfect competition and the growth of mass welfare no longer allow measuring economic success by the standard of monetary incomes, then a new moralization in the form of a new social contract becomes necessary, which must be negotiated outside the market. In such a social contract, it is not probable that the liberation of the individual from moral obligations can be maintained. It is also not very probable that the new obligations can be limited to a minimum. This is because the emerging structure of negotiations creates great incentives for those participating in these negotiations to overcome difficulties in applying new regulations just by enacting new regulations, very similar to the growth of state classes.

The market is a-moral. There are doubts that there is greater possibility of individual development within a more moral system which is more or less consciously agreed upon by negotiation. This does not mean that the return to capitalism of perfect competition is possible. It implies, however, that the impending end of the bourgeois age with its a-moral market provokes regret.

References

Afheldt, Horst. 1995. Ausstieg aus dem Sozialstaat? Gefährdungen der Gesellschaft durch weltweite Umbrüche. Aus Politik und Zeitgeschichte 25/26: 3–12.

Afheldt, Horst. 1996. Standortbestimmung zwischen Zollschranken und schrankenlosem Wettbewerb. Vorwärts (January): 12–15.

Bhaduri, Amit. 1986. *Macroeconomics. The Dynamics of Commodity Production*. London: Macmillan.

Elsenhans, Hartmut. 1976. Die Neue Internationale Wirtschaftsordnung – Chancen für die Überwindung von Unterentwicklung oder die letzte Karte im Kampf der Industrieländer um die Aufrechterhaltung der ungleichen Spezialisierung? Das Beispiel des Integrierten Rohstoffprogramms und der exportorientierten Industrialisierung. *Internationale Entwicklung* 2: 13–27.

Elsenhans, Hartmut. 1979a. Gesellschaftsreform und Wirtschaftswachstum. Akkumulationsprobleme in der Bundesrepublik. *Forum DS. Zeitschrift für Theorie und Praxis des demokratischen Sozialismus* 4 (8): 135–170.

Elsenhans, Hartmut. 1979b. Grundlagen der Entwicklung der kapitalistischen Weltwirtschaft. In *Kapitalistische Weltökonomie. Kontroversen über ihren Ursprung und ihre Entwicklungsdynamik*, ed. Dieter Senghaas, 101–148. Frankfort on the Main: Suhrkamp.

Elsenhans, Hartmut. 1980. Gesellschaftliche Reformen in der Dritten Welt gegen Konzessionen in der Weltwirtschaftsordnung. *Wirtschaftsdienst* 60, 10 (October): 482–485.

Elsenhans, Hartmut. 1981. Social Consequences of the NIEO. No Change for Continued Reformist Strategies in the Centre without Structural Change in the Periphery. In *Elements of World Instability: Armaments, Communication, Food, International Division of Labour*, ed. Egbert Jahn and Yoshikazu Sakamoto, 86–95. Proceedings of the Eighth International Peace Research Association Conference. Frankfort on Main, New York: Campus.

Elsenhans, Hartmut. 1983a. Égalité et développement. L'expérience européenne et le monde sous-développé d'aujourd'hui. *Cultures et développement* 15 (2): 187–215.

Elsenhans, Hartmut. 1983b. Rising Mass Incomes as a Condition of Capitalist Growth. Implications for the World Economy. *International Organization* 37 (1): 1–38.

Elsenhans, Hartmut. 1987. Absorbing Global Surplus Labor. *Annals of the American Academy of Political and Social Science*, 492: 124–135.

Elsenhans, Hartmut. 1989. Public Administration in Developing Countries: Specificities of the Notions of "Public" and "Administration" in Market Regulated Developing and Capitalistic Societies. *Indian Journal of Public Administration* 35 (1) (January–March): 16–26.

Elsenhans, Hartmut. 1991. Economie sous-développée et société civile: surcharge du système politique et possibilités de pluralisme politique. In *Actes du Colloque: Pluralisme social, pluralisme politique et démocratie. Cahier du CERES, Série Sociologie No. 19* (Tunis), ed. CERES, 23–52.

Elsenhans, Hartmut. 1992. Ein neues internationales System. In *Staat und Demokratie in Europa*, ed. Beate Kohler-Koch, 244–268. 18. Wissenschaftlicher Kongreß der Deutschen Vereinigung für Politische Wissenschaft. Opladen: Leske und Budrich.

Elsenhans, Hartmut. 1994. Rent, State and the Market. The Political Economy of the Transition to Self-Sustained Capitalism. *Pakistan Development Review* 33 (4): 393–428.

Elsenhans, Hartmut. 1996a. Gegen das Gespenst der Globalisierung. In *Jahrbuch Arbeit und Technik 1996: Zukunft der Industriegesellschaft*, ed. Werner Fricke, 25–36. Bonn: Dietz.

Elsenhans, Hartmut. 1996b. Mythos Weltgesellschaft. *epd Entwicklungsdienst* 18 (September): 15–23.

Elsenhans, Hartmut. 1996c [1981]. *State, Class and Development*. New Delhi, London, Columbia, MO: Radiant; Sangam; South Asia Books.

Elsenhans, Hartmut. 1997a. Das Gespenst der Globalisierung: Grenzen der Internationalisierung des Kapitalismus für die Herausbildung transnationaler Gesellschaftsstrukturen (1). *IWVWW Forschungsberichte* 7 (56) (March): 11–34.

Elsenhans, Hartmut. 1997b. Das Gespenst der Globalisierung: Grenzen der Internationalisierung des Kapitalismus für die Herausbildung transnationaler Gesellschaftsstrukturen (2). *IWVWW Forschungsberichte* 7 (57) (April): 22–30.

Elsenhans, Hartmut. 1997c. Über Bedingungen und Chancen zu einer sozial verträglichen und dann auch vertieften Globalisierung der Weltwirtschaft. In *Jahrbuch Arbeit und Technik 1997: Globalisierung und institutionelle Reform*, ed. Werner Fricke, 147–158. Bonn: Dietz.

Göcke, Matthias. 1996. Formen ökonomischer Hysteresis. Zeitschrift für Wirtschafts- und Sozialwissenschaften 116 (1): 31–58.

Habakkuk, Hrothgar J. 1972. Fluctuations and Growth in the 19th Century. In *Studies in Economics and Economic History*, ed. by H. M. Robertson and M. Kooy, 259–279. London: Macmillan.

Irsch, Norbert. 1979. Lohnbestimmungsmechanismen bei restringierten Substitutionsbeziehungen. Kritische Analyse grenzproduktivitätstheoretischer Verteilungsaussagen. Aachen: Rheinisch-Westfälische Hochschule Aachen.

Kazancigil, Ali. 1992. La démocratisation des sociétés musulmanes. Le cas de la Turquie. NAQD – Revue d'Études et de Critique Sociale (2): 32–46.

Keynes, John Maynard. 1939. Relative Movements of Real Wages and Output. *Economic Journal* 49 (193): 34–57.

Kothari, Rajni. 1986. NGO's, the State and World Capitalism. *Economic and Political Weekly* 21 (50): 2177–2183.

Meade, James E. 1963. The Rate of Profit in a Growing Economy. *Economic Journal* 73 (292): 665–674.

Montgomery, Arthur. 1938. *How Sweden Overcame the Depression*. Stockholm: Alb. Bonniers Boktryckeri.

Richardson, H. W. 1967. *Economic Recovery in Britain, 1932–1939*. London: Weidenfeld & Nicolson.

Roepke, Wilhelm. 1936. *Crises and Cycles*. London et al.: William Hodge.

Rosenberg, Hans. 1934. *Die Weltwirtschaftskrise von 1857–1859*. Stuttgart, Berlin: Kohlhammer GmbH.

Say, Jean-Baptiste. 1972. *Traité d'économie politique* [1803]. Paris: Calmann-Lévy.

Sinn, Hans Werner. 1975. Das Marx'sche Gesetz des tendenziellen Falls der Profitrate. *Zeitschrift für die gesamte Staatswissenschaft/Journal of Institutional and Theoretical Economics* 131 (4): 647–696.

Sohn-Rethel, Alfred. 1973. *Ökonomie und Klassenstruktur des deutschen Faschismus*. Frankfort on Main: Suhrkamp.

Tönnies, Ferdinand. 1935. *Gemeinschaft und Gesellschaft* [1887]. Grundbegriffe der reinen Soziologie. Berlin: Curtius.

Tucker, Rufus S. 1936. Real Wages of Artisans in London, 1729–1935. *Journal of the American Statistical Association* 31 (1): 73–84.

Woytinsky, Wladimir. 1936. *Les conséquences sociales de la crise*. Geneva: International Labour Office.

CHAPTER 4

Individualist Household Strategies for Future Security: A Basis for the Decline of Welfare Capitalism

Hartmut Elsenhans

A widely shared conviction emerged with the fall of the Berlin Wall that the existing and newly dynamized capitalist world economy can assure almost indefinite growth. The only noticeable criticism has come from environmentalists, who see a limit to economic growth in the exponential destruction of nature. The warning calls of the 1930s have been silenced. Keynesianism, the theoretical underpinning of the mixed economy which responded to the challenges of the 1930s and the 1940s, has been supplanted by new forms of neoclassical economics, which have even

Originally published as: Elsenhans, Hartmut (1999): Individualistische Strategien der Haushalte zur Zukunftssicherung. Grundlage für den Niedergang des wohlfahrtsstaatlichen Kapitalismus. In: *Comparativ. Leipziger Beiträge zur Universalgeschichte und vergleichenden Gesellschaftsforschung* 9 (3), pp. 114–142.

H. Elsenhans (✉)
University of Leipzig, Leipzig, Germany
e-mail: helsen@rz.uni-leipzig.de

© The Author(s), under exclusive license to Springer Nature Switzerland AG 2021

H. Warnecke-Berger (ed.), *Development, Capitalism, and Rent*,
https://doi.org/10.1007/978-3-030-62605-1_4

appropriated major post-Keynesian findings, such as the absence of a rise of the capital-output ratio, and integrated them into a new, supply-side-oriented version of neoclassical economics, the theory of endogenous growth (Elsenhans 1999, 2000b, 2002).

In opposition to this optimistic view about the future of capitalism, I argue that the Keynesian warnings about capitalism being threatened by a lack of demand are still quite pertinent. In demonstrating this danger, I draw on previous works dealing with the relation between capitalism and growing mass incomes (Elsenhans 1983a, b, 1997b). But the focus of this contribution will be on the impact of the increased propensity of households to save, a mechanism which can potentially cause a crisis for capitalist growth if households do not have enough trust in the future to deter their preference for amassing savings.

I argue that, in a purely individualistic society where individuals can protect themselves against unknown future dangers only by saving, rising household incomes discourage consumption in the present in favor of the future potential for consumption, hence savings, which are expected to increase when household savings rise more rapidly than household incomes.

I examine the effects of the increase in total savings on economic growth in the cases both of a constant capital productivity and of a declining capital productivity. There are several possibilities for coping with the challenges which emerge in both cases. The redistribution of assets in the business sector through declining profits because of falling demand and hence falling prices in the wake of increased household savings cannot dispossess business. Increasing wages beyond productivity increases leads to stagflation. The creation of a new outlet for savings by enlarging the markets for financial assets will crowd out employment-creating investment in the real economy. I conclude that each of these potential solutions to underconsumptionist tendencies caused by increasing household savings will lead to underemployment and a slow-down of economic growth. Finally, I will discuss some of the political-economic implications that my economic model has on the perspectives of capitalist systems.

The implications that the necessity of increasing mass incomes and mass spending can have on the international competitiveness of an economy are not discussed in this contribution, as I have shown elsewhere that the price competitiveness of an economy does not depend primarily on the level of its real wages but on its exchange rate (Elsenhans 2000a, 2002).

The paper is organized as follows. Section 4.1 provides statistical evidence for the importance of private household savings in a major industrialized economy, Germany, where, most likely due to historical reasons, the level of confidence in continued prosperity is much lower than in the United States.

Section 4.2 of the paper contains a description of the basic structure of the model. I have deliberately chosen the simplest possible model in order present as clearly as possible the impact of the assumed trend toward increasing household savings.

Section 4.3 comprises a discussion of the impact increased savings have on growth under the assumption of a constant capital-output ratio, the most likely empirical relation between capital and output according to new endogenous growth theory, the leading school of neoclassical economics. The conclusion of this section is that, with rising propensities to save and productivity-oriented wage increases, explosive growth with (unrealistically) high increases in the rate of growth of labor productivity, hence the rate of technical progress, will ensue.

In Sect. 4.4, I remove the assumption of a constant capital-output ratio. In this case, the stock of fixed capital will rise more rapidly than national income. Even if the stock of business-owned-capital net of indebtedness rises at a lower rate than the total stock of fixed capital, the ultimate decline of the profit rate ($\pi = P/B$) is inevitable (where $[P]$ is business-profit net of amortization and $[K]$ the total accumulated business-owned fixed-capital net of amortization and indebtedness). Overaccumulation and underconsumption appear to be only two variants of the same crisis scenario. They are distinguished only by the varying capacity of business to anticipate the inevitable future crisis.

In Sect. 4.5, I discuss the competition between private savings and business profits for financing reduced amounts of investment if total demand decreases below the level of full capacity utilization of the productive apparatus. I conclude that in any theory which explains productivity increases not only by physical capital, but also by unknown, but enterprise-specific, or known, but not completely mobile, enterprise-specific complementary factors, the solution, proposed by Meade (1963: 673), of dispossessing business from its assets by driving down profits (via decreasing prices) through private household savings cannot work. Instead, underconsumptionist unemployment will emerge.

In Sect. 4.6, I examine the possibility of wages increasing more rapidly than productivity leading to a rise in consumption in line with the increase of the productive potential. I conclude that this will lead to stagflation.

Furthermore, the creation of new outlets for savings by means of booming financial markets, dealt with in Sect. 4.7, will crowd out investment yielding low profit rates due to lack of demand.

The paper takes the position that capitalism—especially if it is characterized by increasing capital productivity, as assumed in the new economy—requires a social and political set-up where individualism is complemented by a reliable social-security network, which can only be guaranteed by the institution of the state.

4.1 Increased Savings of Private Households

The savings of private households are becoming an important macroeconomic element, at least in some countries of Continental Europe. In Germany, middle-income households with one gainfully employed member save between one-sixth and one-eighth of their monthly incomes.

Accumulated net savings of private households in 1998 amounted to 158% of annual household incomes and 86% of the accumulated fixed assets of the enterprise sector (excluding housing rental).[1]

Due to the efficiency of capitalist entrepreneurs in using scarce financial resources, the total amount of productive property is limited. Capitalism is not a system whose main characteristic is the accumulation of capital. If a capitalist economy with constant employment and a constant capital-output ratio were to be described on the basis of synchronized labor costs (von Weizsäcker and Samuelson 1971) engaged in the production of its different components, there would be no capital accumulation at all. At a constant capital-output ratio, which is the normal case for capitalist growth, the stock of fixed capital does not increase in relation to national income, so that with constant levels of employment this economy would not grow, but only become more productive, if measured in such labor "values (Table 4.1)."

Businesses may use the additional financial resources generated by additional household savings to accelerate the formation of fixed capital,

[1] See Table 4.1.

Table 4.1 Savings, investment and monetary assets in Germany 1991–1998 (in billion DM if not otherwise noted)

	1991	*1992*	*1993*	*1994*	*1995*	*1996*	*1997*	*1998*
Disposable household incomes	1,878.2	2,014.7	2,084.1	2,156.3	2,238.1	2,311.3	2,354.7	2,410.5
Private savings	247.9	259.2	254.8	250.3	262.8	264.9	259.9	254.3
Total accumulated monetary savings (net)	2,304.4	2,455.8	2,719.9	2,815.7	3,048.0	3,234.2	3,522.3	3,800.0
Total gross investment of enterprises	409.2	403.8	354.9	357.2	395.0	371.9	428.5	496.6
Total monetary investment of enterprises	128.9	138.8	159.1	111.5	131.2	127.5	92.3	237.4
Non-distributed profits	31.0	14.4	26.2	24.6	46.9	27.4	57.2	74.4
Amortization	253.9	276.6	294.1	301.6	310.0	314.7	320.3	327.2
Degree of self-finance of gross investments (%)	62.0	72.1	90.3	91.3	90.3	94.0	88.1	80.8
Accumulated net investment apart from housing	3,598.4	3,868.9	4,019.2	4,159.3	4,260.7	4,305.3	4,398.7	n.a.

Data from Monatsberichte Deutsche Bundesbank (1999); Statistisches Jahrbuch für die Bundesrepublik Deutschland, various volumes which also implies employment-creating demand. If technical progress, however, is not a linear function of the amount of capital spent on investment, it may be too limited in relation to the available fixed capital which has to be accumulated in order to maintain full-employment demand, so that the profit rate ultimately falls. In a Keynesian perspective, an entrepreneur may stop the process of accumulation before the profit rate falls because he anticipates this type of future crisis, so that total demand decreases before the profit rate declines for lack of technical progress (although it declines ex post in this case for lack of demand in the wake of too limited spending on new investment). The importance of expanding mass demand as a counterweight to both types of crisis—falling profit rates because of overaccumulation and lack of outlets—will be advanced below.

4.2 Basic Assumptions of the Model

This paper avoids dealing with conflicts between different economic schools where these conflicts are deemed irrelevant to the argument at hand. The following assumptions are considered uncontroversial or at least permissible for the construction of the model:

- An inverse causal relationship exists between the level of employment and the bargaining power of labor. Wage increases in line with productivity increases cannot be realized via market mechanisms without a scarcity of labor. Only the reciprocal relationship is controversial.
- The net investment of business is equal to the savings of business if there is a balanced external sector, a balanced government sector and zero net savings of private households. The ex-post net profit of business corresponds to gross investment minus amortization.
- Private households' propensity to save is positive and increases with rising real household incomes.
- Net investment of business which corresponds to the technically feasible growth path of the economy and which is supposed to create full employment depends on the expectations of business, i.e., on its perceptions of the future development of profitability and demand.[2]

[2] The center-left social-democratic government of Germany was warned by a leading German business journal against cutting wages too severely with the argument that

The model is run under the assumption that total labor supply is constant. Technical progress is assumed to be a function of time. It is also assumed that spending on technical progress may accelerate technical progress, but not indefinitely. Although the model cannot predict a ceiling for the increase in labor productivity through technical progress, technically leading economies have not been known to have had growth rates beyond ten percent per annum, whereas growth rates of around five percent per annum have been characteristic for extremely dynamic epochs of capitalism.[3]

National income (Υ) comprises investment goods production (I) and consumption goods (C). Income is distributed to households as wages (W) and to business as profits (P).

Households use their incomes for savings (SH) and consumption (C). Business uses its incomes (P) for savings. Total savings (S) is the sum of (P) and (SH). The following definitions hold:

$$Y = C + I = W + P = C + SH + P \tag{4.1}$$

National income is a function of the total amount of capital K utilized in production and its productivity β, so that the following also holds:

$$Y = \beta K \tag{4.2}$$

Capital productivity, with is inverse to the capital-output ratio (K/Υ), determines the relation between the rate of growth (k) of the capital stock (K) and the rate of growth (y) of the national income (Υ).

$$y = k\left(\frac{\beta_{t-1}}{\beta_t}\right) \tag{4.3}$$

declining or stagnating real wages will not necessarily lead to innovation, cf. Mundorf (1999: 2).

[3] If there are no limitations to the financial surpluses available for investment because of the absence of rising mass incomes, the profit rate in the business sector invariably declines if rises in factor productivity are not equal to the increase in capital stock. If rises in capital productivity are equal to rises in capital stock, the growth rate of the overall system and its component parts increases in an explosive manner until the share of wages in total national incomes tends to zero, cf. Elsenhans (1995), Chapter 5 in this volume; 1994).

The profit rate is defined as

$$\pi = \frac{P}{K} \tag{4.4}$$

The share of net profit in national income is (P/Y).
An at least constant rate of profit (π) depends on an at least constant rate of growth (p) of profit (P), with

$$p \geq \pi \tag{4.5}$$

If capital productivity (β) declines, the first derivative of (β) will become negative $(\beta' < 0)$. The growth rate (y) of national income becomes lower than the growth rate of the stock of capital (k) (which is equal to the rate of growth of profit $[k = \pi]$). Hence

$$\pi = k > y, \tag{4.6}$$

so that because of (4.5)

$$p > y \tag{4.7}$$

Under the same condition, a constant rate of profit $(\pi = P/K)$ requires an increase in the share of profit in net national income (P/Y).[4] In this case, wages (W) grow less rapidly (at the rate $[w]$) than national income (y), corresponding to the slower growth of total factor productivity. The model does not imply a specific rate of wage increase. But, for reasons not implicit in the model, real wages have to rise.[5]

In this model, we also introduce an assumption about the development of private household savings (SH).

$$f_{SH}(W);\ f'_{SH} > 1;\ f''_{SH} > 1 \tag{4.8}$$

We assume that private households increasingly opt for the satisfaction of future needs if the financial resources at their disposal increase. Marginal

[4]This is similar to the basic equation of the theory of accumulation of Helmstädter (1969: 51). From $i/i_{t-1} > y/y_{t-1}$ and $i = p$ follows $p/y > p_{t-1}/y_{t-1}$.

[5]From von Bortkiewicz (1907) it follows that unit costs have to decrease for known products and products which substitute until then consumed products. New products which satisfy new needs imply increasing demand, hence—under the assumption that consumption is realized only through spending out of wages—rising real wages.

utility of current needs decreases due to their increasing satisfaction so that with constant marginal utility of future needs the preference of private households for future needs increases. The model does not make any assumptions about the reasons for an increased propensity of private households to save. Plausible reasons which can be mentioned here are the fear of joblessness during the period of gainful activity, concerns about the imponderability of old age which intensify as the average period of retirement increases, etc.

4.3 Increased Savings and Unrealistically Explosive Growth in Contradiction Even with Endogenous Growth Theory

The readiness of entrepreneurs to invest on the basis of credit depends on their readiness to bear risk in order to increase profits. It decreases with an increase of borrowed capital in their total financing and increases with rising differentials between the rate of profit and the interest rate (z). The capital stock is composed of two parts: (K_B) constitutes the business-owned-capital-stock net of private business debt; the (K_{SH}) is owned by business but financed from debt.

If we assume that entrepreneurs want to limit risk, then they will incur debt for financing investment if profits are promising. Their readiness to take loans increases with the share of their own capital in the stock of their assets and hence a low level of indebtedness and decreases with higher interest rates in relation to expected profit rates. The readiness of entrepreneurs to incur debt, measured by the variable (L) (loan capital), in order to finance additional investment beyond the increase in (K_B) can be defined as

$$L = f_L\left(\pi - z, \frac{K_B}{K}\right) \tag{4.9}$$

where (K) indicates the value of the accumulated stock of fixed capital, only part of which (K_B), is owned by the business sector.

Full-employment demand is reached if the following condition is fulfilled:

$$f_L\left(\pi - z, \frac{K_B}{K}\right) = SH \tag{4.10}$$

The growth of the system can be defined on the basis of Eq. (4.1) as follows:

$$i\frac{I}{Y} = p\frac{P}{Y} + sh\frac{SH}{Y}; \; y = sh\frac{SH}{Y} + p\frac{P}{Y} + c\frac{C}{Y} \tag{4.11}$$

At constant capital productivity (Y/K), productivity-oriented wages imply ($y = w$), so that according to Eq. (4.8) ($sh > w$), and ($sh > y$). The rate of growth of profits (p) can be constant according to Eq. (4.11) if ($i > y$), as with ($i = y$) and ($sh > y$) it necessarily follows that ($p < y$). Upholding the condition that profits (P) increase in line with national income (Y) implies a rate of growth of investment (i) higher than the rate of growth of national income (y). If ($i > y$), the rate of growth of profit (p) and the rate of profit (π) as well as the identical rate of growth (k_B) of the business-owned capital stock (K_B) can remain equal to the rate of growth of national income (y), a situation which implies that business can maintain at least its share in national income.[6]

But with constant capital productivity (β), and ($i > y$), the rate of growth of investment (i) cannot remain constant over time, but has to rise, so that the rate of growth of national income (y) also has to rise.

With ($p = y$) and a constant capital productivity, an increasing propensity of private households to save can be accompanied by full employment if the rate of growth of investment increases. Hence, the rate of growth (k) of the stock of capital (K) has to increase. If capital productivity (β) is constant, the following holds: ($y = k_{t-1}$, $y_{t-1} = k_{t-2}$), etc., so that ($y > y_{t-1} > y_{t-2}$).

The rate of growth of national income is equal to the rate of growth of labor productivity under the condition of a constant supply of labor. With constant capital productivity, an increase in the rate of growth of capital stock requires an explosive increase of labor productivity.[7]

[6] Annual profits P and the corresponding growth rate p and the total accumulated stock of business-owned capital K_B and its growth rate (because the rate of profit $\pi = P/K$ is identical with the rate of growth of the stock of capital owned by business if profits are reinvested) are interdependent: $\pi = (1 + p)(P_{t-1}/K_{t-1})$. If $p > \pi$, π approaches p until $p = \pi$, cf. Elsenhans (1994: 423–425).

[7] Based on the values proposed by Emmanuel of (π) around ten percent and the capital-output ratio of about three, the model shows that the rate of profit goes up to values between 30 and 60 between the fourth and sixth period, so that because of ($\pi = k = y_{t+1}$) the rate of growth of labor productivity has to reach similar values. This level of

Its unlikeliness is supported by the arguments of neoclassical endogenous growth theory, which tries to defend the neoclassical theory against the counterclaims of Keynesianism. Endogenous growth theory[8] explains the relative stability of the capital-output ratio, a phenomenon observed by Keynesians.[9] Keynesians, in line with Bortkiewicz, have taken the stability of the capital-output ratio as an indicator of the necessity of rising mass incomes. Endogenous growth theory argues that the capital-output ratio remains constant because of supply-side processes resulting from a link between technical progress and factors of productivity growth which are complementary to capital accumulation. If the capital-output ratio can remain constant because of the supply of additional, unmeasurable factors of technical progress, such as skill formation, scientific research, "human capital," inventions, it is highly improbable that a mere increase in the amount of annually invested physical capital would automatically increase the supply of these supplementary factors.[10]

4.4 Increased Savings May Lead to Underconsumptionist "Overaccumulation" with an Inevitably Declining Rate of Profit

Let us drop the assumption of a constant capital-output ratio. The rate of growth of national income (y) is assumed to be lower than the rate of growth of the stock of fixed capital (k). I have shown elsewhere that for any ($k > y$) the share of consumption (C/Y) has to fall if the profit rate is to be maintained, and that, because of this, the possibility of unlimited growth on the basis only of growing capital spending (and of growing demand for investment goods) does not exist (Elsenhans

technical progress has never been observed. Emmanuel (1982: 168) and Elsenhans (1986: 272).

[8] Cf. e.g., Romer (1986, 1994) and Pack (1994).

[9] Kendrick (1961: 166), Fabricant (1959), Helmstädter (1969), and Gillman (1957: 38).

[10] This argument can be substantiated by arguing that rising mass incomes limit an increase in the capital-output ratio on the basis of two mechanisms: The scope for financing additional investment decreases so that the rate of capital accumulation decreases (less money is available for the exploitation of new technologies, only the relatively productive ones are used), whereas, on the other hand, economies of scale raise the rate of technical progress, cf. Elsenhans (1999).

1994: 423–426). We then introduce private household savings, which are assumed to be supplied to investors at very low costs with the purpose of preserving their currently owned resources for future purchasing power. These savings are assumed to be supplied at a zero interest rate.

If ($k > y$), capital productivity (β) has to decline. My intention is to prove that the profit rate (π) then has to decrease, even if the share of savings of private households in total savings ($SH/(SH + P)$) increases and households do not get interest (as assumed here).

The stock of capital (K) grows at the rate (k). It is assumed that the part of the capital stock which is owned by business (K_B) and which is financed out of profit grows at the rate ($k_B = \pi < k$), and that the rate of growth of the share of capital stock which is financed out of savings (K_{SH}) grows with ($k_{SH} > k$). Because of ($k > y$), the following holds: ($k_{SH} > y$). The growth of the capital stock and its component parts can thus be described as follows:

$$k = sh\frac{SH}{I} + \pi\frac{P}{I}; k_{SH} > \pi, k_{SH} > k > y \tag{4.12}$$

We introduce β_t/β_{t-1} as the rate of change of capital productivity β', with $\beta' > 1$ signifying an improving capital productivity and $\beta' < 1$ a falling capital productivity. The growth of the various components of national income can be described as follows:

$$y = sh\frac{SH}{Y} + p\frac{P}{Y} + c\frac{C}{Y} = i\frac{I}{Y} + c\frac{C}{Y} \tag{4.13}$$

$$\beta' k = \beta\left(k_{SH}\frac{SH}{I} + \pi\frac{P}{I}\right) = y = sh\frac{SH}{Y} + p\frac{P}{Y} + c\frac{C}{Y} = i\frac{I}{Y} + c\frac{C}{Y} \tag{4.14}$$

Because ($k_{SH} > k > y$), it follows that ($sh > y$) and (SH/Υ) increases. How (P/Υ) will change cannot be determined from the model. The growth rate (π) of (K_B) may be higher or lower than (y). Because ($k > y$), the rate of growth (i) of annual investment outlays, and hence also the rate of growth of the sum of ($SH + P$), has to be higher than (y), so that ($i > y$). A rise in the share of investment in total national income is only possible as long as ($C/\Upsilon > 0$), but with decreasing shares of consumption due to increasing savings, the value of (C/Υ) approaches zero. The process of accumulation in this model can only be maintained as long as (C/Υ) decreases. If $(cC/y\Upsilon \leq 0)$, hence if the share of consumption in national income can no longer be lowered for physical or political reasons, this process of accumulation is blocked. This process of accumulation can continue as long as $(cC/y\Upsilon)$ is high, hence as long as there is a large share of consumption in national income, and $(c > 0)$, hence a positive growth rate of consumption, so that the increase of $(i > y)$ can be compensated by $(0 < c < y)$. The model accommodates a decreasing propensity to consume which, at particular levels of the share of consumption in national demand, can be compensated by capital intensive growth. Such a process is blocked when the share of consumption in national income declines beyond a critical level, where a further decline in (C/Υ) can no longer compensate the higher rate of growth of investment (i) relative to the growth of national income (y). This threshold depends on the possibility of consumption growth having negative values, which, however, is a limited option politically. It is clear that the borderline case of $(c = 0)$ depends on a variety of factors, possibly non-economic ones too. In the model presented here, this threshold can exist at any level of the share of consumption. There are no assumptions about a specific level or rate of growth of consumption that has to be maintained, although $(c < 0)$ seems unacceptable in a democratic society, at least in periods of peace, or even in a totalitarian society if there are no non-economic factors working against this tendency.

The decisive factor is that $(c < 0)$ will occur even if capitalists refrain from increasing the rate of their capital accumulation beyond the rate of growth of national income, so that (12) can be modified with all earnings from accumulated capital going to business. There is no income accruing from interest. (SH) is financed, at least in the borderline case, only from savings.

The borderline case is characterized by the following relationship: The rate of growth of household savings (sh) has grown more rapidly than the rate of growth of wages (w), so that it reaches a share (SH/W) that cannot be further increased. At this level of private household savings $(sh = w)$. According to (4.12), $(k_{SH} > k > \pi)$ can no longer hold, as the rate of expansion of private household savings (k_{SH}) and of (K_{SH}) is reduced to the rate of growth (w) of wages (W), which cannot grow more rapidly than national income (y) if the rate of growth of profits (p) is at least as high as the rate of growth of national income (y). In the borderline case, $(k_{SH} = y = w)$ with $(k > k_{SH})$ because of a declining capital productivity (β). The profit rate has to decline with a declining (k_{SH}) because, due to a declining (k_{SH}), (k) and, hence with a declining capital productivity (β), (y) also decline. A constant or, for a limited period, rising (y) was possible despite declining capital productivity, because households supplied additional investable funds for which they received only little interest (in the model, no interest at all). Thus, despite declining capital productivity, the growth rate of profits (p) and hence the rate of profit (π) could be maintained, as all additional surplus went to the capitalists. When ($k_{SH} > y$) is no longer possible, the components of the capital stock (K_B) and (K_{SH}) grow at a maximum at the same rate as national income for the previous period: (k_B) because of the assumption made in this part of the discussion that capitalists are wise enough not to increase their own stock of capital beyond the rate of growth of national income, and (k_{SH}) because the rate of growth of private household savings (SH) can no longer be higher than (w), which, if ($p = y$), is equal to (y).

Either the economy returns to the golden-rule rate of growth, with the rate of growth of national income and capital stock being equal, or capitalists opt for increasing their own accumulation of capital by raising the rate of growth of profit to above the level of the rate of growth of national income, with the implications described above on the decline of the rate of profit. As the effect of the decline in capital productivity (β) is initially weaker than the effect of the rise in investable sources due to an increasing (sh), the economy seems to grow at first through the additional investible resources supplied by households which have been "disciplined" enough to save for growth, but the economy ultimately suffers from the overaccumulation of financial resources, even if disproportionately growing savings are not expected to yield additional returns. With an ever increasing share of investment in national income, the process of accumulation is inevitably blocked at some point because of a lack of technical progress. Thus, if accumulation goes unchecked, unemployment occurs and, because of a decline in the rate of accumulation, the profit rate declines.

The growth of the resources available for accumulation beyond the growth of national product and technical progress eventually leads to a decline of the rate of profit, either due to lack of consumption or to overaccumulation.[11]

[11] Roepke (1936: 90) "There exists in fact a close connection between the fundamental ideas of the underconsumption theory and the overcapitalization doctrine presently described, even if this connection may be difficult to acknowledge in the face of the unscientific formulation of the popular variety of the underconsumptionist theory."

Whether entrepreneurs stop the process of growth when the profit rate falls due to an oversupply of financial resources in relation to technical progress or whether the process stops due to the expectation of entrepreneurs that the decline of the rate of profit is inevitable (Hicks 1982: 41; Harrod 1952: 273) is probably not such a relevant question.

The two elements which, according to Eq. (4.9), determine the propensity of business to attempt transforming private household savings into business investment will decline in approaching crisis. The profit rate (π) will decline, and with the usual limits to a decline in the rate of interest (z), the relation ($\pi - z$) has to decline. As the profit rate ($\pi = P/K_B$) is also the rate of growth of business-owned fixed-capital net of debt, a declining profit rate also implies a decline in the ratio (K_B/K) if all other variables remain equal.

According to Eq. (4.9), the decline in the rate of profit (π) will lead to a change in investment behavior of entrepreneurs, as (L) decreases.

A decrease in the propensity to finance investment from borrowed funds implies the emergence of a demand gap if (SH) does not also decrease, and, in any case, a decline in the rate of profit, which may also lead to a demand gap. It is highly improbable that households will increase their spending on consumption in periods of diminished job security.

4.5 The Impossibility of a Redistribution of the Stock of Fixed Capital Through Savings

From Sects. 4.3 and 4.4 it follows that the redistribution of assets between business and private households by means of savings is extremely difficult, because it implies rapid and accelerating growth, especially growth of labor productivity. If capital productivity declines because labor productivity no longer rises in line with capital accumulation, the inevitable decline in the rate of profit ultimately leads to unemployment.

With increasing private household savings tensions emerge on the demand side. Equation (4.9) shows that in a credit-financed process of accumulation the risk factors increase up to a level where the accumulation process is stopped, either because the profit rate has to fall due to overaccumulation or because entrepreneurs refuse to engage in overaccumulation and turn to liquidity preference so that the share of their own property in their assets increases.

Decreasing demand due to savings implies that enterprises can no longer sell their products at prices which secure a profit, the sum of all profits (P) of the business sector equaling net investment (I) minus private savings (SH) (Kalecki 1971: 13). This perspective implies that households will not only reduce their demand by means of savings, but may also force entrepreneurs to devalorize their own capital and accept lower, perhaps even zero profit rates. The implied microeconomic equation of ($I = S = P + SH$) is, however, a simplification in an economy with book money, which may have no real counterpart in the form of assets in the real economy. This becomes evident in the reaction of entrepreneurs to slackening demand; entrepreneurs will react by cutting back production. This mechanism was described by Sohn-Rethel with respect to German big industry during the Great Depression of the 1930s and was presented as proof for the end of the Pigou effect (Sohn-Rethel 1973: 47–51). During the Depression prices no longer fell more rapidly than nominal wages (which had been one major effect of maintaining demand during crises in the nineteenth century).[12]

The following two assumptions seem to correspond to reality: Not all enterprises suffer to the same extent from low or even negative average profit rates; the costs of financing fixed capital differ from enterprise to enterprise according to the degree of self-financing. Less efficient enterprises are the first to close their doors. Even at identical levels of technical efficiency, enterprises do not all go bankrupt at the same time in the case of falling profit rates; the first to do so are those with a low rate of self-financing. As enterprises withdraw from the market, supply decreases and prices can be defended. Similar mechanisms result from the (possibly increased) importance of enterprise-specific knowledge for increasing productivity.

The theory of endogenous growth has borrowed from post-Keynesian growth theory the notion that the contribution of physical capital to technical progress is only of relative importance. Newcomers do not have the knowledge of established enterprises at their disposal, even if markets are otherwise perfect (Romer 1987, 1990; Grossman and Helpman 1994). Research on human capital, knowledge, disembodied technical progress and other elements of technical innovation show that at least some parts

[12] Tucker (1936), Keynes (1939), Richardson (1939), Habakkuk (1972: 275), Rosenberg (1934: 185), Woytinsky (1936), Mowat (1968: 452, 493), Montgomery (1938: 52), and Rostow (1938).

of these additional and complementary productivity-increasing factors are not mobile between enterprises. Labor skills are not only the result of the time spent in formal training institutions, but are also the result of learning by doing. Such learning is enterprise-specific. The effects of learning by doing can be compared with a soccer team where each member is used to playing with the others.

Because of complementary factors of technical progress established enterprises can keep their prices above the costs of production of new entrants, even with otherwise perfect competition. No enterprise can be forced by other enterprises in comparable situations to dispense with a minimum profit rate. Only newcomers which for one reason or another would be willing to accept long-term losses and at the same time are highly productive could push prices below the accepted minimum profit rate of competitors.

With stable capital-output ratios and moderate growth rates of productivity, amortization has become the most important source of finance for investment. In Germany, up to 80% of gross investment in the business sector is financed from amortization (see Table 4.1). The factors of technical progress characterized as complementary to physical capital depend on gross investment—as technical progress is linked to the replacement of old investment goods with new ones—and not on net investment. The higher the share of amortization in gross investment, the higher the advances of established enterprises in relation to newcomers in the creation and reproduction of these complementary factors of technical progress.

Private households will not be able to undersell established enterprises except in totally new branches where the factors associated with learning by doing do not play an important role. The so-called new economy could be cited as an example of such an exception.

4.6 Short-Term Solutions Aggravate the Problem: The Demand Gap Cannot Be Closed by Rising Real Wages if There Is a Rising Propensity to Save Out of Household Incomes

With increasing household savings, wage increases sufficient for the clearing of commodity markets and which create incentives for net investment have to be higher than the rise in labor productivity and thus lead to stagflation. With a rising propensity to save, real wages would have to increase more rapidly than national income if consumption is to keep pace with productivity growth. This implies a cost-push inflationary effect which compensates the demand-pull deflationary effect of less consumption in relation to wages paid.

By definition, real wages would then grow more rapidly than labor productivity (y). Both definitions imply, by definition, a rising share of wages are put into savings.

$$w > y, c = y, c < w < sh \tag{4.18}$$

Different forms of labor incomes directly channeled into investment have been the subject of considerable discussion in Western Europe. The underlying thought is that the financial resources paid out by an enterprise or a group of enterprises as wages but not used by the beneficiaries for their consumption or their own strategies of financial accumulation are given back to the enterprises as risk capital, e.g., for old-age pensions. These constitute tax-free retained earnings until the old-age pensions are paid out.

If the argument presented in Sect. 4.5 of this paper holds, enterprises can limit the share of this loan capital in total financing because they are able to raise prices due to productivity-increasing complementary factors acquired through learning by doing as well as due to amortization. The cost push caused by wage increases being higher than productivity increases can be passed on to the customers without established enterprises running the risk of being undersold by new start-ups, as the new start-ups have to pay similar wage rates without enjoying the productivity-increasing effects of having already engaged in production.

For the reasons outlined in Sect. 4.5, the deflationary tendencies originating from household demand increasing less rapidly than the incomes received by households from the business sector will not compensate the inflationary tendency, but contribute to unemployment. In the model, the net effect of inflationary and deflationary tendencies will depend on the value of (f_{SH}) at the respective level of real wages and on (f_L) at the level of ($\pi - z$) and (K_B/K) achieved.

As increasing shares of capital financed from debt and a lower difference between ($\pi - z$) are assumed to reduce the propensity to finance investment from loans, any effort of the monetary authorities to curb inflation (caused by wage increases higher than productivity) by raising (z) will reduce (L).

The model implies a possible explanation for stagflation, which cannot be elaborated here. With full employment, inflation is inevitable if household savings increase. With price stability, unemployment is inevitable because and to the extent that households do not use their incomes for effective demand.

4.7 The Transfer of Household Savings to Financial Markets Leads to the Intensification of Deflationary Tendencies in the Real Economy

It could be argued that households have no real interest in taking over the real assets of current business owners. It is reasonable to assume that they only want to buy assets which allow them to hoard purchasing power for an unknown future.

We therefore introduce financial markets where assets are traded, the amount and value of which do not directly depend on the growth of the stock of physical capital, but on expectations and the supply of fresh money. The supply of fresh money is assumed to be provided by the increase in household savings (SH).

As long as financial markets are supplied with such additional financial resources, the value of shares will not decrease as a result of low dividends. Expectations about the development of the value of shares are no longer determined by the capacity of businesses to earn profits but by expectations concerning the future development of share values. Demand for such financial assets grows as long as there are financial resources available which accrue to the financial markets. The buyer of options for future purchasing power interprets the higher prices of shares as an accrual to his property, hence as an earning. Increasing dividends become less important for the purchasing of shares than the predictions of analysts about the future prices of these shares.

As assets increase their value due to speculation, it is possible that the volume of financial assets held by portfolio holders grows much more rapidly than the stock of real capital in the economy. The increase in the German stock market value from 1992 (498.3 billion DM, 80.4 billion DM from private households) to 1998 (3,286.9 billion DM, 491.9 billion DM from private households, Deutsche Bundesbank 1999) is far greater than the increase in the value of fixed capital of the enterprise sector in Germany, roughly 800 billion DM from 1991 to 1997 (see Table 4.1) and of property and the participation of German companies abroad (293 billion DM in 1992, 609 billion DM in 1999, 50; 2001: 62).[13]

The opportunities for investment on growing financial markets are attractive because they liberate profits from the fetters of the real economy of goods and services. Profits no longer depend on the expansion of demand for goods and services created by net investment spending,[14] but only on the supply of financial markets with cheap money.

Cheap money is normally considered a source of inflation, especially if it overheats the real economy. In the model presented here there is not necessarily an inflationary tendency on the markets for goods and services. The additional supply of money promotes saving and does not manifest itself on the markets for goods and services. The only inflationary process which takes place is the rise of share prices, which the central bank and the portfolio holders interpret as an increase in wealth.

The deflationary tendencies triggered by the slow growth of real consumption in combination with increasing shares of savings in private household spending work in favor of cheap-money policies. Investment projects have to have expected rates of return which are at least as high as the returns from future increases in the price of assets on financial markets.

Financial resources will be shifted to financial markets if profit expectations in the real economy are low or negative. With high earnings on financial markets, investment becomes impossible in areas of the real economy where profit rates are low. The effect of falling prices due to low demand is blocked.

4.8 Conclusion

The paper has focused on the impact of household savings on growth and effective demand. The model is based on the assumption of post-Keynesian and endogenous growth theory about factors complementary to the formation of fixed capital being decisive for maintaining capital productivity. It introduced an additional source of finance, household

[13] All data from Monatsberichte der Deutschen Bundesbank, various issues.

[14] Cf. Glyn (1997: 608), on growing profits despite lower net investment in Great Britain in the 1980s.

savings, which is assumed to grow more rapidly than wages and national incomes. The shift of financial resources from consumption to investment in the model does not necessarily constitute a lack of demand which triggers an underconsumptionist tendency with negative employment effects, as usually argued. Problems arise, however, as soon as we consider the possibility that the factors complementary to fixed capital formation and considered responsible for maintaining capital productivity may not be supplied in a completely elastic manner.

The benign case, with its assumption of a constant capital-output ratio, demonstrates that increasing shares of national income supplied for investment can be absorbed only if there is rapidly growing labor productivity. If we drop the assumption of a completely elastic supply of technical progress, capital productivity, by definition, decreases in the model. As long as enterprises continue to borrow despite possibly, but not immediately, declining profit rates, and households continue to restrict consumption and, thus, the share of consumption in national income, a pattern of growth of this sort can be self-supporting for quite some time, but cannot continue indefinitely despite increases in national income and capital stock.

We can therefore argue that the observed constant capital-output ratio is not the result of the supply of complementary factors of production such as skills and human capital highlighted in endogenous growth theory, but the consequence of a limited availability of financial resources for additional investment.[15] The mechanisms which maintain a constant capital-output ratio observed by post-Keynesian economics and neoclassical new endogenous growth theory are linked to the scarcity of labor and the increase in consumption accompanying this scarcity which justifies capacity-increasing net investment, the basis of profit.

In neoclassical theory, consumption is not considered a support for growth. But at low enough wages all available resources are invested. This inevitably leads to full employment and scarcity of labor. With labor scarcity, profitable enterprises compete for labor until the marginal cost of labor has risen to the (decreasing) level of marginal product of labor. Post-Keynesian economics will certainly not disagree with neoclassical

[15] This may be complemented by the productivity-increasing effects of this scarcity of resources and labor, such as intensified competition due to rapidly expanding and relatively homogeneous markets, and increased possibilities for standardization and process innovation.

economics about the positive effect of rising real wages in a growth process which leads to labor scarcity. I myself have shown that this assumption is based on specific economic conditions which do not apply to all national economies of the capitalist world economy (Elsenhans 1994: 394–399). Underdeveloped economies are characterized by a structurally low level of marginal product which causes structural unemployment (Elsenhans 1997a). Post-Keynesians would, however, disagree with the automaticity of reaching full employment through investment implied in the neoclassical model.

By introducing household savings as a source of investment, investment is no longer simultaneously supply and demand-driven. There are additional supplies of resources for investment, but not all wages paid to labor are spent on consumption.

In none of the variants of the model does an increase in financial resources for investment lead to more stable long-term growth. If technical progress is characterized by elastic growth due to disembodied complementary factors, full employment can be maintained with very high growth rates of invested financial resources, which are effectively transformed into physical capital. If we abandon this unrealistic assumption, a decline in capital productivity, and ultimately the profit rate, is inevitable. If factors complementary to physical capital are important for productivity, households cannot take advantage of the reluctance of enterprises to commit new financial resources (originating from household savings) for investment in order to appropriate assets from the business sector. According to the Bortkiewicz criterion, the capital-output ratio also cannot grow indefinitely (Elsenhans 2000a: 9–12). Thus, the amount of fixed capital necessary for a certain volume of production is limited in a capitalist system by the growth of effective demand; the increase in capital is ultimately a result of the increase in effective demand, of which consumption demand is an essential part. This paper tends to support the view that, because of this limit to production, the amount of assets which can be owned as property rights in capitalism is restricted. This implies that the amount of property rights, which is the source of future incomes, is also limited.

So-called overaccumulation and underconsumptionist crises are thus merely two sides of the same coin: insufficient increases in mass consumption. Insufficient increases in mass consumption cannot be compensated by additional spending on investment, because this would ultimately lead to a decline of the profit rate. Increasing wages more rapidly than productivity in order to compensate private household savings leads to stagflation. The possibility of acquiring assets, the amount of which is not dependent on the fixed capital employed in the goods and services sector, depends on a lavish monetary policy and money creation in the financial markets which ultimately raise the rate of profit to levels where full-employment investment levels in the real economy are not achieved.

The desire for future security, which was considered the main motive of households to increase their savings when current needs are largely satisfied, therefore, requires another solution apart from private savings, i.e., a guarantee for access to future purchasing power which is not based on a reduction of current consumption, but on property rights to a national income which has to be produced in the future at a time when the holders of these property rights are no longer capable of delivering goods and services in exchange for these property rights.

The paper therefore implies that without an alternative structure to deal with unknown future risks, individual private households will increase their propensity to save with increasing household incomes because of a shift in preferences, the reasons for which are not further investigated here. If this argument is correct, the survival of a capitalist system will depend on finding new avenues for satisfying the need for security in the face of unknown future risks.

4.9 Perspectives

For post-Keynesians, the private ownership of means of production is a matter of delegated rights. These rights are delegated in the interest of society to produce goods and services at the lowest possible costs. But even in Keynes' day, investment spending was considered too important a factor for maintaining employment to be left only in the hands of entrepreneurs (Keynes 2018 [1936]: 30–38; Richardson 1939). When private households become so prosperous that they develop a preference for future security over the satisfaction of their current needs, the role of coordinator and initiator assigned to the state acquires a new dimension.

The model presented here reveals the class character of a capitalist society. There is a limited amount of assets. Households may become prosperous and refuse to spend their incomes—at least a substantial part of them—on goods produced in the present and supplied by the business sector. Instead, they develop an interest, comparable to that of the property-owning class, in assets which can guarantee future incomes. Yet by increasing their savings they only disempower themselves through unemployment.

The political embeddedness of capitalism can no longer be limited to the state guarantee of a legal order which only secures the property rights of existing goods and services. It has to be extended to welfare-state-style social rights.

As individualistic solutions cannot provide the more prosperous households with enough assets for securing future incomes, the needs felt by these households have to be satisfied outside the market-regulated part of the economy. Society itself has to direct this process and ensure that it is democratic. The market is left to regulate where it is capable of this task; society regulates where the market falls short. The perception of capitalism implied here is different from the Anglo-Saxon one, a representative example of the latter being North's (1988) contributions on institution-building. In the Anglo-Saxon perspective, capitalism is a "natural" system, even if it has to be developed by society on the basis of incentives for economic gain. In the Rhenish (Albert 1991) conception, capitalism is a manmade institutional set-up which is permanently endangered, particularly by the very classes which stand to benefit the most from it, i.e., the rich. The richer classes of a capitalist society do not so much strive for profit, appropriated under competitive conditions on the basis of additional demand created by investment spending, but rent. The system can only be maintained if surpluses for investment are reduced to the level required for financing innovation and the capacity expansion triggered by rising mass incomes. Thus, the overall system depends on the capacity of the masses to assert their interest in rising mass incomes,[16] as well as on the acceptance of this form of class struggle by the richer classes. The question of the impact of savings on the capitalist growth process is therefore not merely a technical one; it is an element of the overall struggle to maintain capitalism.

[16] Rising mass incomes are also possible in an era of "globalization," because with international price competition exchange rates matter more than real wages, so that wage restriction will lead to global underconsumption and the import of rentier structures into the West from the South. This argument is developed in Elsenhans (1981, 1987, 1992: 260; 2000a, 2002).

4.10 List of Symbols

$L = f_L(\pi - Z, K_B/K)$	Loan as absorption of private savings of households depending on the difference between the rate of profit π and the rate of interest z, as well as the development between the share of capital stocks owned by private business and total capital stock
B	Y/K
β'	Change of β/β_{t-1}
C, c	Consumption and its growth rate
I, i	Investment and its growth rate
K, k	Capital stock (net) and its growth rate
K_{SH}, k_{SH}	Capital stock (net) financed from private household savings and its growth rate
K_B, k_B	Capital stock owned by business and its growth rate
L	Loan capital
P, P	Profit and its growth rate
SH, sh	Private household savings and their growth
$f_{SH}(W)$	Savings of private households as a function of their real incomes
W, w	Sum of wages and its growth rate
Y, y	Net national income and its growth rate
Z	Interest
Z	Interest rate
π	Profit rate

Acknowledgements I would like to thank Prof. Hubert Hieke (then Lugano, now Warsaw) for his many instructive comments.

References

Albert, Michel. 1991. *Capitalisme contre capitalisme*. Paris: Editions du Seuil.

Deutsche Bundesbank. 1999. Die gesamtwirtschaftlichen Finanzierungsströme im Jahr 1998. *Monatsberichte der Deutschen Bundesbank* 51 (6).

Elsenhans, Hartmut. 1981. Social Consequences of the NIEO. No Change for Continued Reformist Strategies in the Centre without Structural Change in the Periphery. In *Elements of World Instability: Armaments, Communication, Food, International Division of Labour*, ed. Egbert Jahn and Yoshikazu Sakamoto, 86–95. Proceedings of the Eighth International Peace Research Association Conference. Frankfort on Main, New York: Campus.

Elsenhans, Hartmut. 1983a. Égalité et développement. L'expérience européenne et le monde sous-développé d'aujourd'hui. *Cultures et développement* 15 (2): 187–215.

Elsenhans, Hartmut. 1983b. Rising Mass Incomes as a Condition of Capitalist Growth. Implications for the World Economy. *International Organization* 37 (1): 1–38.

Elsenhans, Hartmut. 1986. Der Mythos der Kapitalintensität und die notwendig falsche Technologiewahl der Entwicklungsländer. In *Technik und internationale Politik*, ed. Beate Kohler-Koch, 267–290. Baden-Baden: Nomos.

Elsenhans, Hartmut. 1987. Absorbing Global Surplus Labor. *Annals of the American Academy of Political and Social Science*, 492: 124–135.

Elsenhans, Hartmut. 1992. Ein neues internationales System. In *Staat und Demokratie in Europa*, ed. Beate Kohler-Koch, 244–268. 18. Wissenschaftlicher Kongreß der Deutschen Vereinigung für Politische Wissenschaft. Opladen: Leske und Budrich.

Elsenhans, Hartmut. 1994. Rent, State and the Market. The Political Economy of the Transition to Self-Sustained Capitalism. *Pakistan Development Review* 33 (4): 393–428.

Elsenhans, Hartmut. 1995. Überwindung von Marginalität als Gegenstand der Armutsbekämpfung. In *Bevölkerungsdynamik und Grundbedürfnisse in Entwicklungsländern*, ed. Hans Bernd Schäfer, 193–221. Schriften des Vereins für Socialpolitik 246. Berlin: Duncker und Humblot. Chapter 5 in this volume.

Elsenhans, Hartmut. 1997a. The Relevance of the Principles of Keynesian Economics for the Transition to Capitalism in Today's Underdeveloped World. In *Improving the Global Economy. Keynesianism and the Growth in Output and Employment*, Paul Davidson, and Jan A. Kregel, 283–303. Cheltenham, Lyme: Edward Elgar.

Elsenhans, Hartmut. 1997b. Rent and the Transition to Capitalism. *Asien – Afrika – Lateinamerika* 25 (6): 651–686.

Elsenhans, Hartmut. 1999. Wirtschaftswachstum und institutionelle Entwicklung. Korreferat zum Beitrag von Rainer Klump. In *Neue Wachstums- und Außenhandelstheorie – Implikationen für die Entwicklungstheorie und –politik*, ed. Renate Schubert, 115–128. Schriften des Vereins für Socialpolitik, Band 269. Berlin: Duncker und Humblot.

Elsenhans, Hartmut. 2000a. Globalisation in a Labourist Keynesian Approach. *Journal of Social Studies* (89): 1–66.

Elsenhans, Hartmut. 2000b. Political Economy or Economic Politics? The Prospects of Civil Society in an Era of Globalization. *Indian Journal of Public Administration* 46 (4): 567–600.

Elsenhans, Hartmut. 2002. Macroeconomics in Globalization. Productivity, Wages, Profits, and Exchange Rates in an Era of Globalization. *Brazilian Journal of Political Economy* 22, 1 (85): 53–78.

Emmanuel, Arghiri. 1982. Reply to Hartmut Elsenhans. In *Appropriate or Underdeveloped Technology? Followed by a Discussion with Celso Furtado and Hartmut Elsenhans*, ed. Arghiri Emmanuel, 158–186. Chichester et al.: Wiley.

Fabricant, Solomon. 1959. *Basic Facts on Productivity Changes*. Occasional Paper 63. New York: National Bureau of Economic Research.

Gillman, Joseph Moses. 1957. *The Falling Rate of Profit; Marx's Law and Its Significance to Twentieth-Century Capitalism*. London: Dobson.

Glyn, Andrew. 1997. Does Aggregate Profitability Really Matter. *Cambridge Journal of Economics* 21 (5): 593–619.

Grossman, Gene M., and Elhanan Helpman. 1994. Endogenous Innovation in the Theory of Growth. *Journal of Economic Perspectives* 8 (1): 23–44.

Habakkuk, Hrothgar J. 1972. Fluctuations and Growth in the 19th Century. In *Studies in Economics and Economic History*, ed. H.M. Robertson and M. Kooy, 259–279. London: Macmillan.

Harrod, Roy Forbes. 1952. *Economic Essays*. London: Macmillan.

Helmstädter, Ernst. 1969. *Der Kapitalkoeffizient. Eine kapitaltheoretische Untersuchung*. Stuttgart: Gustav Fischer.

Hicks, John. 1982. *Money, Interest and Wages. Collected Essays on Economic Theory*. Oxford: Basil Blackwell.

Kalecki, Michal. 1971. *Selected Essays on the Dynamics of the Capitalist Economy 1933–1970*. Cambridge: Cambridge University Press.

Kendrick, John W. 1961. *Productivity Trends in the United States. A Study by the National Bureau of Economic Research*. Princeton, NJ: Princeton University Press.

Keynes, John Maynard. 2018 [1936]. *The General Theory of Employment, Interest, and Money*. Cham: Palgrave Macmillan.

Keynes, John Maynard. 1939. Relative Movements of Real Wages and Output. *Economic Journal* 49 (193): 34–57.

Meade, James E. 1963. The Rate of Profit in a Growing Economy. *Economic Journal* 73 (292): 665–674.

Montgomery, Arthur. 1938. *How Sweden Overcame the Depression*. Stockholm: Alb. Bonniers Boktryckeri.

Mowat, Charles Loch. 1968. *Britain Between the Wars 1918–1940*. London: Methuen.

Mundorf, Hans. 1999. Becks Rezepte sind zu einfach. *Handelsblatt*, July 16/17: 2.

North, Douglas C. 1988. Theorie des institutionellen Wandels. Eine neue Sicht der Wirtschaftsgeschichte. Tübingen: J.C.B. Mohr.

Pack, Howard. 1994. Endogenous Growth Theory. Intellectual Appeal and Empirical Shortcomings. *Journal of Economic Perspectives* 8 (1): 55–72.

Richardson, Henry. 1939. Real Wage Movements. *Economic Journal* 49 (195): 425–441.

Roepke, Wilhelm. 1936. *Crises and Cycles*. London et al.: William Hodge.

Romer, Paul M. 1986. Increasing Returns and Long-Term Growth. *Journal of Political Economy* 94 (2): 1002–1037.

Romer, Paul M. 1987. Growth Based on Increasing Returns Due to Specialization. *American Economic Review* 77 (2): 56–62.

Romer, Paul M. 1990. Endogenous Technological Change. *Journal of Political Economy* 98 (5): 71–102.

Romer, Paul M. 1994. The Origins of Endogenous Growth. *Journal of Economic Perspectives* 8 (1): 3–22.

Rosenberg, Hans. 1934. *Die Weltwirtschaftskrise von 1857–1859*. Stuttgart, Berlin: Kohlhammer GmbH.

Rostow, Walt Whitman. 1938. Investment and the Great Depression. *Economic History Review* 8 (2): 136–158.

Sohn-Rethel, Alfred. 1973. *Ökonomie und Klassenstruktur des deutschen Faschismus*. Frankfort on Main: Suhrkamp.

Tucker, Rufus S. 1936. Real Wages of Artisans in London, 1729–1935. *Journal of the American Statistical Association* 31 (1): 73–84.

Bortkiewicz, Ladislaus von. 1907. Wertrechnung und Preisrechnung im Marxschen System (3). *Archiv für Sozialwissenschaft und Sozialpolitik* 25 (2): 445–489.

Weizsäcker, Carl C.von, and Paul A. Samuelson. 1971. A New Labor Theory of Value for Rational Planning Through Use of Bourgeois Profit Rate. *Proceedings of the National Academy of Sciences, USA* 68 (6): 1192–1194.

Woytinsky, Wladimir. 1936. *Les conséquences sociales de la crise*. Geneva: International Labour Office.

PART II

Rent, Marginality, and Pitfalls of Development

CHAPTER 5

Overcoming Marginality as an Objective of the Struggle Against Poverty

Hartmut Elsenhans

Underdeveloped economies can be defined as economies structured by marginality of large masses of the population. Essential mechanisms of capitalist economies as described in mainstream economics do not work in these economies: At low levels of development, a substantial part of the available labor force adds less to production than necessary for physical survival. Additionally, while average income is higher, marginal income is lower due to decreasing returns in agriculture. Not all types of technical progress contribute to removing rent and marginality, such

Originally published as Elsenhans, Hartmut. 1995. Überwindung von Marginalität als Gegenstand der Armutsbekämpfung. In *Bevölkerungsdynamik und Grundbedürfnisse in Entwicklungsländern. Schriften des Vereins für Socialpolitik 246*, ed. Hans Bernd Schäfer, 193–221. Berlin: Duncker und Humblot.

H. Elsenhans (✉)
University of Leipzig, Leipzig, Germany
e-mail: helsen@rz.uni-leipzig.de

© The Author(s), under exclusive license to Springer Nature Switzerland AG 2021

H. Warnecke-Berger (ed.), *Development, Capitalism, and Rent*,
https://doi.org/10.1007/978-3-030-62605-1_5

as a general increase in productivity or an intensification of competition. Marketization does not necessarily overcome marginality. In the labor surplus theory of underdevelopment, the possibility of mobilizing such labor surpluses for "capitalist" investment was modeled. It did not realize its goals because real wages, and hence internal demand, did not substantially increase, owing to these economies' high degrees of marginality. These contradictions explain the tendency toward increased state interventionism as a plausible result.

If such economies open up to a world economy that is dominated by developed capitalist economies, additional tendencies to reduce employment emerge. To escape the marginality trap, instruments of the non-market economy are necessary, such as income redistribution or "nonprofitable" investment. The deepening of the integration of underdeveloped economies into the world economy launched spontaneous tendencies which reduce the incentives to apply such instruments, i.e., income redistribution or "nonprofitable" investment. Within underdeveloped countries, it follows that rents shall emerge; however, the political structures of these underdeveloped countries do not promote the utilization of these rents toward pushing economic growth and employment—nor do they expand mass demand. In such a situation, export subsidies are justified. Successful export orientation can be understood as being based on the same material conditions as state-planned restructuring of the productive apparatus by non-market oriented investment spending. Both are characterized by the channeling of rent. In both cases, increasing productivity of agriculture is decisive. In state-planned restructuring of the economy, raising marginal productivity of agricultural labor is decisive. In case of export orientation with export workers subsidized from local food production, raising average productivity is sufficient.

The struggle against marginality—by means of increasing average and especially marginal productivity of labor in agriculture—must be the decisive goal of strategies aiming at the overcoming of poverty by means of market regulation.

Policies characterized by "help for the poor" should be rejected when they are not embedded in appropriate macroeconomic strategies that do not consider the overcoming of poverty as a condition for market-regulated economies. Only overcoming poverty renders possible market-regulated growth processes—which in that case do not require particular political interventions for poverty eradication outside of agriculture. This will allow us all to propose limits and new definitions of the role of the non-market economy in the process of transition to capitalist growth.

5.1 The Emergence of Marginality and Rent in the Transition to Capitalism

5.1.1 A Basic Model with Marginality in Agriculture

An underdeveloped economy is characterized by a still low level of technical development.[1] The law of diminishing returns in agriculture applies: Fertile land is scarce. In case of demographic growth, food production must be increased. Available agriculturally useful land must be cultivated more and more intensively, or less fertile land must be put into cultivation. In case of decreasing marginal returns, marginally productive workers will tend more and more to produce less than they require for their survival and the survival of their nuclear families (so-called subsistence income or barebones income).

The following graph is based on the assumption of agricultural production being represented by one single and uniform product, and productivity of factors of production is measured in units of factors of production employed and units of production achieved.

The argument can be represented as follows Fig. 5.1.

Production is described by the function $Y = f(O)$, with $f' > 0$, and $f'' < 0$ beyond A.[2]

Factors of production engaged in agriculture are only labor services, measured as number of substance units produced by active workers. All active workers (O for occupied) receive only subsistence incomes (w) independently of the marginal product of their labor. The cost of these active workers is $W = wO$ as represented by the straight line. The production of these active workers is represented by the curve in the upward graph, which has the form of a lying parabola ($y = x^2$). In case of capitalist means of production, production would increase until the point A_1 where $f'(Y) = w$. Tax amounts to a maximum of 50% of the surplus and

[1] For similar approaches refer to: Georgescu-Roegen (1960: 32–40), and Bai (1982). Nearly all labor surplus models are based on similar assumptions, and concentrate however on praxeological recommendations for planners, cf. as examples among many Fei and Ranis (1964: 13–18).

[2] $f_1 = 10\sqrt{x}$, $f_2 = 10\sqrt{x} - 12,5$ $f_3 = 10\sqrt{x} - 18,75$.

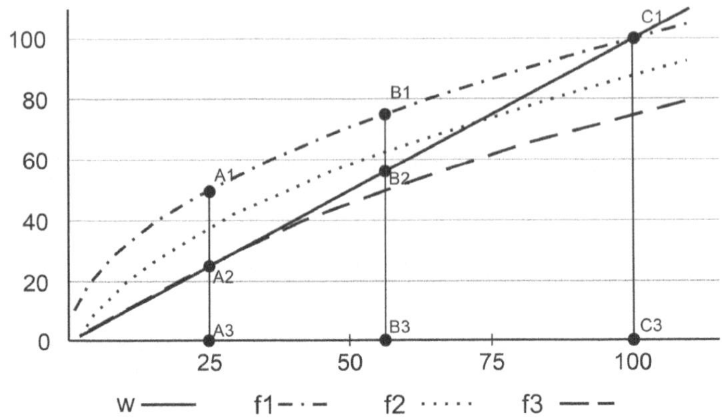

Fig. 5.1 The Marginality-Cum-Rent Model. Citation: own elaboration

subsequently decreases as shown by the difference between function f_2 and the straight line. The total amount of the surplus in the hands of the landlords is maintained. It is possible to reach employment beyond A_3 by subsidizing marginal labor. In our case, total employment more than doubles (represented by B_2). Total employment in our case more than doubles (represented by B_2).

Beyond C_1 no society can exist on its own. If society is divided between privileged ones who own the fertile land and the propertyless workers, the maximum employment corresponding to the production level C_1 cannot be reached. Beyond A_1, the surplus of agriculture—defined as the difference between production and labor costs in agriculture—decreases. I call this level of production the threshold of marginality. Any additional worker consumes more than he contributes additionally to production and is therefore marginal. His being marginal implies that, in case of surplus maximizing owners of land, he must be shed. There is a maximum level for productive activity in agriculture. At that level, a surplus of agriculture emerges by necessity.

This maximum level of surplus in agricultural production is to be distinguished from the food surplus of the agricultural economy, defined as commercially available surplus for nonagricultural consumers. Those who are active in agriculture also consume non-food items. Their spending for non-food items is financed from the sales of food which is not appropriated as economic surplus by the owners of land, or the state.

These parts of the food production are exchanged at their production value for products of the non-food economy. This commercialized food surplus is defined as the sum of food not consumed by the agriculturally active workers and the lords. This food surplus of agriculture is assumed to feed labor which produces goods and services for the privileged ones and for the agricultural producers. The food surplus of agriculture is larger than the surplus of agricultural production. It comprises both food exchanged by agriculture with the nonagricultural sectors of the economy and the exchange of food for mass consumption goods for the agriculturally active workers.

In case of class separation between owners of land and landless workers in the closed economy, maximum employment is the sum of those whose marginal production in agriculture is still higher than the cost of labor and those who satisfy their demand for nonagricultural goods and services and the sum of those who are paid by the owners of land for their luxury goods and services. These elements of demand depend on the consumption habits of the landowners.

Not all elements of demand which are part of this maximum employment are determined in the same manner by social structures. Those elements can be considered as being part of the basic volume of activity:

1. Maximum in agriculture before reaching the threshold of marginality as labor produces a surplus above subsistence level;
2. Those employed in the production of non-food goods and services for those employed in agriculture;
3. Nonagricultural active workers engaged in the supply of nonagriculturally active workers which supply nonagriculturally active workers with nonagricultural necessities.

Employment on the basis of the surplus of agricultural production accruing to the privileged ones depends on their consumption habits and may be instable. All those who do not belong to one of these three groups can be marginalized—and hence can be shed off and are kept from becoming proletarians (in the Marxist sense) who can at least sell their labor power.

If there is marginality, there are always laborers who are ready to work at subsistence wages.[3] As long-term skill levels do not differ greatly, marginalized unemployed workers cannot outcompete those workers who are employed and produce a marginal product at least equal to their subsistence costs. Only the readiness of providing non-economic goods—such as submissive behavior or the readiness to accept dependency—can be used for getting preferred status in relation to fellow workers. The model can therefore account for the readiness of the marginalized ones to enter relations of clientelist dependency.[4] They can protect their survival only with the help of the not marginalized part of the population or by acting against the productive part of society—the latter being achieved either in the collective form or in the form of stealing. In societies which are characterized by marginality, social movements take the form of violent rebellion, wherein the marginalized struggle against the productive part of society and economy. Consequently, the possibilities for compromise and reform remain limited. The form which marginalized classes wage their struggle against the established order becomes most visible in South Asia via actions called *Bandh* or *Hartal*. Local social science considers them as equivalent to strikes, but the issue is not the refusal to work. Rather, they employ the occupation of all strategic points of the cities which those who are ready to work must use in order to move to their workplaces, including a total blockage of all means of transport. The goal is not the rejection of the own work of the marginalized, and therefore the refusal to produce a surplus but rather the blockage of work of all those others who might supply such a surplus to their employers. Clientelist dependency deepens already organizational weakness of horizontally defined interests. Marginality further contributes to this weakness and therefore to the absence of experience in political conflict regulation on the basis of the rule of law and rising mass markets.

As long as the surplus population in agriculture is appropriate for maximizing the "unproductive" employment of marginal ones in luxury

[3] This assumption is justified because labor cannot survive without at least a subsistence wage. In the real cases of transition to capitalism, especially in Latin America, there are however arrangements under which entrepreneurs pay less than subsistence wages for that part of production which they commercialize themselves—in exchange for rights in using land, the production of which is less certain, cf. Knight (1986: 49–51), Lynch (1992: 71–75).

[4] Elsenhans (1994: 183; 1995), Fafcamps (1992), Scott (1972), Singelman (1974: 52–53), and Tilly (1971).

production, the privileged ones are in favor of population growth. In a "rich" society with a high surplus of agricultural production and a highly unequal income distribution, a regular level of demographic growth must be expected where the share of those who depend on the luxury consumption of the privileged is high. If precapitalist social or political obligations for feeding the unemployed do exist, population may grow beyond the level of marginality as agricultural production still grows beyond this level. This population is employed although it does not produce more than it consumes.[5]

These obligations regularly get weaker in the wake of increasing competition on the market or in case of internal troubles. This is because the privileged are no longer able to maintain their luxury consumption, whereas hunger or vagabondage increase (as was the case in the initial phase of European capitalism).[6] When capitalist competition intensifies, marginality can only be avoided if the disappeared demand for luxuries could be compensated by the demand for investment goods.

5.1.2 *The Results of Increasing Productivity*

We have to ask: Do market-triggered developments in the emerging capitalist sectors compensate for intensified marginalization of labor in the wake of intensified competition? Therefore, we examine the results of different types of technical progress and competition on the level of employment:

1. Increasing labor productivity in the production of luxuries does not influence the cost of the agriculturally employed and hence also does not affect the level of marginality. Additionally, the surplus of agricultural production does not increase. Artistically higher-performing workers produce simply more or better luxuries.
2. Any increase in labor productivity in nonagricultural wage goods reduces the cost of workers engaged in agriculture. The slope of the straight line—which represents here the costs—decreases. Landholders perceive this as a wage reduction, even if real wages remain

[5] Similar model with differing conclusions regarding opportunities for technical development, using the example of China: Chao (1986: 8–12).

[6] Even a highly intensive analysis of the problem of the poor avoids, such as does Geremek (1980), quantitative evaluations of the phenomenon of marginality.

constant. The result of an increase in employment in agriculture is however limited by the limit of the maximum surplus of food production. This limit for diminishing the cost of agricultural labor is reached when industrial wage goods are produced with zero costs in the wake of productivity increases. A shift in the level of marginality in agriculture by increasing productivity in industrial wage goods production can be more important the higher the share of such products in mass consumption. This means that climatically colder countries with high shares of textiles and shelter in total mass consumption can benefit more than hot countries from fighting marginality via industrial progress and increasing productivity in industrial wage goods production.

Increasing productivity in industrial wage goods production implies deteriorating terms-of-trade for the industrial sector. Productivity increases in industrial wage goods production reduce the quantity of labor per unit produced in this sector. Employment might increase in agriculture in the wake of a lower necessary wage there. In total, employment increases.

3. Technical progress with rising productivity in agriculture may have two different outcomes: Productivity of already active workers may increase, or the threshold of marginality and productivity of those who are not yet productively active for big landowners may increase. Both effects can be combined to different degrees. If the surplus from the work of already productively active agricultural workers increases, then growth and employment for the masses will depend on spending habits of the owners. If technical progress raises the threshold of marginality, then agricultural employment increases together with employment in nonagricultural activities in the wake of additional demand of additional agricultural workers for industrial products.[7]

[7] Mingay (1963: 92), Grabowski (1991: 11–14), and Minami (1986: 388). In such a scenario the terms-of-trade between agriculture and industry may deteriorate. This is compatible with constant real incomes and increasing purchasing power for industrial products. I showed elsewhere the link between economic growth and increasing mass incomes as a condition for capitalist growth (and not as a result of it). This link may appear in the form of improving terms-of-trade between hours worked in agriculture and industrial products together with stagnating nominal but also under certain conditions stagnating real incomes. In the transition to demographic growth and the implied transformation of agriculture which faces increasing demand, there is the possibility of

Technical progress can remove the barrier constituted by marginality against a breakthrough of capitalist growth only to a rather limited degree. Technical progress may increase the amount of surplus available. Under capitalist conditions, this increase in surplus can lead to growing employment outside agriculture, if the capitalist sector achieves accumulation and growth with increasing mass employment—even without increasing real wages.

5.1.3 *The Analysis of the Industrial Sector*

At the threshold of marginality, the level of employment in agriculture does not necessarily trigger employment in industrial mass consumption production to a level where this industrial employment would provoke net investment goods production. The demand for investment goods therefore may be lower than the amount of surplus achieved by the owners of assets. We examine therefore the possibility that the industrial sector itself increases employment by its own demand for investment goods. In this modeling, the relations between industry and agriculture are neglected.

I define

$$Y_1 = P_1 + W_1 = \pi_t \cdot K_{t-1} + W_t = \beta_t \cdot K_t \text{ and} \tag{5.1}$$

$$\pi_t = \frac{P_t}{K_t}, \beta_t = \frac{Y_t}{K_t} \tag{5.2}$$

Y stands for net production, *P* for profits, *K* for the amount of fixed capital, *W* for the cost of labor and in case of stagnating real wages also the volume of labor, π for the profit rate, and β for capital productivity. In order to counterfactually reject the necessity of rising real wages for the transition to capitalism, I assume that real wages, the volume of employment, and hence also the total sum of wages remain constant. We neglect the impact of amortization. The lifetime of capital goods is assumed to be

increasing costs of agricultural production. In such a case, real incomes in relation to products may not have increased, but stagnating incomes reflect increases in relation to a deteriorating average productivity, Elsenhans (1976, 1983, 1983). Position confirmed by Broadberry and Gupta (2006: 3–7). When different spending components are distinguished, real wages increased slowly in comparison with increases in average productivity, because productivity in agriculture initially decreased: Less productive agricultural land had to be put into cultivation. In the same time purchasing power for industrial consumption goods increased.

unlimited because I assume that the machines are always repaired. Investments are always net investment. In addition, it is assumed that all profits are invested, and all wages are consumed.

On the basis of the implied saving functions

$$K_t = (K_{t-1})(1 + \pi_{t-1}) \tag{5.3}$$

From (5.3) equation (5.4) results

$$\frac{W_t}{K_{t-1}} = (\beta_t - \pi_t)(1 + \pi_{t-1}) \tag{5.4}$$

The wages and the volume of employed labor stagnate with continued capital accumulation. As all profits are reinvested, W_t/K_t tends to 0. Equation (5.4) can be fulfilled only by a permanently increasing the rate of profit π or a permanent deterioration of capital productivity β (Elsenhans 1986: 267–276).

Two cases may be distinguished:

(1) β is constant
(2) β decreases because if $\beta = f(K)$; $f'(K) < 0$.

The difference between both cases can be tracked to different interpretations of the causes of technical progress, which leads to increasing labor productivity with different patterns of the development of capital productivity. Capital productivity can rise or fall in case of technical progress. Technical progress can be understood as the result of a systematical research for innovation by entrepreneurs. This would justify its being interpreted as depending on capital accumulation, as expressed by the assumption of $f'(K) = 0$. Particular progress can also the interpreted as independent of the rate of capital accumulation. This is because being the result of a permanently undertaken innovative activity of such a society, so technical progress is dependent on time. Depending on the rate of capital accumulation which equals the profit rate, W_t/K_t tends more or less rapidly toward 0 (all profits but only profits are reinvested). The rate of technical progress can be higher or lower than the rate of capital accumulation. One possible consequence is that the rate of capital accumulation accelerates beyond the rate of technical progress.

If capital productivity does not decline, the rate of growth of profit increases more rapidly than the rate of growth of national income.[8] From period to period, the resources available for investment increase more rapidly than the national income, as wages are assumed to remain constant. Without rising real wages, there must be rising rates of growth of production and capital stock. With W_t/K_t tending to 0, π_t must increase. With constant capital productivity β this results in a proportional increase of the rate of increase of production. Both the rate of growth of production and the profit rate increase to unrealistic heights. This process ends when the share of labor incomes in national income tends to 0. This also is an unrealistic scenario.

We drop the assumption of constant capital productivity and admit declining capital productivity in line with an increasing stock of capital and constant amount of labor engaged. We admit also that the share of profits in total incomes increases. Even in that configuration, the rate of profit rate reaches an unrealistic maximum value and subsequently declines.[9]

Both conditions of a constant volume of labor and constant real wages can be dropped in two manners. When the profit rate risks falling, individual enterprises can reduce the rate of growth of capital stock by abandoning the introduction of more capital-intensive technologies which lower the profit rate. They could try to profitably exploit their capital by luring away labor from other enterprises using known technologies which do not reduce the profit rate. In that case, obstacles to economic growth as described in this situation would be removed by means of increasing real wages.

[8] The text was written in 1994. So, it could not consider Piketty (2014). To the difference to Piketty, I do not consider these different growth rates as a condition of capitalism but as a deviation of capitalism to a rent-based structure. Therefore, I write about the rent-oriented decline of capitalism (Elsenhans 2015). I consider that for getting majorities in the West one does not have to show, as Piketty does, that this difference in growth rates is unjust, but that it destroys capitalism. This is because very few people want to abandon capitalist regulation for state regulation if it is not inescapable.

[9] This is not identical with the Marxist tendency of the profit rate to fall. In case of appropriately rising real wages, which diminish the speed of accumulation to the level of the possibilities of technical progress, this tendency of the profit rate to fall would not occur. Such a configuration would correspond to capital accumulation parallel to the rate of technical progress and could be called capital accumulation in line with the exogenously (outside capital accumulation) generated technical progress. This was interpreted here as being time-dependent, provided that factors like competition facilitate this time depending discovery process. Cf. also Nadiri and Schankerman (1981: 318).

The other solution would be growth with constant K/W as described by Tugan-Baranowski 1901: 21–25). Such a pattern of growth would be characterized by the worldwide absorption of all available labor in the capitalist sector so that there would be ultimately no further growth of employment. During this process of absorption, all additional workers must be employed at the same level of labor productivity as the already employed ones.

It is an empirical observation that such a worldwide extension of capitalism has not yet taken place. When interpreting this empirical observation, the causes of technical progress are of central importance. If technical progress is linked only to the means of production (especially machines), the physical counterpart of capital—technical progress—is geographically mobile. With entirely mobile technical progress, such a worldwide extension of employment can be reasonably expected. Consider that those theories which link technical progress to the skills of labor—such as Denison's (1967: 298) theory of the residual factor of technical progress—are correct. This would mean that the expansion of employment requires that the cost of that labor rises which is already "transformed" and disposes of higher skills in the wake of economic growth. This would support the argument that such a process of expansion of employment is easier in early phases of worldwide industrialization: Differences between already transformed and not yet transformed labor were less in those times (late eighteenth and nineteenth centuries). As accumulation intensifies on a global scale, an element of technical progress which cannot be transferred geographically becomes more and more important. Because of this increasing weight of non-capital-bound technical progress, new labor which is still blocked in the not modernized sectors becomes competitive only after considerable increases in real wages in the more advanced economies.

The theory of the product cycle—with its insistence on differential costs of the transfer of technologies (Vernon 1966: 202) and the observation of relatively low productivity differences between industrial and developing countries in mature but capital-intensive technologies (according to their degree of maturity)—would support this hypothesis.[10]

[10] On relatively low productivity differences in case of capital-intensive technologies: Amsden (1983: 355), Clague (1967: 489; 1991), and Siggel (1984).

5.1.4 Growth of the Industrial Sector by Luxury Consumption

We still must examine the solution proposed by Sombart (1913: 114–118) of solving the problem of absorption of an increasing surplus of agriculture by expanding luxury consumption, since net investment and the subsequent increase in employment lead to this result without increasing real wages. There is no doubt that the expansion of luxury consumption can create markets for an increasing production of the capitalist sector. Often the argument is voiced that redistribution in favor of the Third World may, however, contribute to the destruction of the capitalist sector because of the aim of increasing export markets. The respective authors argue against redistribution in favor of the poor, as that consumption out of lower incomes is said to be import intensive and even often capital intensive.[11]

Independently of better chances for technical development through mass consumption as shown in nineteenth-century Germany[12] or in the perfect example of the United States (Brady 1964: 177–180; Williamson 1960: 144), luxury consumption promotes transition to capitalism if it does not block capitalist competition. Luxury consumption, therefore, is interpreted as promoting capitalist development by Nef (1958: 137; also, Heckscher 1933: 719) only because of its possible role as a demonstration which triggers rapid imitation through mass consumption. The following question is therefore of major interest: Are capitalists capable of imposing by economic means on non-capitalist owners of assets capitalist forms of interaction—especially competition—in case of accumulation on the basis of luxury consumption? Or will capitalists be co-opted into the non-capitalist class of owners of assets by economic and non-economic means?

Non-capitalist owners of assets may well constitute markets for capitalists and contribute to the absorption of surplus by their luxury consumption. But for maintaining their purchasing power, these non-capitalist

[11] The literature on the subject is relatively old and, the counterargument is dismissed by the mainstream as having been definitively rejected: Raveau and Vossenaar (1972: IV), Cline (1975: 395), Tokman (1975: 58). The opposing argument about a positive link between redistribution and growth has been reformulated, but it is not discussed by the mainstream following Murphy et al. (1989: 534). Cf. also Dutt (1991).

[12] The only author who to my knowledge has proposed this argument is Howard (1907: 91–92). This created comparative advantage in such products for Germany. Cf. Buchheim (1981).

owners of assets need monopoly on their markets for goods and services. Otherwise capitalists outcompete them and destroy their possibilities to articulate such a demand for luxuries. Big landlords can always return to less market orientation if their terms-of-trade deteriorate; they can use their own surplus, in the physical form of food, to employ labor on various stages for producing their own luxuries (Thrupp 1980: 146–147). This argument holds especially in case of low advances in productivity within the capitalist sector, a probable configuration because of low degrees of mechanization in luxury production, at least in times of early industrial development.

The non-capitalist big landlords can also invest part of their surplus in labor, which they use in political strategies, perhaps in the form of fighting capitalist owners with non-economic means, such as political warring or use of gangs for plunder.[13]

Possibilities of defense of rent generating monopolies or the financing of non-economic forces for defending non-capitalist forms of appropriation of surplus trigger reactions of the capitalists. They may themselves develop tendencies to invest in non-capitalist forms of appropriation of surplus because here the relation between future income streams and actual costs of investment may be better than in case of capitalist investments, for example because of lower risks. Many early capitalists bought landed estates. Similarly, long-distance merchants bought land or public office.[14] In order to defend themselves against non-economic force, as against Marx's "dull compulsion of economic relations," capitalist may feel forced to defend the possibilities of access to surplus by investment into political instruments, possibly even private armies (Steensgard 1981: 272). If there is a surplus which cannot be absorbed by profitable net investment spending, the possibility and the necessity of appropriating rents emerge. Both tend to transform the capitalists into precapitalist owners of assets for surplus appropriation.

When the capitalist sector has already become important, non-capitalist landlords will perceive incentives to invest in their own estates or into the

[13] On the decline of the campaign fairs in the fourteenth century cf. Chaunu and Gascon (1977: 4). On the development of the Italian city states: Chittolini (1989). There are parallels outside Europe as well: Praskash (1971: 215).

[14] On England, see: Jones (1974: 176–180). Other cases Kamen (1984: 127); Genovese and Fox-Genovese (1979: 8), Nicholas (1976: 6), Le Mené (1977: 89), Romano (1968: 736), Sheldon (1983: 483), and Aymard (1982: 191–195).

industrial sector in two scenarios. In one scenario, the real incomes of workers in the industrial sectors increase because of scarcity of labor, and the challenge of marginality is overcome. The other option is if the costs of political compulsion increase because of the technical advance in the capitalist sector.

5.2 International Exchange of Surplus Sharpens the Marginality Trap

When more backward economies are opened to more advanced economies via the world market, rent and marginality increase. There are new possibilities of spending surplus which is appropriated as rent; no longer does rent have to be used to employ local labor (already Smith 1976 [1776]: 433, 437). This opening to more advanced, capitalistically organized economies may transfer capitalist forms of regulation into less-developed economies without marginality being removed. Forms of capitalism are transferred, but the basic mechanism of capitalism is not. In the closed and predominantly precapitalist economy, access to surpluses exceeding the financial needs of capitalist enterprises for net investment may lead to wasteful consumption of financial resources, which creates employment but may block the transition to capitalism.

Suppose an economy with predominant appropriation of surplus by big landlords. If it opens up to more developed capitalist economies, the previously existing precapitalist limits on surplus utilization are removed. All profitable possibilities of investment spending on the world market are available. Besides luxury consumption goods, all sorts of property titles with their future income streams can be bought. Surplus available in the backward economy is no longer used for employment of labor on the estate which is marginal in agriculture. It is used for the purchase of property titles in capitalist economies (capital exports) or luxury consumption goods from abroad.[15]

The amount of employment decreases by the amount of labor previously marginalized but employed on the basis of being subsidized from the surplus either in agriculture or employed in luxury production for the rentier lords, if foreign luxuries are preferred. Marginal labor was

[15] Whether the privileged consume luxury goods produced locally or imported luxury goods is important. Felix (1989: 1466) repeats his earlier observation (1977: this 201–204) on the importance of the propensity to import in case of luxury consumption.

originally paid from the surplus is shed, whether it was employed in agriculture or in the production for the landlords. The result of the activity of this labor had been the physical counterpart for the surplus previously appropriated by the privileged.

5.3 The Impact of Income Redistribution

Redistribution of income can promote growth even if the surplus of agriculture decreases. In that case, the amount of employment increases. In the heartland of the Industrial Revolution in Europe, claims to consumption emanating from the poor had been reduced to minimum levels by means of repression. They were however not entirely removed through unemployment as is the case of the marginalized in today's Third World. The English poor had to work for wages below subsistence cost for capitalist entrepreneurs. The difference between these subsistence cost and their wages were, however, compensated by benefits distributed by the parishes. These benefits could be financed only from the surplus of agriculture which would have accrued to the rich in case of absence of the corresponding taxes. Taxes on buildings and land or other assets imposed on the privileged ones at fixed rates were independent from employment achieved through these assets. Subsidizing workless people out of such taxes (Elsenhans 1992 [1980]: 136–143) can cause lower wages than their subsistence costs. Entrepreneurs can employ such workers because their wage costs are lower than the cost of subsistence and possibly also their (declining) marginal product. Employment increases by hiring workers who receive less wage from their employers than their barebones subsistence costs, because of their low marginal product. The fact that the entrepreneurs must pay themselves for the cost of subsidy by paying tax has no effect on the level of employment. The threshold of marginality as defined by equality of subsistence costs and marginal product estimate is moved, because subsistence costs for the employing entrepreneur are reduced below the actual subsistence costs. In addition, the tax allows increasing agricultural production (but not the surplus of agriculture). Even labor with lower marginal product than de facto subsistence costs still produces a positive marginal product. A long as the share of agricultural products is high in the subsistence level of consumption of workers, more workers can be financed in agriculture than in nonagricultural production. Workers in agriculture produce also food, however less than they consume. Only part of their subsistence has to be provided by spending out of the surplus of agriculture. Nonagricultural labor has to be fed entirely from the surplus of agriculture. In the above diagram the total production is represented by the lying parabola. A parallel dotted lying parabola represents the production available to the big landlords in case of introduction of a single rate tax, which is independent from the level of employment and the level of production. The tax is used beyond the threshold of marginality to subsidize otherwise marginal labor which does not produce as much as it must consume. The marginal cost of labor decreases as a result of the subsidy. The tax does not diminish the amount of labor which can be used without subsidy. However, it pushes the employment to the right despite an unchanged threshold of marginality because the cost of reproduction decreases "artificially," as long as the subsidy is sufficient to complement the declining marginal product and to provide at least subsistence income to marginal workers.

There are many indications that a lower share of investment in national income—as might result from redistribution—is easy to manage and leads to higher efficiency. The English poor laws demonstrate that redistribution reduces the surplus of agriculture but may increase profit against non-capitalist forms of surplus appropriation, such as the purchase of luxury goods which are produced without investment goods or without locally produced investment goods. By redistribution, the demand for industrial mass consumption goods, however, increases. These products tend to be produced with locally produced investment goods.

Agrarian reform—which leads to an egalitarian distribution of agriculturally useful land—has similar results (Elsenhans 1979: 552–555). Marginal labor is internalized within the family farm. For his first hours of work any owner-operator achieves already high yields per labor time engaged, but the total result for these highly productive hours is not sufficient for the needs of his nuclear family. Because of the generally low level of productivity there are no alternative possibilities of employment for the low yielding not yet used additional hours of work. In order to increase the available means of subsistence for his family, such a farmer cannot avoid engaging more labor—even the non-highly productive labor—on his farm. This still holds true even if increases in production are low but still positive. He proceeds to supply this marginal labor. This is reinforced by the fact that this additional supply of labor time does not proportionately increase the consumption of calories by himself or by his family (Dandekar 1962: 71–72; Sen 1966: 437–440).[16]

Surplus of agriculture (surplus over costs of agricultural workers) may decrease as well as agricultural surplus (surplus of food not consumed by agricultural workers), if government-sponsored reforms force big landlords to transfer their land to their peasants if these peasants do not receive surfaces large enough like middle peasants. Too small tracts of land do not guarantee a positive marginal product above marginal costs even for their "last" hour of work. Reduction of both types of surplus may lead to increasing employment and subsequent increasing mass demand—and similar to the impact of the poor laws—to economic growth.

5.4 Late-Comers' Investing of Rents in Case of Low Productivity Backlog

There is no doubt that rent can be used in order to proceed to investment via the non-market economy. Such investment may benefit productivity growth later on. But the condition for such investment is that non-capitalist "elites" have an interest in such use, perhaps because they do not have an alternative for defending their surpluses by political means. Maintaining a country's relative military rank is such a motive. But their spending on armament leads to the purchase of locally produced investment goods only if their production requires such investment goods.

Railway construction in the nineteenth century, which for military reasons was inevitable, had such consequences, especially in those cases where the local availability of iron ore and coal accelerated growth in heavy industries. In Great Britain, but also in France, Germany, Belgium and even in the United States, railway construction created employment on a massive scale. Railways were also the largest market for iron, coal and machine construction (Cootner 1963: 518; Kocka 1990: 68; Spree 1977: 286).

[16] Consequently, the share of this additional income in total income of our farmer is lower than the share of this additional labor time in the total time he is working.

Technical developments have changed the pattern of infrastructural investment since the nineteenth century: In present-day developing countries, there is no more railway or multipurpose infrastructure construction. Instead, pipelines are constructed. Even in the case of the construction of railways—but also in the case of the construction of roads—the construction of the new routes, and especially the procurement of rolling stock, is characterized by high import intensity. Imports can only be paid, however, from surplus of the agriculture produced by those workers which produce surplus. The local construction of infrastructure by the local workers in nineteenth-century Europe, however, absorbed all those workers which could still be fed from the surplus of agriculture—even if their marginal product in agriculture was lower than their wage costs.[17]

A similar observation should be made for armaments: In some industrially more advanced countries of the Global South, spending on armament increases; however, the majority of the armaments is still imported also in case of these countries.[18] Workers in export production have to be fully supported from the surplus, in our model, from agriculture. Reduced exports may limit imports and also employment in export production, but less than the increase in employment by subsidizing marginal workers out of the surplus, as long as they produce a positive marginal product.

State rivalry has contributed to employment through changes in the internal power structure of the leading powers. These states needed soldiers. They could use locally available marginal labor for armaments and infrastructure if their backwardness in relation to the technically leading economies was not too great. In this case they could produce the physical counterpart for their military consumption and the military infrastructure by local labor and use for that purpose rents as investment in the non-market sector with positive employment effects. But even in this case, the importance of mass markets is demonstrated by the bad quality of German industrial consumption goods in the last third of the nineteenth century. They were produced for local mass markets and clients with low incomes (Weiher 1987: 177–182; Pollard 1987: 182–192). Their quality was so bad that the label "made in Germany" was

[17]Deane (1965: 69), Fishlow (1965: 100), Wagenblass (1973: 77), and Fremdling (1977).

[18]On import intensity of armament spending in today's Third World: Brauer (1991) and Terhal (1982).

imposed (Buchheim 1981). Additionally, French capitalism had a comparative advantage in the production of luxury consumption goods, which explains the lack of dynamism. This is not contradicted by the observation of a high labor productivity in nineteenth-century French industry (O'Brien and Keyder 1978: 162).

5.5 No Rents in Case of Plentiful Agriculturally Useful Land

There were special conditions for the transition to capitalism in the European settlement colonies. There can be no marginality in agricultural production if there is enough agriculturally useful land, where able-bodied workers can produce a surplus under the prevailing technical conditions. This is an important reason for the neglect of the problem of the emergence of rents in the transition to capitalism in today's development discussion, where rents are explained exclusively by the political behavior of elites (i.e., rent seeking).[19] This results in the demand for intensifying market competition, which in turn results that there is no interest in the theory of a possible positive contribution of the non-market economy to the transition to capitalism. European history is full of examples of empowerment of labor in their relation to the privileged ones when land is plentifully available for colonization. German eastern colonization has contributed considerably to the improvement of labor's position in the areas of outmigration.[20]

With the existence of an open frontier, as in the nineteenth-century United States, marginality and agriculture could not emerge: Shed workers without employment outside agriculture could move to the frontier, where high incomes were paid even for wage. High labor incomes reduced surplus and increased profit because of investment spending for nonagricultural mass consumption goods: In the nineteenth century and the period of the two world wars of the twentieth century, those among the capitalist societies became dominant where marginality was avoided—very often without explicit intention, but with the instrument

[19] This applies also to the more recent contributions of US-American theory of rent seeking as in the edited book of Rowley et al. (1991).

[20] Brenner (1985: 27), Gimpel (1976: 44), Bolton (1980: 29), Reynolds (1961: 97), and Malowist (1966: 19).

of settlement laws (i.e., the Homestead Act).[21] This is entirely different from the artificially created shortage of land in most of Latin America.

The experience of the settlement colonies and their interpretations by Western academia have largely determined the development debate. Today's Third World must face the problem that the real challenge of overcoming underdevelopment, i.e., the emergence of rent and that the necessity of its best possible use for growth is suppressed. The reason the Third World must face this problem to the difference of the United States is because in America another Third World population, the North American Indians, was deprived of their property rights and utilization rights to their land, which today is part of the United States.

5.6 Marginality and the External Sector

The problem of rents is one aspect of structural heterogeneity which is pushed by the integration of underdeveloped economies into a world economy that is dominated by technically more advanced economies. Structural heterogeneity is increased by integration into the world market.[22]

Against neoclassical theory of specialization, I show that marginality and low productivity in agriculture with low food production hinder or even block perfect specialization.

It is quite possible that increases in productivity in agriculture in the capitalist industrialized countries may lag behind the increase in productivity in industrial production, especially in manufacturing. Backward economies should therefore enjoy comparative cost advantage in agriculture. In comparison with manufacturing, the obstacles for the transfer

[21] von Nardroff (1962: 137–140), Turner (1966: 28), and Shannon (1966: 41). This discussion is characterized by the lack of integrating the problem of marginality. In its center it deals with the absolute volume of the unemployed who migrated out of the cities. The fact that any additional farmer family created jobs by its demand for nonagricultural products in the cities and that the more that its productivity allowed higher consumption of industrial products is rarely investigated. After this theoretically cut short discussion, the American debate concentrated on property concentration. Cf. as examples Pessen (1971, 1982). Inequality is however secondary when the growth of mass consumption was assured by rising real wages. The struggle of American labor for free access to land credits it with more insight into the real interdependencies than on the part of academic social sciences, Commons (1918: 5).

[22] On structural heterogeneity see Nohlen and Sturm (1982: 99–100), Elsenhans (1996 [1981]: 92–95).

of technical progress in agriculture are however high. In general, technical innovation does not allow increasing management efficiency and labor control. The uncontroversially low work discipline in the underdeveloped world can be raised in agriculture but this is not comparable to the ability to raise the discipline in the industrial sector. Obstacles to the acceptance of modern technology are higher in agriculture than in industry. Most importantly, progress in agriculture, however, is linked to the natural conditions of production. These natural conditions of production differ much more between the northern industrial countries and the underdeveloped countries of the South than the conditions for industry. This often results in comparative advantage in application of imported technology in manufacturing as compared to agriculture.

The process of devaluation—in order to cheapen local factors of production—faces an absolute barrier and an additional problem which results from the poverty trap. The international cost of local factors of production, especially of local unskilled labor, can be cheapened by means of devaluation only if the majority of wage goods is locally produced. Suppose food must be imported for labor which has newly acquired comparative advantage. The result is that competitive advantage in the export-oriented industries cannot be attempted by currency devaluation. The cost of labor is then based on the international cost of labor and therefore can decrease only to a limited extent.

Because of rising marginal cost in agriculture, there is a threshold of marginality. It may be reached already at a level of the exchange rate where, due to decreasing export earnings, the total availability of imports and local production of food becomes lower than in case of a higher exchange rate. Total food availability decreases at low levels of the exchange rate. Suppose that the elasticity of imports in relation to the exchange rate is higher than the price elasticity of local production. An improving exchange rate may increase imports and discourage local production. A deteriorating exchange rate may go with less import reduction compared to the possible increases in local food production.

I assume inelastic demand for exports of the underdeveloped economy. Demand for exports can therefore be described in the following equation:

$$Xm_i = (a - bq) = O_{ex};\ O'_{ex}(q) = -b;\ q \geq 0 \tag{5.5}$$

with q for the international price of an export good i, which hitherto marginalized workers can produce in case of devaluation without additional land or capital, such as labor-intensively produced industrial products; O for employment; and Xm_i for the exported quantity of manufactured product i. I assume constant labor productivity in the export sector. The external demand for the exported product determines also the demand for labor in the export sector $\alpha Xm_i = O_{exp}$. I assume $\alpha = 1$. The parameters $a > 0$ and $b \geq 0$ describe the demand function and therefore, according to our assumption, also describe the demand for labor in the export sector in relation to the price of this export product on the world market. Tendentially, the price of labor in the export sector in international currency follows the price for the export product.

Sale proceeds (Xs_i) for these exports are determined by the volume and the price, so that

$$Xs_i = (a - bq)q = aq - bq^2;\ Xs_i^{'} = a - 2bq \tag{5.6}$$

I assume that the country cannot influence international prices for food, because the volume of its demand is assumed to be too low. In that case, all depends on the relation between $2bq$ and a. If $2bq < a$, then marginal sale proceeds increase. Depending on the parameters, however, it is not excluded that marginal export earnings decrease before full employment is achieved. A lower volume of exports can go with lower employment in the export sector and higher export earnings. Lower local prices for agricultural products in the wake of food imports may lead to a decrease of local food production. In case of an exchange rate which is too high for new exports, a decreasing local food production can be compensated by higher total export earnings in case of high exchange rates for traditional products, like raw materials. "Wrong" exchange rates can be rational in case of price inelastic supply of the local agriculture.

Within such parameters, a correction of income distribution in favor of agriculture fails. Investment in agriculture is not promoted. The transformation of agriculture—which is so important for the transition to capitalism in today's leading capitalist countries—is not realized (O'Brien 1985: 77). Without incentives for increasing agricultural production and productivity, marginality will persist.

5.7 The Central Importance of the Agricultural Question for Poverty-Oriented Policies

In most of the recent development debate, removal of marginality was not a central question. The debate focused on industrialization. What was overlooked was the fact that comparative advantage did not only discriminate against local technology production but also against local agricultural wage goods productions (Elsenhans 1984: 552). Rent was used for financing industrialization for the middle and higher incomes and became import intensive. Due to the neglecting of the absorptive capacity of agriculture, marginality tended to increase. If the channeling of rents into investment projects which reduced marginality fails, then increasing exports in the wake of devaluation of the exchange rate below purchasing power parity may increase employment. This is even the case if devaluation exceeds a level where those employed in the export sector are still able to buy (with their wages) their subsistence on the world market (including the food necessary for the local workers who produce the nonagricultural wage goods to be consumed by export sector workers). The limit for employment is defined by the possibility of the productive apparatus to produce locally wage goods and/or to have access to such wage goods on the basis of export earnings. This implies the possibility of subsidizing exports out of the surplus of agriculture. Export production can be subsidized to the detriment of the local surplus and therefore the luxury consumption of the privileged.[23]

$$Y_{agr} - W_{agr} > (w_{unit} - q)(a - bq) \tag{5.7}$$

Equation (5.7) says that marginal productivity in agriculture can be considered as irrelevant in case of specialization on high-technology products with high prices on the world market, because of $q > w_{unit}$, the wage cost per unit produced. For an economy which attempts to increase employment by exports with low price elasticity of demand, however, marginal productivity of agriculture becomes decisive. Employment creation by means of export orientation is facilitated by an increase in the surplus of agriculture because according to (5.7) more resources for subsidies toward more labor in the export sector are available.

[23] Y_{agr} = net production of agriculture, W_{agr} = labor costs in agriculture, wage multiplied by volume of employment, w_{unit} = wage per unit.

Employment increases even if marginal product is lower than the marginal cost of labor provided that marginal product is still positive, that (import-dependent) luxury consumption is reduced, and the national currency devalued. Employment decreases only when marginal product becomes negative. Both export-oriented and self-centered development are promoted by an increasing surplus of agriculture. A decision on the choice between either strategies, export orientation or internal market driven industrialization, or their combination—in both cases with agricultural growth being the priority—depends on the growth potential of long-term economic development triggered by those activities which are financed out of the surplus of agriculture. This surplus may be used for internal market activities without provoking learning about technology, if only additional personal services are consumed. In that case, subsidizing manufactured exports is preferable even if these exports lead only to the formation of a working-class, hence social modernization and perhaps only some technical learning.

The option of industrial production of mass consumption goods for the internal market requires rising mass incomes and therefore redistribution or raising the threshold of marginality. If rents cannot be channeled in such activities, additional exports may provoke more increase in mass incomes than a self-centered development strategy. From Eq. (5.7) it follows that a particular society and economy do not naturally dispose of this choice. In case of unfavorable export demand with negative marginal earnings from exports, it cannot use additional exports for subsidizing labor. Employment may increase without redistribution by the simple increase in marginal productivity of agriculture and export orientation by more devaluation. Redistribution, however, promotes overcoming marginality not only by higher levels of employment in agriculture, as shown in the analysis of agrarian reform, but also in the form of intensified export orientation, as demonstrated by the possibility of subsidizing labor in the export sector out of additional farm incomes. If the surplus of agriculture increases, rising mass incomes and growing exports are possible despite declining terms-of-trade.

The learning curves in manufactured exports and in internal market-oriented industries determine the optimal mixture of both strategies. My model shows that in a backward country, the position of the production curve of agriculture, the resulting surplus of agriculture, and the marginal productivity in agriculture are decisive for removing poverty and joblessness. What is not decisive is the wage rate as expressed in international currency, if side entry based on modern technology is not available as an option.

Concentrating on the problem of marginality in agriculture is the condition not only for the removal of poverty but also for the support to development policies based on more export orientation. Following the argument of W. A. Lewis (1978: 8, 10–16) on the link between terms-of-trade and productivity in agriculture, I argue that the backlog in productivity in relation to the industrial countries (lower skills, position of the learning curve) can be compensated by using less skilled but (in international currency) cheaper labor. The decisive aspect of cheapening this labor consists in increasing local food supply, as these unskilled workers have high propensities to consume food, with high shares of food in their total spending. The strategy of low exchange rates in order to diversify the economy and increase employment is promoted by a high surplus of agriculture. Suppose that productivity in agriculture increases and the threshold of marginality is raised. If marginal earnings in export decrease, the local market-oriented wage goods production will increase, initially in agricultural production and then, given low exchange rates, in the production of industrial wage goods. Promoting productivity in (agricultural) wage goods production and international competitiveness support each other.

All attempts for raising the threshold of marginality will fail if the reproductive behavior of the populations of the South does not change. It might be possible that the Green Revolution would have solved the problem of marginality in India at the level of population achieved around 1900. The argument is therefore topical, because the industrial countries in their transition to capitalism had already enjoyed much lower demographic growth, even "degrowth" (population losses during the great plague, fourteenth and fifteenth centuries),[24] which stands much in contrast to the continued population growth in today's Third World.

If raising the threshold of marginality and the surplus of agricultural can be realized, many other programs can be dropped. More employment in agriculture automatically increases the demand for industrial goods which can be manufactured with low import intensity.

With respect to the widely shared demand for promotional programs for small and medium industries, I argue that sufficient demand from the

[24] Jones (1981: 56), Bridbury (1973: 583; 1974: 551), Bolton (1980: 215), and Dyer (1968: 33).

poor and an appropriate exchange rate largely allow such programs to be dropped.

Should such a concentration on subsidizing programs for raising the threshold of marginality be impossible to realize, then simple transfers of the type of the creation of an "artificial" industry[25] are preferable to other forms of subsidizing. This is because they are immune to strategies of enrichment on behalf of the rich, which can use subsidies for increasing their import-intensive consumption, as well for appropriating rents in the export-import business.

In the alternative between raising the surplus of agriculture and raising the threshold of marginality, the fact should be taken into consideration that any distribution of the surplus by political instruments requires controls for the political management of rents. Raising the threshold of marginality directly addresses, however, the market-regulated sector, as the number of those who directly operate on the market increases. This is because they dispose of higher incomes as they have become capable of producing a surplus and therefore receive higher incomes in relation to their status as marginalized people.

References

Amsden, Alice H. 1983. 'De-skilling', Skilled Commodities and the NICs's Emerging Comparative Advantage. *American Economic Review* 73 (2): 33–337.

Aymard, Maurice. 1982. From Feudalism to Capitalism in Italy. The Case That Doesn't Fit. *Review (Fernand Braudel Center)* 6 (2): 31–132.

Bai, Moo-Ki. 1982. The Turning Point in the Korean Economy. *Developing Economies* 20 (2): 117–140.

Bolton, J.L. 1980. *The Medieval English Economy 1150–1500*. London, Totowa, NJ: J.M. Dent & Sons; Rowman & Littlefield.

Brady, Dorothy. 1964. Relative Prices in the Nineteenth Century. *Journal of Economic History* 24 (2): 145–203.

Brauer, Jürgen. 1991. Military Investments and Economic Growth in Developing Nations. *Economic Development and Cultural Change* 39 (4): 873–884.

Brenner, Robert. 1985. Agrarian Class Structure and Economic Development in Pre-Industrial Europe. In *The Brenner Debate, Agrarian Class Structure and*

[25] Cf. my recent proposals to this committee (Ausschuß für Entwicklungsländer, Verein für Socialpolitik), Elsenhans (1991a: 281–283; b: 127–129).

Economic Development in Pre-Industrial Europe, ed. Trevor H. Aston and C.H.E Philpin, 10–63. Cambridge: Cambridge University Press.

Bridbury, A.R. 1973. The Black Death. *Economic History Review* 26 (4): 577–592.

Bridbury, A.R. 1974. Sixteenth Century Farming. *Economic History Review* 27 (4): 538–556.

Broadberry, Stephen N., and Bishnupriya Gupta. 2006. The Early Modern Great Divergence: Wages, Prices and Economic Development in Europe and Asia, 1500–1800. *Past and Present* 59 (1): 2–31.

Buchheim, Christoph. 1981. Aspects of Nineteenth-Century Anglo-German Trade Rivalry Revisited. *Journal of European Economic History* 10 (2): 273–299.

Chao, Kang. 1986. *Man and Land in Chinese History*. Stanford, CA: Stanford University Press.

Chaunu, Pierre, and Richard Gascon (eds.). 1977. *L'Etat et la Ville. Histoire économique et sociale de la France Tome I: de 1450 à 1660*,, vol. 1. Paris: Presses Universitaires de France.

Chittolini, Giorgio. 1989. Cities, 'City-States', and Regional States in North Central Italy. *Theory and Society* 18 (5): 689–706.

Clague, Christopher. 1991. Relative Efficiency, Self-Containment and Comparative Costs of Less Developed Countries. *Economic Development and Cultural Change* 39 (2): 506–530.

Clague, Christopher K. 1967. An International Comparison of Industrial Efficiency. Peru and the United States. *Review of Economics and Statistics* 49 (4): 487–493.

Cline, William R. 1975. Distribution and Development. A Survey of Literature. *Journal of Development Economics* 1 (4): 359–400.

Commons, John R. (ed.). 1918. *History of Labour in the United States*. London: Macmillan.

Cootner, Paul H. 1963. The Role of Railroads in the United States Economic Growth. *Journal of Economic History* 23 (4): 477–521.

Dandekar, V.M. 1962. Economic Theory and Agrarian Reform. *Oxford Economic Papers* 14 (1): 69–80.

Deane, Phyllis. 1965. *The First Industrial Revolution*. Cambridge: Cambridge University Press.

Denison, Edward F. 1967. *Why Growth Rates Differ. Postwar Experience in Nine Western Countries*. Washington, DC: Brookings Institution.

Dutt, Amitava Krishna. 1991. Stagnation, Income Distribution and the Agrarian Constraint. A Note. *Cambridge Journal of Economics* 15 (3): 343–351.

Dyer, Christopher. 1968. A Redistribution of Incomes in Fifteenth Century England. *Past and Present* 39: 11–33.

Elsenhans, Hartmut. 1976. Lohnerhöhungen. Wachstumschance für den Kapitalismus. Eine Kritik am Gesetz vom tendenziellen Fall der Profitrate. In *Forum DS. Zeitschrift für Theorie und Praxis des demokratischen Sozialismus* 1 (2): 78–133.

Elsenhans, Hartmut. 1979. Agrarverfassung, Akkumulationsprozeß, Demokratisierung. In *Agrarreform in der Dritten Welt*, ed. Hartmut Elsenhans, 505–652. Frankfort on the Main, New York: Campus.

Elsenhans, Hartmut. 1983. Rising Mass Incomes as a Condition of Capitalist Growth. Implications for the World Economy. *International Organization* 37 (1): 1–38.

Elsenhans, Hartmut. 1984. Endettement. Echec d'une industrialisation du Tiers Monde. *Tiers Monde* 25 (99): 551–564.

Elsenhans, Hartmut. 1986. Der Mythos der Kapitalintensität und die notwendig falsche Technologiewahl der Entwicklungsländer. In *Technik und internationale Politik*, ed. Beate Kohler-Koch, 267–290. Baden-Baden: Nomos.

Elsenhans, Hartmut. 1991a. Problems Central to Economic Policy Deregulation in Bangladesh. *Internationales Asienforum* 22 (3/4): 259–286.

Elsenhans, Hartmut. 1991b. Reforming the Economic System of Bangladesh. Main Fields of Action. In *Wirtschaftspolitische Reformen in Entwicklungsländern*, ed. Hermann Sautter, 109–133. Schriften des Vereins für Socialpolitik 209. Berlin: Duncker und Humblot.

Elsenhans, Hartmut. 1992 [1980]. English Poor Law and Egalitarian Agrarian Reform in the Third World. In *Equality and Development,* ed. Hartmut Elsenhans, 130–162. Dhaka: Center for Social Studies.

Elsenhans, Hartmut. 1994. Politökonomische Restriktionen und Grundlagen für die Reform des Managements in der Entwicklungsverwaltung. In *Neue Entwicklungen im Management*, ed. Michael Hofmann and Ayad Al-Ani, 165–199. Wien: Physica Verlag.

Elsenhans, Hartmut. 1995. Die Rolle internationaler Entwicklungszusammenarbeit unter veränderten wirtschaftlichen und gesellschaftsstrukturellen Rahmenbedingungen. In *Die Dritte Welt im Rahmen weltpolitischer und weltwirtschaftlicher Neuordnung*, ed. Dietrich Barsch and Heinz Karrasch, 140–157. Stuttgart: Franz Steiner.

Elsenhans, Hartmut. 1996 [1981]. *State, Class and Development*. New Delhi, London, Columbia, MO: Radiant; Sangam; South Asia Books.

Elsenhans, Hartmut. 2015. *Saving Capitalism from the Capitalists. A Contribution to Global and Historical Keynesianism*. Beverly Hills, CA, London, New Delhi: Sage.

Fafcamps, Marcel. 1992. Solidarity Networks in Preindustrial Societies. Rational Peasants with a Moral Economy. *Economic Development and Cultural Change* 41 (1): 147–174.

Fei, John C.H., and Gustav Ranis. 1964. *Development of a Labor Surplus Economy. Theory and Policy*. Homewood, IL: Irwin.
Felix, David. 1977. The Technological Factor in Socioeconomic Dualism. Toward an Economy of Scale Paradigm for Development Theory. In *Essays on Economic Development and Cultural Change*, ed. Manning Nash, 180–211. In Honour of Bert F. Hoselitz. Chicago, IL: University of Chicago Press.
Felix, David. 1989. Import Substitution and Late Industrialization. Latin America and Asia Compared. *World Development* 17 (9): 1455–1469.
Fishlow, Albert. 1965. *American Railroads and the Transformation of the Antebellum Economy*. Cambridge, MA: Harvard University Press.
Fremdling, Rainer. 1977. Railroads and German Economic Growth. A Leading Sector Analysis with Comparison to the United States and Great Britain. *Journal of Economic History* 36 (3): 583–604.
Genovese, Eugene D., and Elizabeth Fox-Genovese. 1979. The Slave Economies in Political Perspectives. *Journal of American History* 66 (1): 7–23.
Georgescu-Roegen, Nicholas. 1960. Economic Theory and Agrarian Economics. *Oxford Economic Papers* 12 (1): 1–40.
Geremek, Bronislaw. 1980. *Inutiles au monde. Truands et misérables dans l'Europe moderne (1350–1600)*. Paris: Editions Gaillard; Julliard.
Gimpel, Jean. 1976. *The Medieval Machine. The Industrial Revolution of the Middle Ages*. Harmondsworth: Penguin.
Grabowski, Richard. 1991. Economic Development and the Traditional Sector. A Comparison of Japanese and African Experience. *Developing Economies* 29 (1): 1–17.
Heckscher, Eli F. 1933. The Aspects of Economic History. *Economic Essays in Honour of Gustav Cassel*, 705–719. London: Allen & Unwin.
Howard, Earl Dean. 1907. *The Cause and Extent of the Recent Industrial Progress of Germany*. Cambridge, MA: Houghton Mifflin.
Jones, Eric L. 1974. *Agriculture and the Industrial Revolution*. Oxford: Basil Blackwell.
Jones, Eric L. 1981. *The European Miracle: Environments, Economies and Geopolitics of the History of Europe and Asia*. Cambridge: Cambridge University Press.
Kamen, Henry. 1984. *European Society, 1500–1700*. London: Hutchinson.
Knight, Alan. 1986. Mexican Peonage. What Was It and Why Was It? *Journal of Latin American Studies* 18 (1): 41–74.
Kocka, Jürgen. 1990. *Arbeiterverhältnisse und Arbeiterexistenzen*. Grundlagen zur Klassenbildung im 19. Jahrhundert. Bonn: J.H.W. Dietz Nachf.
Le Mené, Michel. 1977. *L'économie médiévale*. Paris: Presses Universitaires de France.
Lewis, William Arthur. 1978. *The Evolution of the International Economic Order*. Princeton, NJ: Princeton University Press.

Lynch, John. 1992. The Institutional Framework of Spanish America. *Journal of Latin American Studies* 24 (1): 69–81.

Malowist, Marian. 1966. The Problem of Inequality of Economic Development in Europe in the Later Middle Ages. *Economic History Review* 19 (1): 15–28.

Minami, Ryoshin. 1986. *The Economic Development of Japan: A Quantitative Study*. Houndsmill et al.: Macmillan.

Mingay, Gordon. 1963. *English Landed Society in the Eighteenth Century*, 92. London and Toronto: Routledge and Kegan Paul.

Murphy, Kevin M., Andrei Shleifer, and Robert Vishny. 1989. Income Distribution, Market Size and Industrialization. *Quarterly Journal of Economics* 104 (3): 537–564.

Nadiri, M. Ishaq, and M.A. Schankerman. 1981. Technical Change, Returns to Scale and the Productivity Breakdown. *American Economic Review* 71 (2): 314–319.

Nef, John Ulrich. 1958. *Cultural Foundations of Industrial Civilization*. Cambridge: Cambridge University Press.

Nicholas, David M. 1976. Economic Reorientation and Social Change in Fourteenth Century Flanders. *Past and Present* 70: 3–29.

Nohlen, Dieter, and Roland Sturm. 1982. Über das Konzept der strukturellen Heterogenität. In *Handbuch der Dritten Welt (1). Unterentwicklung und Entwicklung – Theorien, Strategien, Indikatoren*, ed. Dieter Nohlen and Franz Nuscheler, 92–116. Hamburg: Hoffmann & Campe.

O'Brien, Patrick Karl. 1985. Agriculture and the Home Market for English Industry. *English Historical Review* 100 (397): 773–800.

O'Brien, Patrick Karl, and Çaglar Keyder. 1978. *Economic Growth in Britain and France 1780–1914. Two Paths to the Twentieth Century*. London: Allen & Unwin.

Pessen, Edward. 1971. The Egalitarian Myth and the American Social Reality. Wealth, Mobility, and Equality in the 'Era of the Common Man'. *American Historical Review* 76 (4): 989–1034.

Pessen, Edward. 1982. The Beleaguered Myth of Antebellum Egalitarianism. Cliometrics and ... to Rescue. *Social Science History* 6 (1): 111–128.

Piketty, Thomas. 2014. *Capital in the Twenty-First Century* (Electronic Version). Cambridge: Belknap.

Pollard, Sidney. 1987. 'Made in Germany'. Die Angst vor der deutschen Konkurrenz im spätviktorianischen England. *Technikgeschichte* 53 (3): 183–195.

Prakash, Buddha. 1971. The Genesis and Character of Landed Aristocracy in Ancient India. *Journal of the Economic and Social History of the Orient* 14 (2): 196–220.

Raveau, M.E., and R. Vossenaar. 1972. *Distribución del ingreso, estructura de la demanda y ocupación. Estudios de algunos vinculos en tres paises latinoamericanos*. Santiago de Chile: Nacional Unión Catalogue.

Reynolds, Robert L. 1961. *Europe Emerges. Transition Towards an Industrial World-Wide Society*, 600–1750. Madison, WI: University of Wisconsin Press.
Romano, Ruggiero. 1968. L'Italia nella crisi del secolo XVII. *Studi Storici* 9 (34): 723–741.
Rowley, Charles K., Robert D. Tollison, and Gordon Tullock. 1991. *The Political Economy of Rent-Seeking*. Boston, MA et al.: Kluwer Academic.
Scott, James. 1972. The Erosion of Patron-Client Bonds and Social Change in Rural Southeast Asia. *Journal of Asian Studies* 32 (1): 5–37.
Sen, Amartya Kumar. 1966. Peasants and Dualism with or without Surplus Labour. *Journal of Political Economy* 74 (5): 427–450.
Shannon, Fred E. 1966. Not Even an Indirect Safety Valve Attracting Eastern Farmers. In *The Frontier Thesis. Valid Interpretation of American History?*, ed. Ray Allen Billington, 41–50. New York, et al.: Holt, Rinehart & Winston.
Sheldon, Charles. 1983. Merchants and Society on Tokugawa Japan. *Modern Asian Studies* 17 (3): 477–488.
Siggel, Eckhard. 1984. On the Nature of Technology Shelves Facing Less Developed Countries. Some Hypotheses and Case Studies. *Journal of Developing Areas* 18 (2): 227–246.
Singelman, Peter. 1974. Campesino Movements and Class Conflicts in Latin America. The Functions of Exchange and Power. *Journal of Interamerican Studies and World Affairs* 16 (1): 39–72.
Smith, Adam. 1976. *An Inquiry into the Nature and Causes of the Wealth of Nations* [1776]. Oxford: Clarendon Press.
Sombart, Werner. 1913. *Luxus und Kapitalismus*. Munich, Berlin: Duncker und Humblot.
Spree, Reinhard. 1977. *Die Wachstumszyklen der deutschen Wirtschaft von 1840 bis 1880 mit einem konjunkturstatistischen Zusammenhang*. Berlin: Duncker und Humblot.
Steensgard, Niels. 1981. Violence and the Rise of Capitalism. Frederick C. Lane's Theory of Protection and Tribute. *Review (Fernand Braudel Center)* 5 (2): 247–273.
Terhal, Peter. 1982. Foreign Exchange Costs of the Indian Military 1950–1972. *Journal of Peace Research* 19 (3): 251–259.
Thrupp, Sylvia L. 1980. Das mittelalterliche Gewerbe. In *Europäische Wirtschaftsgeschichte. Die europäische Volkswirtschaft im 20. Jahrhundert*, ed. Carlo M. Cipolla and K. Borchardt, 141–176. Stuttgart, New York: Gustav Fischer.
Tilly, Louise A. 1971. The Food Riot as a Form of Political Conflict in France. *Journal of Interdisciplinary History* 2 (1): 25–57.
Tokman, Victor E. 1975. Income Distribution, Technology and Employment in Developing Countries. An Application to Ecuador. *Journal of Development Economics* 2 (1): 49–80.

Tugan-Baranowski, Michael Iwanowitsch von. 1901. *Studien zur Geschichte der Handelskrisen in England*. Jena: Gustav Fischer.

Turner, Frederick J. 1966. Statement of the Frontier Thesis. In *The Frontier Thesis. Valid Interpretation of American History?*, ed. Ray Allen Billington, 9–20. New York, et al.: Holt, Rinehart & Winston.

Vernon, Raymond. 1966. International Investment and International Trade in the Product Cycle. *Quarterly Journal of Economics* 80 (2): 190–207.

von Nardroff, Ellen. 1962. The American Frontier as a Safety Valve—The Life, Death, Reincarnation and Justification of a Theory. *Agricultural History* 36 (3): 120–142.

Wagenblass, Horst. 1973. *Der Eisenbahnbau und das Wachstum der deutschen Eisen- und Maschinenbauindustrie 1835–1860. Ein Beitrag zur Geschichte der Industrialisierung Deutschlands*. Stuttgart: Gustav Fischer.

Weiher, Sigfried von. 1987. 100 Jahre 'Made in Germany'. Absicht und Auswirkung eines britischen Gesetzes. *Technikgeschichte* 53 (3): 175–182.

Williamson, Harold F. 1960. Mass Production, Mass Consumption, and American Industrial Development. In *Première Conférence Internationale d'Histoire Economique. Contribution A: L'industrialisation comme facteur de la croissance économique depuis 1700. Contribution B: Etude comparée du grand domaine depuis la fin du Moyen Age*, ed. Fernand Braudel, Moisei M. Postan, and E. Söderlund, 137–148. Paris, The Hague: Mouton.

CHAPTER 6

Global South: The Transition to Capitalism Against Rent

Hartmut Elsenhans

6.1 The Ubiquity of Rent

This contribution aims at demystifying rent in order to facilitate overcoming its nefarious consequences at political and social levels. In this perspective, the current task for the forces of progress in the Global South consists of the transition to market economies based on the welfare state: This means as much market as possible together with as much planning as necessary. In this perspective, monopoly capitalism and finance capitalism appear as anticapitalist deviations which emerge because of too little political and social embeddedness of the respective market economies.

Originally published as: Elsenhans, Hartmut. 2018. Global South. La transition vers le capitalisme contre la rente. *NAQD—Revue d'Études et de Critique Sociale* 36, 33–74.

H. Elsenhans (✉)
University of Leipzig, Leipzig, Germany
e-mail: helsen@rz.uni-leipzig.de

© The Author(s), under exclusive license to Springer Nature Switzerland AG 2021

H. Warnecke-Berger (ed.), *Development, Capitalism, and Rent*,
https://doi.org/10.1007/978-3-030-62605-1_6

This contribution will therefore follow Hobson's (1938 [1902]) position, which Lenin (1964 [1916]) not only criticized but ridiculed.

To begin, I insist on the ubiquity of rent in all social systems. Rents, for example, are not only appropriated in exporting certain goods that are easy to produce in the South.[1] Until the rise of capitalism, rent was the normal form of appropriation of surplus. In the modes of production which preceded capitalism, surpluses were appropriated by political means in order to benefit the ruling groups—which emerged on the basis of the most varied forms of gangs and clans. The political framework within which they are active is called a state, despite its fragmentation and the discretionary exercise of power. The Mughal Empire (sixteenth century to eighteenth century in Northern India) had been corroded by internal struggles, similar to the feudal systems in medieval Europe (Brara 1994). In these precapitalist systems, the distinction between rent and tax is difficult to discern (Neale 1957: 231). The argument of Teschke (2003: 158) about the difference between a precapitalist proprietor state and the bourgeois regulatory state is therefore important here.

I suggest that the most appropriate definition of rent resides in its general character as a form of appropriation of surplus. It is determined by the political character of the instruments of appropriating it which can go from simple and pure violence to the influencing of political structures and the creation of market imperfections, such as the control of markets or the exclusive ownership of certain possibilities of production. One can mention here the ownership of fertile land with high speculative incomes or which contains minerals that are easily exploitable or exist in high content as another method of rent appropriation.

In my contribution I want to show that rent and profit have structurally different economic bases. Profit does not depend on attitudes or social cultural values from the past, taken from social cultural heritage. It depends on politico-economic structures which at least partially emerge without conscious action of the principal social actors. In order to face the challenge of these structures, all those who aspire to have access to economic surplus must develop precisely defined behaviors. In this way,

[1] This reduction dates from Mahdavy (1970), taken up and popularized by Beblawi (1987). Rent has become understandable for an audience which is fundamentally opposed to political economy because of its rejection of interdisciplinarity such as the Anglo-Saxon social sciences, exemplified by Karl (1997). What is interest in these discussions is that the most developed and pertinent analysis—by Sid Ahmed (1989)—is not even taken note of.

profit determines fundamental aspects of the behavior of social classes independently of their ideological or sociocultural heritages.

From here it can be shown that profit implies controls by those who are excluded from the appropriation of surplus by their purchases of goods on the market and the investment in innovation or plant expansion which they trigger with their purchases. Rent, however, can always be appropriated by the privileged classes, if they have enough political power and if surplus is available. Yet quite to the contrary, there may be only small profits—despite the potential availability of large surpluses which are either not produced or not realized as surpluses on the market.

Because profit depends on increasing mass incomes, the transition to capitalism consists of making possible the bargaining power of the masses. This is, however, never the intention of the privileged classes.[2] Capitalism emerges on the basis of the political rise, economic improvement and cultural development of the popular masses—in spite of the desires and the interests of the dominant classes, which nevertheless continue to maintain their privileged position in the exercise of power.

Transition to capitalism is therefore obviously accidental. Knowing the conditions of its emergence, however, allows for its critical analysis. Under favorable conditions, this can constitute a critical weapon for those who suffer from rent-based structures of domination. Therefore, the debate on the transition to capitalism is all the more important because, in history, those who opposed capitalist expectation did not have the intention to maintain this system—even if their politico-social activities eventually resulted in its (unintended) stabilization. There is therefore a great discrepancy between the conscience of the popular masses and the practical results of their activities. In their daily activities, working-class movements have always been oriented toward reforms, despite all resistance of radical extremist character. This was the case whenever pragmatic class coalitions allowed reinforcing the political tendencies to admit reforms of capitalism, especially by rising mass incomes.

Underdeveloped countries are not capitalist ones. Whatever the market penetration they experience from the outside, market mechanisms paradoxically strengthen rent relations—at least so long as the impact of employment creation is not strong enough for providing the popular masses with bargaining power on the basis of their scarcity on the labor

[2] Elsenhans (1983a: 191–193, b: 3–14, 1992b [1979]: 41–44, 2007 [1976]: 187–192, 2011a: 82, 2012: 67–107, 2015: 37–43).

market (Elsenhans 1997: 287–291). The resulting evils are attributed to capitalism by the critics of capitalism. But these evils stem from the fact that these markets have not undergone any fundamental capitalist transformation: The transformative effects of these external pushes for capitalism are too shallow and do not represent a fundamental capitalist transformation. Market relations alone still do not create capitalism (Elsenhans 2011a, b). The initial tendencies of specialization between the West—which develops capitalism—and South—which suffers only from the penetration of economic and social market relations without the essentials characteristics of capitalism, especially the creation of bargaining power of the world of labor—have only intensified the dispossession of the poor and deepened the blockages against the transition to capitalism.

6.2 Profit Depends on the Expansion of Mass Incomes

My argument in this article disagrees with most of contemporary social sciences, which have abandoned political economy. Mostly they do not distinguish between profit and rent, and if they do, political scientists and sociologists differentiate between those two categories of surplus in associating them to certain classes, even in the precapitalist societies.[3] This allows linking these two types of income to sociocultural patterns of behavior, or "habitus" in the terminology of P. Bourdieu (1991: 10). It is argued that there are big landlords who receive rents on the one side, and other privileged people, who, despite not necessarily being landless, receive the mass of their incomes from other sources, such as profits from long-distance trade, buildings or speculatively landholdings.

Historically these "capitalists" have invested their incomes in landholding in order to receive rents or in political positions within those

[3] For an abundant literature, I recall the example of the discussion on the neopatrimonial estate in the Global South, for example: Bratton and Van de Walle (1994: 462), Erdmann and Engel (2007: 104). On the explanation of the European rentier transition from feudalism to capitalism based on sociocultural attitudes: North (1985: 571), Postan (1967: 580). But there are also reductionist arguments elsewhere: Fanon (1968: 110).

political structures that are called precapitalist states.[4] This pattern of behavior occurs all over the world quite independently of the sociocultural characteristics of the respective countries/classes. Such non-innovative behavior has been critically reported even in the case of developed capitalist countries for the case of (English "gentleman") entrepreneurs facing decreasing possibilities of economic growth.[5]

Rents are appropriated on the basis of market imperfections which—if the rentier wants to continue to receive said rent—requires the rentier to use political means to project power or connections. The rentier receives his income if he succeeds in creating the political conditions necessary for its appropriation. He is unable to economically reproduce anything himself unless he benefits from a political power position, even if this power position is maintained in a very indirect manner. For example, the oil rent would disappear if the OPEC countries would lose the right to limit production. There would be no "subaltern" rentiers without their capacity of self-enriching being more or less explicitly recognized by the dominant political power which arranges or even protect them in exchange of their political services. Capitalists, however, emerged against the political power and created their own economic "power" inside the precapitalist society, without controlling a political power which would protect them.

Regarding the difference of rent, profit is not what is left over after consumption as classical, neoclassical and Marxist theories assume. Its principal characteristic consists in being the result of net investment spending. Profit is appropriated on anonymous markets without political intervention in favor of particular participants (Elsenhans 2014a: 603–606; b: 533). Producers of consumption goods can realize profit only if certain conditions are met.[6]

[4] This investment in monopoly positions is so extensively documented in the literature that is difficult to understand how the argument about an origin of capitalism in monopolistic long-distance trade is still advanced. Some examples of that literature: E. Jones (1974: 176–179), Richards (1974: 427), and Deng (1999: 197).

[5] Evaluations of the falling behind of English capitalism in relation to United States and German capitalism are at the end of the nineteenth century are full of such observations: Wiener (1980: 127), Robbins (1990).

[6] I explain these conditions (with some simplifications which do not change the fundamental relations), cf. Elsenhans (2011b: 11–18; 2015: 7–10).

Simplifying the demonstration, we assume that the external balance of trade (exports/imports) and the government sector (with government spending and tax income) are in balance, that entrepreneurs spend all their income for investment, and that private households spend all their incomes for consumption. All consumption goods are sold to private households. The sales of the consumption goods producers equal the spending of the private households. They will profit if there are households with incomes (wages, salaries) not paid by enterprises in the consumption goods sector directly and indirectly (as are jobs paid by the government and financed by taxes on the consumption goods producing). If there is only a consumption goods producing sector, these government jobs are already costs of production and therefore part of the value formation of the consumption goods sector, as are worn-out investment and primary products. The only possible sector for an additional demand which is not financed by the consumption goods producers themselves is the net production of investment goods, i.e., gross investment goods production minus worn out and replaced investment goods (which is also called amortization).

In a capitalist economy, any technical innovation is realized by improving equipment. The combined investment goods producers therefore know all the technologies which are used in consumption goods production. Consumption goods producers therefore have to accept prices which allow investment goods producers to achieve the same rate of profit as in consumption goods production. Otherwise, they would use their own technologies and enter the production of consumption goods themselves. They must also receive profits in the production of investment goods. Total sales of consumption goods correspond to the totality of the wages. The earnings of the producers of these consumption goods consist of salaries. In this case, the sum of salaries paid in the production of investment goods equals the profit in the production of consumption goods. As a result, total profit in both sectors—the production of investment goods and the production of consumption goods—equals the sales proceeds from new investment goods after amortization (Kalecki 1942).

In a capitalist economy, net investment is possible in case of the emergence of new products (new technologies being required for these products) and of technologies which allow to reduce unit costs of known products. In both cases, even when net spending on investment is increased, this will only lead to (in the midterm) increasing total incomes when also combined with increasing consumption.

This differs from the old theory about the role of purchasing power of salaries, which justifies high salaries for profitable sales. In my demonstration, profit is not supplied by wages. Profit takes its origin from net investment spending, i.e., investment spending that is higher than the cost of replacement of worn-out investment goods. With constant wages, the relation between production and cost of competitive new technology is always better than this relation in an older technology (von Bortkiewicz 1907: 456–459, later: Okishio 1961). A new technology must reduce unit cost per product, and therefore, wage costs must fall to compensate the possibly rising capital costs per unit. This is called rationalization technology. Total demand decreases if the wage rate does not increase.

In the same way, increasing real wages may lead to efforts for substituting labor with capital. This can be interpreted as the replacement of simple work with more complex work, since more complicated investment goods are normally produced by rather skilled workers. This can lead to higher unit costs in relation to unit costs previously achieved when salaries were lower. Such investment I call defensive investment.[7] Positive net investment is possible only in case of increasing demand or in case of increasing real wages.

The costs of a technology are also incomes—which become demand as they are paid to factors of production engaged in a branch of production. If real wages are constant and demand for investment goods is equal to replacement of used up equipment, there is no increase of demand and hence no possibility of the producers of consumption goods to be able to sell products at a profit. Technical innovation for the production of already known products can contribute to profit only if rising wages are imposed by the workers. These rising wages can force entrepreneurs to choose more "heavy" technologies or to increase production.

In case of new products which do not replace already consumed products, at the very least, certain segments of society must enjoy rising incomes in order to be able to buy these new products. Rosa Luxemburg (1951 [1913]: 104) already observed that the great majority of capitalist

[7] Defensive investment does not reduce unit costs in comparison with a preceding period with still low salaries but only in relation to a previous technology which leads to higher unit costs now with higher wage costs. Unit costs in the previous technology increase because of higher wage costs. Therefore, a new, more complex technology which saves on labor can enjoy lower unit costs when wages increase. Such a new technology may have higher capital unit costs but the increase in capital unit costs may be compensated by lower labor inputs even at higher wages.

entrepreneurs cannot increase their own consumption without risking the loss of their own competitiveness in relation to other capitalists. This is observed today in the non-monopolist industrial sector of top industrial economies. Rosa Luxemburg examines the capacity to consume of different segments of the capitalist societies—entrepreneurs, middle-class, and working-class—and demonstrates that in a capitalist system, none of these classes can increase its consumption incomes on its own initiative without first removing competition.

Luxemburg is right about the privileged classes: They can increase their incomes because of higher productivity in relation to the mass of the producers. These higher incomes induce lower-earning people to learn and acquire the necessary skills. At high levels of employment, any innovating entrepreneur can increase his production only by offering higher wages or better working conditions. In case of innovation, capitalists can increase surplus value taken from their workers (and thus their profits) only by increasing wages in order to attract new workers or workers from other activities. In these other, non-innovating activities, production would decrease. In activities which lose workers and face inelastic demand that is difficult to satisfy, entrepreneurs will increase their prices. This will allow them to also increase the incomes of the workers in order to keep them. This process culminates when wages have converged between the innovative activities and the activities without innovation so that average wages emerge differing only according to the physical or psychological workload (Salter 1960: 161). Average wages, i.e., wages which differ little between branches and skill contents, are a fundamental condition for the formation of a working class.

Fordism was not created by a more intelligent entrepreneur than his fellow entrepreneurs. It did not emerge with Henry Ford but as an essential characteristic of capitalism since its inception. Marxists admitted the existence of this type of power relation between labor and capital only during a limited epoch then called Fordism. They did not have to give up their previous discourse on the origin of capitalism in the ever-intensifying exploitation of labor. Some even maintained their claim that real wages had not risen at all.[8] When wage rises could no longer be denied, some of them even engaged in the most extravagant intellectual pirouettes, for example, by pretending that these wage rises did not

[8] Evans (1969: 43), Boyer (1978: 58), Gordon et al. (1982: 9–11), and Lipietz (1982: 35–36).

constitute an improvement of the living conditions of the working class but only reflected an increase in the cost of reproduction of labor (Aglietta 1979: 166).

Profit as the income of a decentralized bourgeois class depends on the rise of investment spending. Hence, the expansion of consumption is a condition of capitalist growth—even if the bourgeoisie ferociously denies this relation and fights against rising wages by pretending that suppressed wages are a necessity to preserve the conditions of well of functioning of capitalism, which such an increase in wages is said to threaten.

Two additional remarks: The better-off classes can certainly contribute to rising demand in capitalism if the better-off classes are protected against competition and have abandoned the capitalist principle of formation of the exchange values on an anonymous market. Rosa Luxemburg did not consider this possibility, ultimately because she believed in some progressive aspects of capitalism. I admit therefore that the capitalists do not need expanding mass incomes if they are able to abolish capitalism. Here I find a reason for the capitalists' lack of interest in making a distinction between profit and rent. In reality, capitalists are always looking to create the economic and political conditions for political appropriation of rents. They themselves want to become new rentiers.[9]

This pattern of consumption has important consequences on the type of technical progress launched. Technical progress can aim either at making products more perfect by improving their quality, or by making products of average quality cheaper by reducing their costs of production. The unique product which excels by its perfection therefore gives its consumer not only satisfaction in his relation with the world of nature but also in his relation with other human beings. The manufacturing of such unique products renders the use of machinery difficult in comparison with the production of mass consumption goods, which attract consumers only by their use values. Even today the production of luxury products uses less machinery than products for mass consumption.

Profit is strengthened by increasing mass incomes. Such an increase of demand for mass consumption goods can be articulated by various social strata but is more prominent in the demand of the lower classes. One nice example is the debate on the imitation of Asian luxury product in Western

[9] Piketty (2014), passim reflects this in his analysis, as well as Salama (1978: 283).

European by the middle and working classes during the seventeenth and eighteenth centuries.[10]

It was in the relatively egalitarian economies that capitalism took its origin. In Western Europe, the Continental aristocracies despised the English ruling class as poor and unsophisticated, miserly and unaccustomed to luxury goods (Wright 1935: 19–20, Ruggiu 2001: 269). The United States had been the bastion of equality during the nineteenth century (Brady 1964: 177). Even Japan was remarkable in nineteenth-century Asia because of the high incomes of its peasants.[11] Contemporary China enjoys a minimum wage as a result of land redistribution by the preceding communist regime. India has accelerated its economic take-off by the extension of ambitious social programs which, at least partially, have been implemented. Brazil has succeeded in its take-off by the defense of the poor with measures of social assistance (Elsenhans and Babones 2017: 56–76).

6.3 Marginality as Founding Mechanism of Underdevelopment and the Permanence of Rents

All successful transitions to capitalism took hold out of the basis of the most diverse social and economic structures. They had, however, one common characteristic: bargaining power of labor for the most diverse reasons, ranging from: demographic crisis in Europe following the great plague of the fourteenth century,[12] the weakening of precapitalist ruling classes (England of the fourteenth and fifteenth centuries), great spending on infrastructure for maintaining military capacity with resulting jobs (Prussia nineteenth century),[13] falling capacity of surplus extraction from the mass of the population such as the inflationary devaluation of monetary rice taxes in Japan because of inflationary overspending of the modernizing state (Hayami 1972: 29, Grabowski 1994: 443), or free

[10] Gilboy (1934), Thirsk (1978: 106–111), Coleman (1977: 119), and Berg (2004: 87).

[11] Akimoto (1981: 57), Hanley (1983: 189), and Yasuba (1986: 224).

[12] Hilton (1978: 279), Clark (2007: 98–99), and Acemoglu and Robinson (2012: 98).

[13] Broadberry et al. (2008: 170), Fremdling (1977), and Kocka (1990: 68).

access to cultivatable land in nineteenth-century regions of new European settlement, resulting often in displacement of the autochthonous population.[14]

Without such supporting factors, a tendency emerges in precapitalist societies which cannot be kept from developing without being counteracted by measures of support to the poor: the emergence of marginality.

I call marginal workers anyone who is part of the average skilled labor force that is unable to produce as much as necessary for their reproduction. This part of the global workforce survives on the basis of redistribution, realized by mechanisms which generally exist in precapitalist societies.

We need only some simple hypotheses: People in precapitalist societies may well know how to control births, but they behave in a way to procreate children in sufficient numbers (also taking account of the survival chances of these children) in order to help them in their old age. This implies regular demographic growth. The relation between available workers, consumers and the agriculturally useful land diminishes in quantity and in quality because less fertile land and more distant land must be put into cultivation. If there are no important technical innovations, the marginal product of active workers in agriculture diminishes at least after some time. There is therefore a level of production where marginal product per worker equals subsistence costs of a worker and his nuclear family. At this threshold, there is a surplus of agriculture to which the only ones who have access are those who are capable of taxing the direct producers, i.e., the state or landowners (Elsenhans 1994: 394–401).

Survival beyond this threshold is possible if some of the surplus (produced by those who produce more than they need for subsistence) is redistributed to the deficit households. The possibility of redistribution depends on the degree of repressiveness of the class which has appropriated the surplus. Political power relations in precapitalist societies are open for redistribution if it is limited to maintaining a minimum level of subsistence of the rural population in their communities. The succession of "good" and "bad" emperors demonstrates this. Religious legitimacy of practically all precapitalist emperors is seriously threatened in case of famine. The existence of a marginal population which does not produce

[14] Coghlan (1918: 425), Engerman and Sokoloff (2012: 27), and Allen et al. (2012: 868).

as much as it has to consume can be admitted as an established fact. This (over-) population does not have the option of "exit," a resistance option so much insisted on by Hirschman (1970).

The very fact that this marginal population exists is proof that it was maintained by means of solidarity among which the grand family, the caste, belonging to ancestors' temples (China), the tribe or in general the village community et cetera supported this marginal population. Such groupings can give up some of their material resources on the basis of privileged relations of some of their members with a/the lord(s) of private and public sectors. I call these members chiefs. Such chiefs have access to important incomes only on the basis of their being accepted and tolerated by the lords. Redistribution implies the respect of these chiefs for the lords and their commitment to support them; furthermore, resistance cannot be organized unless chiefs participate in great number. Resistance is possible if exploitation by the lords has become so ruthless that it become intolerable even for the previously privileged in the rural areas. All over the world, not only in Europe, there were therefore relatively regular peasant revolts—however, they were characterized by the resistance only against overexploitation which threatened the reproduction of the social order. Their objective was not the participation of the rural (and urban) masses in the fruit of rising productivity.[15]

When market relations penetrate such structures, the lords perceive possibilities of increasing their surpluses and realize them, if necessary, by removing redistributive mechanisms: They can exchange a (higher) surplus against new products (luxuries) from abroad. Consequently, they tried to suppress the marginals by sending them out from their estates.

In the European countries, the expulsed marginals appear as vagabonds on whom the governments clamped down with ferocious repression and with forced working, such as the laws against the poor (Elsenhans 1992a [1980]). These poor laws, however, were also a mechanism of substitution to the previous mechanisms of redistribution within primary groups such as tribe or large family. Such systems of redistribution diminish in these non-European economies as they further integrate into the world economy.

Imperialist penetration in the two forms—either by colonization, or the instrumentalization of local elites as bridgeheads of the imperialist

[15] I have no information about any precapitalist peasant movements where the insurgents asked for participation in the increasing wealth of the privileged.

powers—considerably increased the means of repression of the rulers of the South. These rulers did not care much for the danger of expulsion of the marginals. Therefore, the marginals (often called the "subalterns") formed an important element of the national liberation movements. They were, however, rarely able to develop an alternative social project but were instead led by members of other social classes, normally by intellectuals with middle-class backgrounds. These "organic" intellectuals of the resistance movements identified capitalism and imperialism and rejected profit as merely being like rent—both being elements of imperialist exploitation. Increasing mass incomes for supporting profit did not even play a small part in their discourse.

6.4 The Weberian Impasse

All the theories based on Jean Baptiste Say's (1972 [1803]: 103–110) law of the markets do not deduce the emergence of profit from final demand. They are therefore forced to deduce differences in the utilization of rents and profits to noneconomic factors, usually to sociocultural ones. Cultural modernization theory has been able to describe *ex post facto* cultural changes in the developed world. It has, however, been unable to recommend efficient measures for diffusing the same values in the Third World. This creates doubt regarding the practical dimension of these theories. Lavishly financed efforts of social science in United States for modernizing the bureaucracies of the Third World have had little impact in orienting the same bureaucracies of the South toward real development (Riggs 1964; Caiden 1973).

The Weberians' claim—that long before the emergence of a capitalist mode of production there was a (special) rationality of capitalists based in long-distance trade—boils down to the observation that these capitalists could behave economically rationally, ultimately keep files, and properly calculate. The cuneiform script was invented order to keep the accounts of traders. This special rationality of traders therefore had existed like this script for more than 4000 years before European transition to capitalism. During these four millennia, there were dazzling breakthroughs of rationalism in philosophical and religious thought. The axial age can be seen as proof with its foundation of monotheists or deist religions as Jainism, a radically materialist religion born in India at the same time as Buddhism around the sixth century BC (Ruben 1961).

On the one hand, rationalism has never been absent in human history. It could however not be applied to phenomena which were inexplicable. The lower ones never could offer themselves the luxury of neglecting rationality whenever they were lucky enough to know the essence of realities which were important in their concrete situation. On the other hand, patterns of behavior which may be considered as nonrational can be interpreted as perfectly rational. In highly inegalitarian societies, those modes of behavior which strive for satisfying luxury consumption of the privileged can be called rational because they seek to establish clientelist relations with those in power. On the contrary, it would be irrational for those who invest (and therefore contribute to profit) to develop cost-reducing technologies—in order to satisfy the needs of the poor. Here it is rational not to be capitalist in one's orientation toward production. Furthermore, it is in one's best interests to limit one's rationalism to only good management of luxury craftsmanship production or long-distance trade, all of these being described marvelously in the stories of *One Thousand and One Nights*. In an inegalitarian society, it is rational to reserve one's money for the erection of political structures which are conceived for political appropriation of surplus, hence for the defense of rents by appropriate institutions.

The privileged of all sorts—also those privileged called "capitalists"[16]—only exceptionally care (and then for very specific reasons) about the type of surplus they receive. Capitalism is not produced by the capitalists who do not hold capitalism as their historical project of social organization. Rather, capitalism emerges because capitalists cannot impose their goal of maximization of surplus for themselves by means other than competition on anonymous markets.[17]

[16]The application of the concept of capitalist to those privileged which already had succeeded in freeing themselves from the constraints of the market is found in notions as capitalism of the ancient world. More recently Braudel (especially Braudel 1967) has again described the monopolistic traders as capitalist, followed by all the work triggered off by Wallerstein (1974), recently also by Kocka (2013). Cf. my comments in Elsenhans (2014c).

[17]Any other interpretation would imply that capitalists are the first social class in history which not only produces its own history but also which knows the long-term implications of its social and economic practices. If this is correct, the poll-tax-based democracy with suffrage dependent on a certain tax payment of the early nineteenth century should be re-established, since the capitalists have a more correct vision of the good society than the popular masses. The historians of "precapitalist" capitalisms never discussed this implication. The privileged ones of these precapitalist capitalisms, however, strongly persevered

Denying the capitalist character of "precapitalist" capitalisms has a major implication for the discussion of contemporary rent. Sociocultural norms are no safeguard against a new rent-based regression. Capitalist norms may slow down rent-oriented regression, because existing norms entail transaction costs for changes in behavioral patterns, but they are not capable of blocking such changes. There are no differences between the European oligarchies of the seventeenth, eighteenth, and in part of the nineteenth centuries compared to the privileged classes of today's rent-based countries so much decried in contemporary Western writings.

From this perspective, the rise of capitalism is characterized by the rise of small entrepreneurs who may initially be weak but who were able to challenge the big rentiers—be they landlords, traders or holders of government office. Their rise is based on their efficiency in markets and on the levels of standard of living of the population; consequently, there is a great number of consumers who create a demand for average quality products. Capitalists often emerge as small entrepreneurs in weak positions who use competition and performance on markets in order to destroy the de facto monopolies of established rentiers. This explains that the transition to capitalism is realized by successive waves of newly rising entrepreneurs (Pirenne 1914: 494, Mantoux 1905: 34–35). This all remains true, even if, after their initial success, they may eventually also try to become rentiers themselves.

Capitalists appear in their history not as agents who engage consciously in the transformation of precapitalist structures. Rather, they are climbers who attempt to be directly included in the already-existing systems; however, unfortunately for them, these climbers are so numerous that they cannot be integrated into the already existing rentier classes. They

in fighting the enlargement of suffrage also to the poor, under the direction of the richest ones among them and in close alliance with all well-to-do. They opposed the appropriation of these parts of the surplus which cannot be realized on the market and refused these resources even to democratically legitimated states which tried to pursue objectives favorable for the great mass of the population. Colonial Algeria is a good example: the "agrarian capitalists" (i.e., the big landowners who were perfectly integrated into markets) always defended double voting constituencies, one for the tiny number of European settlers, the other one for the great mass of the Muslim population, both electing a same number of representatives. They openly argued (like many early nineteenth-century liberals) that the principle of one-voter-one-vote would give the majority the legal possibility of redistributing their estates to the Algerian Muslim majority, from which they had taken this land.

are orphans without any other alternative than re-falling in the social hierarchy or opting for competitiveness on the market. Marxist literature on the transition to capitalism has great difficulties to explain why the big trading cities of Germany, Italy or the Netherlands once more turned to precapitalist stagnation after their temporary take off during the thirteenth century to eighteenth century (Goldstone 2002: 331). Only when the patricians had given voice to the less privileged classes could capitalist structures emerge.

The "precapitalist" capitalists may have certainly other habits than the other rentiers in their use of their rents, but they all depend on monopolies and organize themselves as "gangs" for imposing political power—even using violence—in order to defend their possibilities of political appropriation of rent against their rivals. Such "gangs" are based on such accidental criteria as caste, ethnical belonging, and religious sects. They are therefore structurally opposed to the expansion of the status of legally equal citizens to the general public, which is so important for capitalism.

Capitalist modernity is not imposed by the "precapitalist" capitalists but by those forces which are able to limit the possibilities of enrichment of the rentiers, even if these rentiers appear to be capitalist. These forces may also comprise "capitalist" forces which, because of their weakness in relation to monopolistic enterprises, themselves engage in maintaining competition and so strengthen themselves against the "precapitalist" capitalists with their better access to surplus.

Specialization on mass consumption goods normally implies rising sales when costs and prices become lower. In this segment of the market, rising sales proceeds are rarely achieved by price increases with reduced quantities, such as in the luxury segment. There are two consequences: relatively weak tendencies of concentration among the entrepreneurs, and a preference for free trade, also internationally.

Entrepreneurs who are specialized in products with high price elasticity of demand—as in the case of mass consumption goods—must satisfy their desire for enrichment by increasing sales instead of coordinating with other exporters or the state (Elsenhans 2001: 37–41). There are historians who are able to show that the political economy of the late eighteenth century and early nineteenth century favored free trade. However, it is very doubtful that these intellectual contributions have caused the adoption of free trade (Morrison 2012). The alternative hypotheses to the adoption of free trade for new ideas, a materialist causality, would imply that the transition to capitalism is due to specific macroeconomic structures which were favorable for mass consumption. It would support my general argument that in today's Global South, the struggle against rent should concentrate on the macrosocial and macroeconomic structures—instead of on the values of the ruling classes.

6.5 The International Dimensional of the Reinforcement of Rent

In addition to the different effects of the positioning in the international economic system, historical context matters. The first countries that transitioned to capitalism have for a long time been favored (in comparison with their followers). Globalization has reinforced blockages, but nowadays it also presents new opportunities. Blockages and opportunities are mediated by the interaction of different prices systems: The structure of the system of relative prices differs at different levels of development (Amin 1973: 186).

The success of developed countries in deepening their internal mass markets inevitably resulted in comparably higher growth of their productivity in mass consumption goods production lines in comparison with productivity increases in products traditionally consumed by the richer strata of society. Without any particular effort, the rest of the world therefore enjoyed comparative advantage in luxuries.

The industrial economies of the West, of Japan later, and of present-day China had or have today comparative advantage in mass consumption goods production. They have risen in the international division of labor and are specialized on mass consumption products. This was not the result of deliberate action or even the intention of their ruling classes. Those who chose the products for the McCartney Mission of Britain[18] to China in the late eighteenth century neglected mass consumption products (where England had comparative advantage) and instead concentrated on sophisticated luxury products which did not catch the admiration of the Chinese rulers (Berg 2006: 271).

In capitalist economies, increases of physical productivity—as measured between the volume of production in relation to the value of factors

[18] In 1793, Britain sent a mission to China with a range of British products in order to persuade the Chinese emperor to open China for British exports.

of production engaged (the latter measured in prices)—vary enormously between production lines. If such economies operate at high levels of employment, however, lines of production with more dynamic growth have to attract workers from other lines in order to increase their production. To do so, they must offer either better incomes or better working conditions—or both. I have already described that this must lead to the convergence of wage costs between innovating productions and non-innovating productions. This convergence of productivity in monetary terms is hence the result of scarcity of labor in capitalist systems.[19]

There is no internal economic reason why relative prices in a technically backward country should have the same structure as prices have in technically more advanced countries. It is only if prices are expressed in terms of more advanced countries will productivities in underdeveloped countries diverge considerably. Underdeveloped economies are normally more backward in high-tech industries than in production lines with relatively low skill requirements where the industrially advanced countries no longer achieve real progress in physical productivity. In advanced countries (despite lagging productivities in low skill activities), wages increase also in these production lines at the average rate. Increases in labor incomes are higher than the line specific increases in physical productivity and hence wage costs in international prices become higher than in technically backward countries.

New products which can be sold to the mass of consumers in richer countries are usually goods which, in the great majority of cases, have higher price and higher income elasticities than older goods. The so often criticized decline of terms-of-trade is based on this mechanism.[20]

[19] Certain European political scientists cherish the illusion that capitalist development is harmonious and transforms all spheres of production in comparable ways. So-called structural homogeneity and hence the flexibility in relation to a changing composition of demand in developed countries can certainly be described as relatively homogeneous productivities in different lines of production (Elsenhans 1992c [1982]: 94–100; Nohlen and Sturm 1982: 99). This homogeneity, however, is the result of economic independence in relation to other economies and ultimately the result of their own capacity to produce investment goods. Structural heterogeneity in the underdeveloped Third World is therefore not a technical phenomenon but the consequence of the transfer of a system of relative prices to the South, which is only appropriate for the West because it is established on the basis of relative productivity levels between different production lines prevailing in the West.

[20] An alternative opposed argument is based on the development of demand in the developed or advanced countries: In the West, increasing mass incomes allow the popular

Due to the specialization of industrial countries on expanding mass markets, technically backward countries have enjoyed comparative advantage in lines of production where the capacity of technical improvement and the growth rate of world demand were both weak. Additionally, technical innovation in the production of mass consumption goods contributes to rendering possible the production of goods which until then had only been imagined in fairy tales, such as the airplane. They replace the older luxury goods of the non-capitalist world which existed in the period of rich tributary modes of production.[21]

Low degrees of backwardness in these lines of production lead to higher incomes in international currency by specializing in these goods. The spontaneous tendencies of backward economies consist in specialization on lines of production with little future possibilities of growth. As such unequal specialization is profitable for the elites, there are only little pressures in favor of economic diversification. Short-term economic rationality discourages the adoption of long-term rationality (Singer 1950: 482). Positive terms-of-trade enrich the elites of underdeveloped economies. They provide the elite with financial resources for financing changes in this pattern of specialization, but at the same time, they reduce all incentives to do so. A different strategy would have been possible only if decision-makers with access to these resources by political means had given priority not to immediate enrichment but to the transformation of their economies and to the know-how of their workers through the acquisition of new knowledge. Such an orientation would have, however,

masses access to certain new products where underdeveloped countries enjoy comparative advantage, such as coffee, tea, or chocolate in the last decades of the nineteenth century. Some raw materials for industry fall into this category, like petrol. In most cases, these goods do not lead to the transfer of technical capacity to their producers via "learning by doing." They use technologies which are either too specific or too complicated to be produced in the South, which is unfortunate because this process might contribute to industrial diversification.

[21]The California School bases its argument about the high level of industrial development in ancient China on these "artistic" productions. André Gunder Frank uses my argument about the importance of simple mass consumption products, which he adopts without quoting me, from my critique of his interpretation of the development of capitalism. He was well aware of my argument as there had been long discussions between us around the publication of Senghaas (1979), where we both contributed (Elsenhans 1992b [1979]; Frank 1979). Frank has qualified my position as extremely dangerous in several private main exchanges, but I am very happy that he has accepted it finally.

implied that those who control the surplus are at the same time sheltered from market competition and short-term maximization of financial surpluses.[22]

The dependency of the South has increased the potentially available financial resources for financing such strategies, but at the same time it has widened the backlogs to be overcome by such strategies.

Finally, in the Global South, unequal specialization has led to the destruction of all lines of production which did not depend on natural conditions. The Global South became specialized on raw materials in two forms, minerals and some agricultural raw materials. The share of the consumption of raw materials in total production decreases with economic development. All these products are therefore characterized by low-income elasticity and normally by low price elasticity of demand. In the production of minerals, however, high prices may be maintained because the industrial countries keep some high cost production sites in the West in strategically important products and contribute to stabilize prices at levels where their own minerals remain competitive (e.g., the international price of oil has to be high enough to keep North Sea oil on the market).

When rich resource deposits near the industrial centers get exhausted, investment in improvement of extraction technologies and/or the adoption of the search for new rich deposits faraway—in the Third World but also in the regions of recent European settlement such as Canada, Australia, and the United States—will commence. These new deposits will also be exploited with the most recent technologies. In comparison with the production sites still operating in the old industrial West, producers achieve differential rents from these new deposits.

In agricultural raw materials, rents do not appear openly but in the form of continuous deterioration of the terms-of-trade. This deterioration of the terms-of-trade is not compensated by a massive expansion of employment in the exporting countries, for the internal markets are not dynamic; therefore, there is no strong economic diversification through incentives from internal demand. Because of the slow expansion of demand for raw materials in the process of economic development of

[22] There are no market prices for the effects produced by transformation. Before reaching results, the limit for financing transformation consists in the exhaustion of all financial resources. This limited availability of financial resources obviously acts as a brake for such strategies.

the industrial West, the societies of the South have not enjoyed a significant impact of these exports on their local labor markets. Their local economic structures were not transformed and did not become economic bases for the transition to capitalism. To the contrary, in some small raw material exporting countries of the West (Scandinavia and Canada, Sandberg 1979: 227; Vries 2013: 173), lower production costs for raw materials have contributed not only to increasing competitiveness of the local manpower but also to the transformation of this competitiveness into rising mass incomes because of a scarcity of workers.

The absence of transformation of labor markets in the South was the result of the absence of capitalist structures, particularly the bargaining power of the masses. This absence is due to a few factors, including: inequality which preexisted in the South, the capacity of the pre-existing "elites" to dispossess the mass of the population in initially even rather egalitarian agrarian societies, and the efforts of capitalist powers to increase the level of exploitation without provoking the resistance of the local rentier classes. The perspectives of transition to capitalism by integrating into the world economy were not blocked by existing capitalism in the developed world but by the absence of capitalism in the South.[23] The political appropriation of rents is the only possibility open to the privileged if there are no structures which favor the masses and their increasing mass consumption, which is the essential condition for the transition to capitalism.

In the Global South, since the 1930s crisis, in the interest of maintaining political stability, the "Center" accepted a limited participation of local elites in already existing rents, i.e., those already existing before political decolonization (e.g., marketing boards, French marketing boards called "Caisses de stabilization des cours," the US acceptation of nationalization of Mexican oil 1938/1939, and the US-Brazil agreement on coffee in 1940, Wickizer 1951: 102).

[23]There are numerous critics of my explanation of the transition to capitalism by the expansion of mass consumption, for example, in the issue of Erwägen-Wissen-Ethik (25, 4, 2014), there are 28 contributions dedicated to critiquing my approach (Elsenhans 2014a, b). In recent literature there have been strong arguments about an equal possibility of growth by rising profits with respect to growth by rising wages. Stockhammer and Onaran (2013: 67) and Pariboni (2016: 216) reach the same conclusion as Elsenhans (1995 [chap. 5 in this volume]: 202–204): a rate of accumulation higher than the rate of growth of consumption rapidly leads to a decline of the rate of profit.

With the exception of the compradors in the import-export business, most of the big landlords as well as the elites which the colonial powers had created (and in the formally independent countries, the local reformers) opted for nationalism in order to preserve their political position in the local context by assuming control of state power which had then become "national." The nationalist movements claimed to use this power for economic and social reforms of various depths following the local conditions in different countries and differences in their social origins. All of them have opted for industrialization based on local demand which, after some initial success, was blocked by narrow markets. Concentrating on the external causation of underdevelopment, these elites were late to recognize that the narrowness of the internal market was the result of social inequality and destitution of the local popular masses.

Tracing industrial backlog back to the lack of financial resources indeed matched well with this external causation discourse. Since the early nineteenth century, Indian intellectuals had attributed the misfortune of India to its exploitation by Great Britain, the so-called drain of India (Chandra 1966: 637). Complaining about the deterioration of the terms-of-trade and their exploitation by colonial commercial or mineral monopolies only add new versions to this discourse.

The use of financial resources appropriated as rents for financing the restructuring of the local economy implies the necessity of orienting investment—and therefore the distribution of available funds—by other criteria than the immediate profitability. The profit rate of realized investment projects cannot be the sole criterion. Profitability early on in development theory was shown to also depend on the success of the construction of complementary lines of production upstream and downstream (Rosenstein-Rodan 1943).

The appropriation of rents and their channeling into not yet directly profitable investment projects required the emergence of centralized ruling classes for two reasons: firstly, free riders had to be kept from increasing supply using slightly lower prices, if necessary, by nationalizing them. Secondly, it was also necessary to create productive capacity for those goods for which the demand would increase in case of rising mass incomes. Many of the production lines required for the satisfaction of the demand of the masses did not yet exist and could not come into existence in the short run because of lack of flexibility of underdeveloped economies. They had to be brought into being before there was purchasing power for them in order to avoid rising mass incomes petering away into inflation.[24]

6.6 Centralization of the Rents by the State

I have bestowed the label "state classes" on the decision-makers which emerge as a social class on the basis of state centralization of the rent (Elsenhans 1996 [1981], 1984). Their access to surplus and privileges are based on the construction and private appropriation of the state.

Rent both provides financial means for restructuring the economy and launches a diametrically opposite process of class creation—but this state-class risks stifling or at least subjugating the capitalist entrepreneurs under their patronage. This limits entrepreneurial dynamism. Excessive financial support induces entrepreneurs to look for the manna distributed by the bureaucracies by getting co-opted at the political level, instead of looking for economic efficiency.

The tendencies toward blockage in development were reinforced by the initial economic choices. In prioritizing accumulation, the extension of the internal mass markets was postponed to a faraway future. The well-to-do had sufficient influence in order to liberate themselves from the constraints imposed by planning; the result was that the demand for luxury products especially increased. Cost reduction via achieving economies of scale was hindered; the use of sophisticated technologies for sophisticated products did not allow launching the local production of investment goods. Agrarian reforms had at best a limited character, resulting often only in increasing the surplus available for commercialization.

Protectionism could be justified for an initial period, but it spurred strong organized interests among enterprises and members of the state classes into blocking any later dismantling of such protectionism. Financial resources were allocated on the basis of political alliances of the most different types, which were financed by the external rent—in the case of Algeria by oil rents. The amounts distributed were so high that the access to these favors paid by the rent was essential for competitiveness. Rent invaded all economic, administrative and political structures.

[24] Such a planned use of financial resources has been first formulated in a more systematic way by the French colonialist development policy during the Algerian war of liberation (Elsenhans 2000 [1974]: 649–652).

Members of these state classes have access to surplus not on the basis of their individual efficiency but rather because of the political alliances which they are able to conclude—as well as to their positions in networks of influence which they help establish within not only the formal but also informal structures of the state (Elsenhans 1984, 1996 [1981]). Despite differences in their particular situations due to differences in the success of investment projects in different production lines, all members of the state classes face similar difficulties with similar failures. They have to avoid being accused of inefficiency and corruption. A climate of keeping secret information emerges (including negotiations on how to block any honest perception of the realities) so long as there are still financial resources which allow for the keeping of these realities from erupting into the public debate (Elsenhans 1987: 83–86). The result is waste and exploitation via collective inefficiency (Elsenhans 1996 [1981]: 144, fn. 89).

The exhaustion of rents lead to morosity, which is characterized by the atomization of the forces of popular resistance by means of police repression. The result of this is uncertain political stability where a minor event could act like a detonator, such as during the Arab Spring.

6.7 The Contemporary Globalization of New Forms of Rent

During the 1980s, the systematic pessimism about exports as a force of development vanished. Rising salaries in the West relaunched delocalization of production into the South—a process which had already started by the end of the nineteenth century. The success of the Green Revolution since the 1940s starting in Mexico and especially from the 1960s onwards in Asia in the wheat and rice producing agricultural sectors (especially of East Asia) allowed local wages to decrease, as measured in international money. Exchange rates could go down below the purchasing power parity. Due to their self-sufficient capacity to feed their own population, such countries could increase employment in new export production lines—even if the additional labor was nourished on the basis of a locally produced food surplus and also of locally produced simple industrial goods in an expanding so-called informal sector.

The strategy of development via manufacturing exports is based on a rent from agriculture. Beyond receiving only sales proceeds, economies oriented to manufactured exports reinforce market mechanisms in their economies, somehow as if they imported market regulation in order to replace their previous highly inefficient and costly planning mechanisms. A possible result is better efficiency. After devaluation and state limitation of the export of food surpluses needed for additional export sector workers, food prices decrease relatively to export earnings. At the same time, the relative rise of workers' incomes in export industries compared to locally produced food constitutes a transfer of a rent which was previously appropriated by local landlords. This corresponds to a channeling of rent type surplus of agriculture to the poor and reduces rentier political structures which favor waste.

Some rents are used for enlarging the range of exported products, technical and economic skills, long-term and export proceedings, and jobs. If the country tries to fix its exchange rate at the level where it earns maximum income, a large part of its workforce may not be competitive enough for starting the production of more sophisticated products. Comparative advantage indicates in which exports of which products an economy will become competitive in case of devaluation—at the earliest with limited rates of devaluation. It does not show at which exchange rate these exports will become competitive. Comparative advantage is not competitive advantage. It does not indicate that an economy has become competitive; rather, it shows where, in the case of a less advanced economy, its relative inefficiency is lowest in relation to more advanced economies. Comparative advantage therefore has to be transformed, as already in the example of Ricardo (1951 [1817]: 135–150), into price competitiveness. In Ricardo's demonstration, the local price level in relation to international prices decreases because of the outflow of specie, i.e., gold and silver bullion. Today the same effect is achieved through deteriorating exchange rates (possibly even below purchasing power parity). Such a massive transformation of comparative advantage into competitiveness often requires the mobilization of local resources as additional workers in export industry do not earn enough in international currency in order to buy their food and other necessities from abroad.

Internally generated rents—which are derived from being able to devalue below purchasing parity—may sometimes have to be very high because devaluation very often only reduces the international price of that small part of sales proceeds from exports which are available for paying the local workforce. In international money, their wage rates may be absolutely insufficient for buying the physical equivalent to the incomes of the new workers in the expanding export sector. The larger part of the consumption by these additional workers in the export sector therefore must come from local production.

The new phenomena in current globalization are not the extent of globalization itself but the possibility of rendering the South's labor competitive on the basis of rents which have emerged as a result of the Green Revolution. In their physical form, these rents consist of additional food and allow the devaluation of exchange rates below purchasing power parity. The consumption basket (locally) necessary for bare bone subsistence can fall to mere fractions of the necessary cost for the purchase of these goods on the world market (Chen et al. 1994).

The basic nonagricultural goods which poor households consume in a typical country of the Third World are up to four-fifths (4/5) simple products, which small and middle industries of these countries, including the informal sector, can manufacture: textiles, cloth, furniture, household instruments and various expenditures like urban transport or cigarettes. Some modern products like TV sets, cellphones or refrigerators are locally produced in most of the countries of Asia and Latin America.

Asia and Latin America have agricultural surpluses and small and middle enterprises with certainly still limited technological capabilities, and this makes them able of choosing the development strategy of manufactured exports. On the contrary, in most cases, sub-Saharan Africa is unable to realize currency devaluation because of the lack of success of its agricultural sectors. The Arab world is unable to produce necessary agricultural surpluses; however, it is kept wealthy by its oil rents. These oil rents discourage any initiative toward economic diversification and impose a subsidized and inefficient limited industrialization for smaller internal markets, which are characterized by high inequality.

There are some production lines which are already competitive even at high exchange rates. The economies of the South are not characterized by equal backlogs in different lines of production in relation to the West. There is the possibility of taxing some exports—as one usually did with the raw materials. The classical case is the blockage of textile machinery imports in South Korea during the middle of the 1970s, when price elasticity of Korean textile exports decreased (Haggard 1983: 83). Textile exporters had to work with local producers of machinery parts they already knew to serve as their suppliers of spare parts. When textile machinery imports were blocked by the government, they had to ask them to produce the entire machinery: Textile exporters had to accept obviously higher machinery costs than for the previously imported ones.

In case of low price elasticity of demand on the world market, the Korean exporters were able to pass on most additional costs within their export prices. The whole mechanism contributed to the launching of the local industry for textile machinery which constituted the point of departure for a diversified machinery industry on the basis of skills acquired in textile machinery production.

Whenever export-oriented economies realize that the initially chosen production lines had limited future growth possibilities, policy makers used taxes on high-income industries with less dynamic prospects. This provided the governments with financial resources for subsidizing new enterprises for diversification into production lines which were not yet competitive (Khan 2000). The West has been successful in eliminating some rules concerning slowly increasing degrees of local content and obligations for foreign direct investors during the negotiations on the World Trade Organization. Such local content rules are appropriate for taking a part of the surplus from production lines with high export incomes because of higher prices on the international market given their already high productivity—as the continued application of these rules to foreign direct investment in the People's Republic of China still shows. These amounts spent on not yet competitive local inputs are rents which are used for financing diversification. The literature on public and private cooperation in national systems of innovation presents illustrative examples on how to mobilize rents intelligently.

The strategy for manufactured exports is based on a rent. Rent is utilized for reinforcing pre-existing tendencies on the market which allow new patterns of specialization. Export-oriented manufacturing production is not conceived in a manner to clearly oppose such tendencies of unequal specialization. For a transitional period, rents are used to allow catching up by devaluation, corresponding to the still low productivity of local industry. This transition will take time until the elimination of marginality.

Manufacturing industries provide much more jobs than raw material industries. They contribute to the launching of internal markets for consumption goods, initially as goods for the poor, who are however less poor than the previously marginalized ones. Exports establish a link between local enterprises and world practices in technologies. This can reduce inefficiency. Such contacts can promote technical learning, because an enterprise which succeeds here will earn more on the world market and therefore has a material incentive to engage in such learning. Levels of learning by doing are normally high because mastering such technologies is not blocked by a hiatus between the skills of the workers and the technical requirements of the equipment—as has been the case for mineral production.

The argument that there are limits to the absorptive capacities of the Center's industrial countries for such exports is important, but we realize today that the first countries to have chosen this strategy—the East Asian Tigers and after this also mainland China—have already delocalized some production lines into countries which are still less advanced. When high levels of employment are achieved, growth promotion by devaluation becomes blocked: tensions on labor markets emerge and launch inflationary tendencies. Eastern China has started suffering from such tendencies—which is the same problem that 1960s Germany was only able to mitigate by considerable appreciation of its currency in the late 1950s and early 1960s.

As long as there is marginality combined with favorable structures for the appropriation of rents by the ruling class (justified by their use for prioritizing certain production lines), then rentier behavioral patterns are inevitable. This can be mitigated by influencing individual styles of behavior of those tasked with the management of the rent. In this perspective, the recipes of administrative sciences of the modernization theory school may have some importance. However, the orientation toward manufactured exports does not imply the end of rents: This is demonstrated by rent-based sociocultural values, the relations between state and enterprise, the generally close links between governments of the emerging countries, and their own transnational companies.

Because of the persistence of rent, the orientation to manufactured exports is always threatened by the danger of these economies becoming rentier systems. This is especially the case if the pressure of the popular masses cannot be maintained. The crises in Brazil of the end of the alliance between the workers' party and the different parties of the industrial bourgeoisie are an example. Providing bargaining power to the popular masses is strategically much more important than the efforts of diffusing sociocultural norms by teaching and disciplining the behavior of the privileged ones. Such bargaining power results in rising mass incomes and strengthens the conscience of the masses regarding their bearing on the political system.

Identifying realistic political steps for reducing the demand of the privileged—and with this the dependency on outside, without neglecting the danger of social shocks in case of redistribution against the middle strata—helps such an approach. Measures which appear as a result of market mechanisms are normally more acceptable than measures more directly imposed by the state. This is the case for devaluation, which increases the price of imports for the better-off and which also offers, through newly emerged more dynamic economic sectors, new opportunities for enriching themselves via productive investment, and even by allowing the privileged classes to participate in increasing exports.

In the struggle against rent and inequalities, influencing the social system by sociocultural instruments is less important than maintaining the course of an egalitarian economic strategy. Economies in transition to a mass needs oriented capitalism will be exposed to rentier temptations for a long time. Such rentier temptations are always present in capitalism—even at later times, though they may be less pronounced in their forms. These rentier temptations are never checked by either the behavior or the sociocultural norms of the capitalists: Instead, they are checked by the pressure of popular mass consumption. Capitalist do not want capitalism; they want money. They will only accept necessary limits for the good operation of capitalism if there is the counterweight of the popular masses which imposes these limits.

Marxist and neoclassical theories have neglected the importance of the bargaining power of the popular masses. The rising incomes of the masses favor the orientation of technical progress to machine-produced products and the refinement of machines in the form of special purpose machinery. They facilitate the transition to capitalism. Marxist theories are therefore rather obstacles for such mass struggles. They do not give an answer to the question of how to utilize rents for achieving the expansion of mass demand and the rise of profit against rents.

What is necessary is a theory of transition which analyses the control of spontaneous tendencies toward inequality when utilizing rents as well as the possibilities of encouraging the local production (using local labor) of goods for popular consumption. This theory must also identify those technologies which can promote the start of local production of investment goods. Because of the ubiquity of rent this task—which was already difficult even for the firstcomers of the Industrial Revolution—this challenge has become more complicated for today's rentier countries because of their integration into the world economy. The dominance of neoliberal positions in the West and its consequent advocation of the end of all state intervention in the economy, also the economies of the South are supplementary hurdles. There are, however, some aspects which allow a bit of hope. The new competitiveness of many countries of the South in sectors of employment in the West deemed key presents a dilemma: The developed industrialized countries might feel pressure to combat this key employment loss by considering the option of closing the boundaries and promoting the globalization of rents (Elsenhans 2006). They might, however, based on a more correct analysis of the frailty of capitalism, opt for participating in the struggle against rent in the countries of the Global South. For most industrialized countries, closing their boundaries would imply technical backwardness at the global level at more or less short delay. There is therefore no other acceptable solution for them but the rapid reduction of marginality by keeping open the markets of the West and by applying social programs for marginality reduction, as shown by the BRICS.[25]

Regarding the amounts to be employed for promoting absorption of the marginalized of the South: Political decisions must be made, and these depend on the mobilization of political support on a global scale. Absorbing the marginals is the condition for good operation of capitalism, particularly to capitalism's extension to those regions and countries where it is blocked by marginality and the absence of bargaining power of the world of labor. Support for such decisions would come more easily if the argument that capitalism can function only on the basis of the expansion of mass demand would become more credible. In contemporary world, there are two or three forces which could enter into this dialogue and which have great difficulties to do so: the remnants of the labor movement in the West, Keynesian positions in economics and the new cultural identitarian movements in the South. Bringing them into this dialogue is more difficult because the West fears identitarian movements in the South, owing to their religious and cultural orientation. For their part, the identitarian political movements in the South mistrust and ascribe malice onto Western reformists not only due to their secularism: They

[25] I have proposed the creation of artificial industries for absorbing unemployed (Elsenhans 1991: 281–286). An increase of the annual income of two billion hungry with annual incomes by about \$500 would cost \$1,000 billion. Already in 2009, losses on the financial markets are estimated to \$4,000 billion: Landler (2009).

also distrust them because of Western reformists' behavior in the colonial conflicts where moderate Western reformists have largely opposed the nationalist forces which mobilized the South.[26]

References

Acemoglu, Daron, and James A. Robinson. 2012. *Why Nations Fail? The Origins of Power. Prosperity, and Poverty*. London: Profile Books.

Aglietta, Michel. 1979. *A Theory of Capitalist Regulation. The US Experience*. London: NLB.

Akimoto, Hiroya. 1981. Capital Formation and Economic Growth in Mid-19th Century Japan. *Explorations in Economic History* 18 (1): 40–59.

Allen, Robert C., Tommy E. Murphy, and Eric B. Schneider. 2012. The Colonial Origins of the Divergence in the Americas. A Labor Market Approach. *Journal of Economic History* 72 (4): 863–894.

Amin, Samir. 1973. *Le développement inégal. Essai sur les formations sociales du capitalisme périphérique*. Paris: Editions de Minuit.

Beblawi, Hazem. 1987. The Rentier State in the Arab World. In *The Rentier State*, ed. Hazem Beblawi and Giacomo Luciani, 49–62. London: Croom Helm.

Berg, Maxine. 2004. In Pursuit of Luxury. Global History and British Consumer Goods in the Eighteenth Century. *Past and Present* 182: 83–142.

Berg, Maxine. 2006. Britain, Industry and Perceptions of China. Matthew Boulton, 'Useful Knowledge' and the Macartney Embassy to China 1792–94. *Journal of Global History* 1 (2): 269–288.

Bourdieu, Pierre. 1991. *Sozialer Raum und Klassen. Leçon sur leçon*. Frankfort on the Main: Suhrkamp.

Boyer, Robert. 1978. Les salaires en longue période. *Economie et statistique* 103: 27–58.

Brady, Dorothy. 1964. Relative Prices in the Nineteenth Century. *Journal of Economic History* 24 (2): 145–203.

Brara, Rita. 1994. Kinship and the Political Order. The Afghani Sherwani Chiefs of Malerkotha (1454–1947). *Contributions to Indian Sociology* 28 (2): 203–242.

Bratton, Michael, and Nicholas van de Walle. 1994. Neopatrimonial Regimes and Transitions in Africa. *World Politics* 46 (4): 453–489.

Braudel, Fernand. 1967. *Civilisation matérielle et capitalisme*. Paris: Armand Colin.

[26] I have published some texts in order to contribute to facilitate such a dialogue, Elsenhans (2017, 2016).

Broadberry, Stephen N., Rainer Fremdling, and Peter Solar. 2008. European Industry 1700 –1870. *Jahrbuch für Wirtschaftsgeschichte* 2: 141–171.
Caiden, Gerald E. 1973. Development, Administrative Capacity and Administrative Reform. *Revue Internationale Des Sciences Administratives* 39 (4): 327–344.
Chandra, Bipan. 1966. *The Rise and Growth of Economic Nationalism in India. Economic Policies of Indian National Leadership, 1880–1905*. Delhi: People's Publishing House.
Chen, Haichun, M.J. Gordon, and Yan Zhiming. 1994. The Real Income and Consumption of an Urban Chinese Family. *Journal of Development Studies* 31 (1): 201–213.
Clark, Gregory. 2007. The Long March of History. Farm Wages, Population, and Economic Growth, England 1209–1869. *Economic History Review* 60 (1): 97–135.
Coghlan, T.A. 1918. *Labour and Industry in Australia from the First Settlement in 1788 to the Establishment of the Commonwealth in 1901*. Oxford et al.: Oxford University Press.
Coleman, D.C. 1977. *The Economy of England 1450–1750*. Oxford et al.: Oxford University Press.
Deng, Gang. 1999. *The Premodern Chinese Economy. Social Equilibrium and Capitalist Sterility*. London and New York: Routledge.
Elsenhans, Hartmut. 1983a. Égalité et développement. L'expérience européenne et le monde sous-développé d'aujourd'hui. *Cultures et développement* 15 (2): 187–215.
Elsenhans, Hartmut. 1983b. Rising Mass Incomes as a Condition of Capitalist Growth. Implications for the World Economy. *International Organization* 37 (1): 1–38.
Elsenhans, Hartmut. 1984. Le développement autocentré contradictoire. *Cahiers du CREAD* 3: 4–47.
Elsenhans, Hartmut. 1987. Dependencia, Underdevelopment and the Third World State. *Law and State* 36: 65–94.
Elsenhans, Hartmut. 1991. Problems Central to Economic Policy Deregulation in Bangladesh. *Internationales Asienforum* 22 (3/4): 259–286.
Elsenhans, Hartmut. 1992b [1979]. Foundation of Development of the Capitalist World Economy. In *Equality and Development*, ed. Hartmut Elsenhans, 21–79. Dhaka: Center for Social Studies.
Elsenhans, Hartmut. 1992a [1980]. English Poor Law and Egalitarian Agrarian Reform in the Third World. In *Equality and Development*, ed. Hartmut Elsenhans, 130–162. Dhaka: Center for Social Studies.
Elsenhans, Hartmut. 1992c [1982]. Overcoming Underdevelopment through Mass Production for Mass Consumption: Evolution of a New Development

Concept. In *Equality and Development*, ed. Hartmut Elsenhans, 80–129. Dhaka: Center for Social Studies.

Elsenhans, Hartmut. 1994. Rent, State and the Market. The Political Economy of the Transition to Self-Sustained Capitalism. *Pakistan Development Review* 33 (4): 393–428.

Elsenhans, Hartmut. 1995. Überwindung von Marginalität als Gegenstand der Armutsbekämpfung. In *Bevölkerungsdynamik und Grundbedürfnisse in Entwicklungsländern*, ed. Hans Bernd Schäfer, 193–221. Schriften des Vereins für Socialpolitik 246. Berlin: Duncker und Humblot. Chapter 5 in this volume.

Elsenhans, Hartmut. 1996 [1981]. *State, Class and Development*. New Delhi, London, Columbia, MO: Radiant; Sangam; South Asia Books.

Elsenhans, Hartmut. 1997. The Relevance of the Principles of Keynesian Economics for the Transition to Capitalism in Today's Underdeveloped World. In *Improving the Global Economy. Keynesianism and the Growth in Output and Employment*, Paul Davidson, and Jan A. Kregel, 283–303. Cheltenham, Lyme: Edward Elgar.

Elsenhans, Hartmut. 2000 [1974]. *La guerre d'Algérie 1954–1962. La transition d'une France à une autre. Le passage de la IV à la Ve République*. Paris: Publisud.

Elsenhans, Hartmut. 2001. Europe's Development and South Asia's Underdeveloped. Globalisation and the Role of the State. In *Contemporary Europe and South Asia*, ed. Bhagavati Panikker Vivekanandan and D.K. Giri, 21–77. New Delhi: Concept Publishing Company.

Elsenhans, Hartmut. 2006. *Globalization between a Convoy Model and an Underconsumptionist Threat*. Münster: LIT Verlag.

Elsenhans, Hartmut. 2007. *Geschichte und Ökonomie der europäischen Welteroberung. Vom Zeitalter der Entdeckungen zum 1. Weltkrieg*. Herausgegeben mit einem Vorwort von Matthias Middell. Leipzig: Leipziger Universitätsverlag.

Elsenhans, Hartmut. 2011a. *The Rise and Demise of the Capitalist World System*. Leipzig: Leipziger Universitätsverlag.

Elsenhans, Hartmut. 2011b. World System Theory and Keynesian Macroeconomics. Towards an Alternative Explanation of the Rise and Fall of the Capitalist World System. *Cahiers du CREAD* 97: 5–61.

Elsenhans, Hartmut. 2012. *Kapitalismus global. Aufstieg – Grenzen – Risiken*. Stuttgart et al.: Kohlhammer.

Elsenhans, Hartmut. 2014a. Capitalism—An Achievement of Labour. Empowerment of Labour and Rising Mass Incomes as a Condition of Capitalist Growth. *Erwägen - Wissen - Ethik* 25 (4): 601–625.

Elsenhans, Hartmut. 2014b. Capitalism and Global History. *Erwägen - Wissen - Ethik* 25 (4): 529–542.

Elsenhans, Hartmut. 2014c. Kapitalismus. In *Die Entwicklung der Menschheit*, ed. Gerd Jüttemann, 291–299. Wiebaden: Pabst Science Publisher.
Elsenhans, Hartmut. 2015. *Saving Capitalism from the Capitalists. A Contribution to Global and Historical Keynesianism*. Beverly Hills, CA, London, New Delhi: Sage.
Elsenhans, Hartmut. 2016. Reconstructing Development Economics. Overcoming Rent for Constructing Capitalism. *Pakistan Development Review* 55 (1): 1–14.
Elsenhans, Hartmut. 2017. Overcoming Political Isolation. The Relevance of Keynesian Fundamentals for Moral Economy Approaches in an Increasingly Multipolar System. *Journal of European Studies (Karachi)* 33 (2): 4–27.
Elsenhans, Hartmut, and Salvatore Babones. 2017. *The BRICS or Bust*. Stanford, CA: Stanford University Press.
Engerman, Stanley L., Kenneth L. Sokoloff. 2012. *Economic Development in the Americas since 1500. Endowments and Institutions*. Cambridge et al.: Cambridge University Press.
Erdmann, Gero, and Ulf Engel. 2007. Neopatrimonialism Reconsidered. A Critical Review and Elaboration of an Elusive Concept. *Commonwealth and Comparative Politics* 45 (1): 95–119.
Evans, Archibald A. 1969. Work and Leisure. *International Labour Review* 99 (1): 35–60.
Fanon, Frantz. 1968. *Les damnés de la terre*. Paris: Maspéro.
Frank, André Gunder. 1979. Über die sogenannte ursprüngliche Akkumulation. In *Kapitalistische Weltökonomie. Kontroversen über ihren Ursprung und ihre Entwicklungsdynamik*, ed. Dieter Senghaas, 68–102. Frankfort on the Main: Suhrkamp.
Fremdling, Rainer. 1977. Railroads and German Economic Growth. A Leading Sector Analysis with Comparison to the United States and Great Britain. *Journal of Economic History* 36 (3): 583–604.
Gilboy, Elizabeth Waterman. 1934. Time Series and the Derivation of Demand and Supply Curves. A Study of Coffee and Tea. *Quarterly Journal of Economics* 48 (3): 667–685.
Goldstone, Jack A. 2002. Efflorescences and Economic Growth in World History. Rethinking the 'Rise of the West' and the Industrial Revolution. *Journal of World History* 13 (2): 323–389.
Gordon, David, Richard Edwards, and Michael Reich. 1982. *Segmented Work, Divided Workers. The Historical Transformation of Labor in the United States*. Cambridge et al.: Cambridge University Press.
Grabowski, Richard. 1994. European and East-Asian Exceptionalism. Agriculture and Economic Growth. *Journal of International Development* 6 (4): 437–451.
Haggard, Stephan Mark. 1983. *Pathways from the Periphery. The Newly Industrializing Countries in the International System*. Berkeley, CA: Dissertation.

Hanley, Susan B. 1983. A High Standard of Living in Nineteenth-Century Japan. Fact or Fantasy. *Journal of Economic History* 43 (1): 183–192.

Hayami, Yujiro. 1972. Rice Policy in Japan's Economic Development. *American Journal of Agricultural Economics* 54 (1): 19–31.

Hilton, Rodney. 1978. Reasons for Inequalities among Medieval Peasants. *Journal of Peasant Studies* 5 (3): 271–284.

Hirschman, Albert O. 1970. *Exit, Voice and Loyality. Responses to Decline in Firms, Organizations and States*. Cambridge, MA, London: Harvard University Press.

Hobson, John Atkinson. 1938. *Imperialism. A Study* [1902]. London: Allen & Unwin.

Jones, Eric L. 1974. *Agriculture and the Industrial Revolution*. Oxford: Basil Blackwell.

Kalecki, Michal. 1942. A Theory of Profits. *Economic Journal* 52 (205–206): 258–267.

Karl, Terry Lynn. 1997. *The Paradox of Plenty. Oil Booms and Petro-States*. Berkeley, CA et al.: University of California Press.

Khan, Mushtaq H. 2000. Rents, Efficiency and Growth. In *Rents, Rent-Seeking and Economic Development. Theory and Evidence in Asia*, ed. Mushtaq H. Khan and Kwame Sundaram Jomo, 21–69. Cambridge et al.: Cambridge University Press.

Kocka, Jürgen. 1990. *Arbeiterverhältnisse und Arbeiterexistenzen*. Grundlagen zur Klassenbildung im 19. Jahrhundert. Bonn: J.H.W. Dietz Nachf.

Kocka, Jürgen. 2013. *Geschichte des Kapitalismus*. Munich: C. H. Beck.

Landler, Mark. 2009. *IMF Puts Bank Losses From Global Financial Crisis at $4.1 Trillion*. New York Times, 21.04.2009. Online available https://www.nytimes.com/2009/04/22/business/global/22fund.html, last proved 15.12.2020.

Lenin, Vladimir Ilyich. 1964. *Imperialism, the Highest Stage of Capitalism. A Popular Outline* [1916]. Lenin Collected Works (22). Moscow: Progress Publishers.

Lipietz, Alain. 1982. Towards Global Fordism. *New Left Review* 132: 33–47.

Luxemburg, Rosa. 1951 [1913]. *The Accumulation of Capital*. London: Routledge & Kegan Paul.

Mahdavy, Hossein. 1970. Patterns and Problems of Economic Development in Rentier States. The Case of Iran. In *Studies in the Economic History of the Middle East. From the Rise of Islam to the Present Day*, ed. Michael A. Cook, 428–467. London: Oxford University Press.

Mantoux, Paul. 1905. *La Révolution industrielle au XVIIIe siècle. Essai sur les commencements de la grande industrie moderne en Angleterre*. Paris: Société nouvelle de librairie et d'édition.

Morrison, James Ashley. 2012. Before Hegemony. Adam Smith, American Independence, and the Origins of the First Era of Globalization. *International Organization* 66 (3): 395–428.

Neale, Walter C. 1957. Reciprocity and Redistribution in the Indian Village. Sequel to Some Notable Discussion. In *Trade and Markets in the Early Empires*, ed. Karl Polanyi, Conrad M. Arensberg, and Harry W. Pearson, 218–238. New York, London: Free Press; Collier Macmillan.

Nohlen, Dieter, and Roland Sturm. 1982. Über das Konzept der strukturellen Heterogenität. In *Handbuch der Dritten Welt (1). Unterentwicklung und Entwicklung – Theorien, Strategien, Indikatoren*, ed. Dieter Nohlen and Franz Nuscheler, 92–116. Hamburg: Hoffmann & Campe.

North, Douglass C. 1985. Transaction Costs in History. *Journal of European Economic History* 14 (3): 557–576.

Okishio, Nobuo. 1961. Technical Change and the Rate of Profit. *Kobe University Economic Review* 7: 85–99.

Pariboni, Riccardo. 2016. Autonomous Demand and the Marglin-Bhaduri Model. A Critical Note. *Review of Keynesian Economics* 4 (4): 409–428.

Piketty, Thomas. 2014. *Capital in the Twenty-First Century* (Electronic Version). Cambridge: Belknap.

Pirenne, Henri. 1914. The Stages in the Social History of Capitalism. *American Historical Review* 19 (3): 494–515.

Postan, Moisei M. 1967. Investment in Medieval Agriculture. *Journal of Economic History* 27 (4): 576–587.

Ricardo, David. 1951. *On the Principles of Political Economy and Taxation* [1817]. The Works and Correspondence of David Ricardo (1). Cambridge et al.: Cambridge University Press.

Richards, Eric. 1974. The Industrial Face of a Great Estate. Trentham and Lilleshall, 1780–1860. *Economic History Review* 27 (3): 414–430.

Riggs, Fred W. 1964. *Administration in Developing Countries. The Theory of Prismatic Society*. Boston, MA: Houghton Mifflin.

Robbins, Keith. 1990. British Culture versus British Industry. In *British Culture and Economic Decline*, ed. Bruce Collins and Keith Robbins, 1–24. London: Weidenfeld and Nicolson.

Rosenstein-Rodan, P.N. 1943. Problems of Industrialization of Eastern and Southeastern Europe. *Economic Journal* 53 (210/211): 202–211.

Ruben, Walter. 1961. L'origine de la pensée rationelle dans l'Inde. *La Pensée* 102: 75–86.

Ruggiu, François. 2001. The Urban Gentry in England, 1660–1780. A French Approach. *Historical Research* 74 (185): 249–270.

Salama, Pierre. 1978. Spécificités de l'internationalisation du capital en Amérique latine. *Tiers Monde* 19 (74): 260–267.

Salter, Wilfried E.G. 1960. *Productivity and Change*. Cambridge et al.: Cambridge University Press.

Sandberg, Lars G. 1979. The Case of the Impoverished Sophisticate. Human Capital and Swedish Economic Growth before World War I. *Journal of Economic History* 39 (1): 225–241.

Saul, Samuel Berrick. 1960. *Studies in British Overseas Trade 1870–1914*. Liverpool: Liverpool University Press.

Say, Jean-Baptiste. 1972. *Traité d'économie politique* [1803]. Paris: Calmann-Lévy.

Senghaas, Dieter (ed.). 1979. *Kapitalistische Weltökonomie. Kontroversen über ihren Ursprung und ihre Entwicklungsdynamik*. Frankfort on the Main: Suhrkamp.

Sid Ahmed, Abdelkader. 1989. *Économie de l'industrialisation à partir de ressources naturelles (I.B.R.) (2) Le cas des hydrocarbures*. Paris: Publisud.

Singer, Hans Wolfgang. 1950. U.S. Foreign Investment in Underdeveloped Areas. The Distribution of Gains between Investing and Borrowing Countries. *American Economic Review* 40 (2): 473–485.

Stockhammer, Engelbert, and Özlem Onaran. 2013. Wage-led Growth. Theory, Evidence, Policy. *Review of Keynesian Economics* 1 (1): 61–78.

Teschke, Benno. 2003. *The Myth of 1648. Class, Geopolitics, and the Making of Modern International Relations*. London: Verso.

Thirsk, Joan. 1978. *Economic Policy and Projects. The Development of a Consumer Society in Early Modern England*. Oxford: Clarendon Press.

von Bortkiewicz, Ladislaus. 1907. Wertrechnung und Preisrechnung im Marxschen System (3). *Archiv Für Sozialwissenschaft Und Sozialpolitik* 25 (2): 445–489.

Vries, Peer 2013. *Escaping Poverty. The Origins of Modern Economic Growth*. Göttingen: V&R unipress.

Wallerstein, Immanuel Maurice. 1974. *The Modern World-System (1). Capitalist Agriculture and the Origins of the European World-Economy in the Sixteenth Century*. New York, Orlando, FL: Academic Press.

Watanabe, Susumu. 1991. The Japanese Quality Control Circle: Why it Works. *International Labour Review* 130 (1): 56–80.

Wickizer, Vernon Dale. 1951. *Coffee, Tea and Cocoa. An Economic and Political Analysis*. Stanford, CA: Stanford University Press.

Wiener, Martin J. 1980. *English Culture and the Decline of the Industrial Spirit 1850–1980*. Cambridge: Cambridge University Press.

Wright, Louis B. 1935. *Middle-Class Culture in Elizabethan England*. Chapel Hill, NC: University of North Carolina Press.

Yasuba, Yasukichi. 1986. Standard of Living in Japan Before Industrialisation. From What Level Did Japan Begin? A Comment. *Journal of Economic History* 46 (1): 217–224.

PART III

The International System Between Capitalism and Rent

CHAPTER 7

Economic Rent: Obstacle to Development or Fuel for Long-Term Growth

Hartmut Elsenhans

The North American rent-seeking school considers rents to be an obstacle to development (Krueger 1974: 290–303; Olson 1982). The critics of imperialism and underdevelopment have based their interpretation of underdevelopment on exploitation, hence finally on a reduction of rents. It is surprising that both schools have never entered into any meaningful dialogue. Indeed, both aspects are intimately intertwined as rent is a source of finance for investment which can allow catch-up industrialization through stepping up the share of investment in total income. But, unlike most mainstream marxist and non-marxist theories of growth, Keynesian views would be based on the Bortkiewicz demonstration that a tendency toward falling rates of profit is impossible (von Bortkiewicz

Article to be presented to Studies in Political Economy, written in 1995 and ultimately rejected as too dense Unpublished paper.

H. Elsenhans (✉)
University of Leipzig, Leipzig, Germany
e-mail: helsen@rz.uni-leipzig.de

© The Author(s), under exclusive license to Springer Nature Switzerland AG 2021

H. Warnecke-Berger (ed.), *Development, Capitalism, and Rent*,
https://doi.org/10.1007/978-3-030-62605-1_7

1907: 454–457; cf. Okishio 1961: 85–90). At least capitalist forms of transition to self-sustained growth do not require additional sources of finance as capitalism does not require what had been called previous accumulation. Raw material and rent rich countries are not among the most successful newly industrializing countries. The degree of their success does not follow from how much they have opened their industries to the world market price system: South Korea, for one, provides a sound example of intelligent rent allocation. So rent extends beyond the raw material sector. Its manipulation and management can be a source of growth. Differences in the volume of rent appropriated, in achievements in the productive investment of rent, in the orientation of the rent-appropriating class and the strategies followed indicate that rent presents an opportunity for additional investment but that it can also keep a country mired in underdevelopment and prevent its transition to capitalism. Rent provides additional sources of finance, but it also reinforces tendencies to waste resources and to render growth-impeding structures and forces more powerful.

Supposing that the microeconomic efficiency of rent-based investment is invariably lower than that of profit-based investment, another aspect has to be added: Why does rent not disappear, as a result of profit-based investment driving it out from the market. At least in the underdeveloped world, rent has become the form of surplus which actually structures the whole political system. One explanation proposed is that rent as the difference between earnings achieved and the opportunity earnings of the same factor of production in any other employment depends on market failure created by the use of political power. The other explanation is that even when political power is absent economic structure creates surplus which cannot be appropriated as profit, but is available in the form of politically appropriated surplus, which I call rent. I will start with this aspect of continuing and reinforced rent since it allows us to get into view the two politico-economic models that are basic to my analysis. They establish that rent can be abolished in the transition to capitalism only after this transition is successfully achieved whereas before reaching such a level of development of productive forces and mass consumption, rent can only be reduced under extremely favorable conditions for international specialization.

Therefore, my contribution will argue that the current mainstream preoccupation with eliminating rent is misplaced. It will lead to new forms of rent, and it precludes considering whether rent can be reasonably managed, which is the most important element in catching up processes. One of the models on which my argument is based relates to the problem of transitioning to capitalism from a low level productivity economy, the other to the long-term results of perfect specialization but with a focus on the typical pattern of evolution of comparative advantage for underdeveloped countries. Both models are integrated into a historically based empirically meaningful explanation of the interaction of internal and external factors of development and underdevelopment. This explanation is capable of providing strategic suggestions toward overcoming underdevelopment within an overall theoretical framework based on Keynesian principles according to which it is the side of deficient demand and investment that especially threatens to undermine capitalist stability.

This Keynesian framework will not be elaborated here.[1] Suffice it to say that net profit is here the result of spending on net investment and not vice versa. In this framework, net investment is taken to depend on expectations of entrepreneurs about future outlets for machine-produced goods at profitable prices, which tend to be purchased by poorer income strata. Their demand pattern allows for improvements in technologies on the basis of economies of scale and specialization of equipment through special purpose machinery. Both tend to keep the capital-output ratio at a constant level through high growth in productivity.[2] The problem that sources of technical progress may be exhausted is not discussed here. The macroeconomic conditions for capitalism and capitalist growth which are indissociable in this model are therefore mass incomes rising in line with labor productivity plus/minus (minor) changes in the capital-output-ratio and in the terms-of-trade.

7.1 The Inevitable Emergence/Persistence of Rent in the Transition to Capitalism

It is assumed that a precapitalist economy whether it historically precedes capitalism or is subject to capitalist penetration emanating from contemporary technically more advanced economies is characterized by low average productivity. This applies especially to agriculture and causes

[1] Kalecki (1942), Kregel (1971: 145), and Robinson, J. V. (1956: 48–55).

[2] Cf. as good introductory texts: Nadiri and Schankerman (1981: 314–319), (Young 1928: 533), and Ruby (1991: 299).

marginal productivity in agriculture to decline with rising employment of labor on limited surfaces of land. Agricultural production is modeled as a function f(E) of employment in agriculture with $f'(E) > 0$ and $f''(E) < 0$. In the case of rising employment, production increases but additional product decreases. Demographic growth at some point will lead to marginal product falling below the inevitable costs of reproduction of producers in agriculture. They either will be shed off by their employers or driven out from the land they use by surplus maximizing landowners, be they capitalist or non-capitalist. There exists a level of marginality, beyond which employment in agriculture can be expanded only to the detriment of surplus. Such excess employment may be possible according to the theory of a social pact which binds a land-owning elite to the direct producers in agriculture if there is no competition. This elite can be centralized as a state class[3] of the type to be found in tributary modes of production or decentralized as in the type of feudal landowners with private property rights in land. At the level of employment and production where marginal product equals the cost of reproduction of a farmworker or peasant, which I call the threshold of marginality, a surplus exists as all agricultural workers/peasants who are employed/active up to this level produce a surplus. The model does not specify the amount of surplus at this level although it indicates that the higher the maximum surplus the more challenging the problem of rent so that relatively poorer societies have greater chances of transition to capitalism. Their technical level of mastery of nature may, however, constitute an economic obstacle for growth in productivity which capitalism also requires. Especially societies in which average and marginal product in agriculture are very close together seem to be extremely favored in the transition to capitalism.

The model implies demographic growth being relatively unchecked at low levels of economic development. If the number of able-bodied average-skilled hands exceeds the number of workers which can be "productively" (i.e., producing a surplus) employed, the only available strategy for members of the exploited class consists in increasing the number of the able-bodied members of their own small (family) unit. This allows them to maximize their number of tickets in this lottery-type labor market. Further, the cost of additional children in relation to additional transfers

[3] On differences between tributary modes of production and European feudalism for example Abrahamian (1975). A similar approach on the basis of such a tributary mode of production is Chao (1986).

from children expected to support parents in their old age is lower for the productive household than the future cost of this labor and its family to society when marginal product decreases in case of demographic growth. The surplus appropriating class (SAC) benefits from larger bargaining power with demographic growth of the underprivileged strata especially because it can use its surplus only if it can find labor which cannot go back into agriculture but has to accept the "stipends" the SAC class hands out.

Only one among four types of technical progress can significantly alter the marginality-cum-surplus configuration (Elsenhans 1994b).

Technical progress which raises the threshold of marginality in agriculture normally associated with labor-intensive forms of production and investment (which are, however, not the only forms) automatically increases total employment in agriculture and nonagricultural employment in wage goods production via the market.

Capital-intensive forms of such progress (e. g., large-scale irrigation) which raise the level of marginality require huge investments normally out of the control of the immediate producers in agriculture. At least at the political level, this will help avoid social consequences of a rise in the threshold of marginality.

Technical progress in agriculture which raises the surplus of the already employed workers increases the surplus and has implications for employment only if the demand of the SAC for services and luxuries increases.

Technical progress in nonagricultural mass consumption goods production which I henceforth call industrial wage goods lowers the cost of labor in agriculture. Fewer nonagricultural workers have to be fed in order to maintain the agricultural labor force at the same level of physical consumption of industrial products. The threshold of marginality rises because the point of equality between marginal product and cost of labor is being achieved at a higher level of employment. This effect is limited if the share of food being consumed by the exploited class is high; it comes to an end at the latest when marginal product in agriculture equals the food consumption of an agricultural worker and his family.

Productivity increases in luxury production have no effect on employment: More or better luxury goods and services will be consumed and produced by a same volume of labor.

There is no pre-established relation in terms of which the surplus at the threshold of marginality can be made to correspond to the financial requirements of capitalist entrepreneurs for investment. The demand for machines derives from the demand for machine-produced products as this latter demand depends on the number of low-income households and their capacity to spend on nonagricultural products. Therefore, a low level of employment in agriculture (threshold of marginality) and a low level of mass incomes due to fierce competition for employment constitute serious obstacles to capital accumulation. The possible surplus of agriculture will however be produced, as the net benefits between production and food consumption do not depend on realization on a market and can be appropriated by any landowner whether there is competition or not.

If the requirements of capitalist entrepreneurs for financing investment are lower than the total available surplus, such entrepreneurs are unable to deprive the precapitalist landlords of their rent, which is the form in which this latter class appropriates surplus. Whatever the efficiency of the capitalists, they are in this case not able to spend as much money on investment as there is surplus. Hence the laborers who are employed in investment goods production are unable to buy all the producible surplus. There is agricultural surplus without workers in the industrial sector capable of buying it. In extremis, the landlords can waste this surplus by employing domestic servants.

Precapitalist landlords can always "realise" the surplus appropriated through domestic production of goods and services, capitalists only in the case where aggregate demand allows the profitable sale of the products. The "weakness" of capitalist entrepreneurs in the case where demand for machine-produced products is absent induces them first to secure for themselves outlets in the SAC and ultimately to buy themselves places in the precapitalist SAC, offices or estates.

The Leninist (Lenin 1960 [1899]: 54–69) solution of accumulation via the demand for investment, a sort of accumulation for the purpose of accumulation, with constant real wages (due to marginality in agriculture keeping the wage rates at the physical level of reproduction) implies geometrically expanding rates of increase in labor productivity. They stand quite outside of any empirically observable dimensions at least if there is no possibility of rapid transfer of technology at low costs (and this implies high priced exportables and hence rents from exports). Such an accumulation for accumulation runs otherwise into rapidly declining capital productivity which brings the accumulation process to a stop (Elsenhans 1994b: 423–426).

The marginality-cum-rent configuration is politically stable for a variety of reasons to be mentioned shortly. The non-surplus appropriating mass of the population is divided into two classes one of which depends on the spending of the SAC. Craftsmen and other urban dependent people favor in periods of disorder the reestablishment of such a class. When the extractive power of the SAC declines, these people have no access to the increasing levels of food endowment provided by the peasantry.

The peasantry/agricultural worker class tend to compete for access to land and employment by providing immaterial services in the form of engaging in relations of clientship with the immediately accessible members of the SAC. These, in turn, need political alliances, hence also clientelist networks in order to preserve their instruments of appropriation of surplus. The structure should normally tend to be hierarchical and closely knit. A culture of dependency develops which explains that even in case of demographic decline military power is normally sufficient to maintain exploitation.

A good example is the so-called second serfdom in Eastern Europe (Richards 1979: 518; Schöffer 1959), but also antique and other forms of slavery. The so-called Atlantic slavery, however, is based on costs of reproduction shifted to technically backward economies with "comparative disadvantage" in all sorts of production with the possible exception of food through which they acquire comparative advantage in labor-intensive productions such as slave hunting (Elsenhans 1977: 60–63).

7.2 Integrating Foreign Trade into the Model

There are two types of benefits from economic specialization: Higher incomes in the form of greater availability of goods, on the one hand, and economic transformation as specialization in the production of goods which require the transformation of infrastructures and skills favorable for maintaining comparative advantage in growth industries of the future, on the other hand. Economies with high prices for their actual exports may experience high exchange rates and hence high international prices of their factors of production which may keep them from achieving competitiveness in goods with future growth perspectives. Increasing incomes and transforming the economy may not coincide.

High incomes precluding specialization in future promising goods are called Dutch disease from the setbacks of Dutch industry after the Dutch currency appreciated in the wake of the country's switch to gas production in the 1960s. It equally could be deduced from the decline of Dutch industry in the wake of Dutch commercial profits in the seventeenth and eighteenth centuries (Vries 1984: 185).

If there is a highly competitive manufacturing sector which does not provide the training for new technologies and new forms of labor organization necessary for new types of products, so that—against received theory of the product cycle—the specialization on most modern products does not entail cost advantages of the same amount in newly discovered technologies, a shift to specialization in these new technologies is precluded. Germany's average productivity was behind Britain until the 1960s although Germany was able to undersell Britain in the industries of the 1890s' second industrial revolution (chemistry, electrical machinery). Germany's backwardness was relatively low in these new industries as compared to the very high backwardness in old industries, such as textiles (Fremdling 1991: 38; Crafts 1989: 134). When Japan launched its export offensive with new high-technology products, its physical productivity in these branches was lower than that of the United States, but its backwardness was here relatively less than on average.[4] The United States was like an oil country which loses competitive advantage because of high exchange rates which were the consequence of its high productivity in old industries, in the oil countries' case a natural resource industry. Germany has attempted in the last 15 years to escape losing absolute cost advantages in high technology branches by wage increases below productivity increases. The main result achieved with respect to national competitivity consisted in the German currency appreciating with respect to its major trade rivals. This was the result of persisting high balance-of-trade surpluses which resulted from the competitivity of Germany in "old" productions such as luxury cars or machine tools.[5]

Whether countries with high actual earnings but low transformative capacity of exports will accept such a pattern of specialization or will try to change it by taxing the highly competitive sectors and subsidizing those sectors which promise technical transformation in the future depends at least initially on the "orientation" of their SACs. A SAC may enjoy the export bonanza by buying luxuries or use it for buying factories which—in case of a "hostile" social environment—may be as unproductive as hours

[4] Dollar and Wolff (1988: 552–554), Watanabe (1991: 58–59), and Audretsch and Yamawaki (1988: 446).

[5] *Handelsblatt* December 29th/30th, 1995; p. 11, August 3rd, 1994; p. 3, August 11th, 1994; p. 2; November 5th/6th, 1993; p. 13.

spent in foreign luxury restaurants. The case of the transition to capitalism seems here to be a limitational case where the reproduction of the capacity to appropriate income depends on continuous reinvestment of surplus. If there is neither a rising internal mass market which limits the rent nor a pattern of specialization which promises high returns in case of reinvestment, the normal result to be expected from integration into a world economy composed of technically more advanced economies is increased rent-seeking.

The marginality-cum-rent model can now be complemented by the traditional models of unequal specialization: Only in case of a pattern of specialization on industrial products with expanding international demand which, for their getting more perfect and cheaper, require reinvestment of surplus under conditions of competition, marginality should be expected to be overcome by intensified specialization.

At the beginning of the industrial revolution, we can assume that the forerunners were enjoying comparative advantage in all industrial productions, as these specializations were linked to transformations in skills and infrastructures not yet available for latecomers. Suppose a rich SAC in a marginality-ridden economy. As long as it has a preference for local luxury products, no foreign trade will occur to any significant degree. Due to the technical advance in foreign countries, mass consumption goods are launched which satisfy luxury needs in the backward one. The preference for foreign luxury increases. The SAC of the backward economy will sell the surplus of agriculture on the world market. Employment will be reduced because the luxuries producing workers are shed off without there being any possibility of their being employed in agriculture or any other nonagricultural activity due to the low level of marginal product in agriculture and the subsequent narrow outlets for nonagricultural mass consumption goods. This corresponds to the often quoted late nineteenth century shedding off of labor in precapitalist societies of Asia and Africa associated with the dissolution of the so-called solidarity pact between landlords and exploited classes.[6]

As export capacity is limited, the SAC class is eager to discover products which can be exported with low levels of industrial advancement. The first sectors where comparative advantage is acquired are tropical

[6] In a more general way, rising productivity of limited factors of production such as land contribute to a shedding off the working population as shown by the Green Revolution, Ladejinsky (1969: 147).

products—due to rising mass incomes and a more diversified demand in technically advanced countries—and minerals. Here, rises in productivity in the technically advanced countries are counteracted by the depletion of cost-effective deposits near the centers of industrial production. Deposits in other areas of the world become cost effective. Still high but decreasing transport costs do not block this specialization. It is intensified as modern technology in mineral production can be transferred to these regions. Technically backward countries are therefore at least initially specialized in products the price and income elasticity of which is low as markets for food are rapidly saturated and markets for minerals are determined by the tendency of capitalism to impose the reduction of raw material consumption per unit of additional product. Dutch disease has to occur for the latecomers in economic development in this initial phase of the constitution of a world economy. It has to be dealt with by societies the SACs of which—outside the labor-scarce regions of European settlement—have—by so-called world market orientation—become increasingly reliant on rents. The initial steps in the integration of these economies into the capitalist world economy have been accompanied by a reinforcement of the rent mechanism.

During the world economic crisis of the 1930s, the terms-of-trade problematique replaced the initial image of their being rich with respect to the discussion about the backward countries. These countries faced declining incomes with faltering external demand because decreasing prices were not compensated by an increasing demand for their exports, be they old or new products. Although this was already felt before the world economic crisis of the 1930s, this tendency was reinforced due to the crisis of the colonial export economies which emerged from the slow-down of economic activity in the industrial centers during this period.

Declining terms-of-trade are but one aspect of this specialization on price-inelastic products; the other one is that there is a possibility to increase prices without incurring the risk of a more rapidly decreasing demand so that non-market intervention into exports is paying. From this there emerged the economic basis of the conflict between the colonial powers and their colonies, i.e., a conflict about the rent. For long periods the colonial powers were not in favor of appropriating rents for development purposes in the colonies, at least not to a large degree. The national movements in the colonies as well as new social forces in the already independent technically backward countries considered however an improvement in the terms-of-trade to be a necessary condition for financing the diversification of their economies in order to become less dependent on instable prices of primary products on the world market.

The development of social movements which favor appropriation of rents in view of their investment into economic diversification is therefore a complementary development to the upfolding of the world economy. The alternative would have been a devaluation of the local currencies which would have brought competitiveness also to manufacturing sectors in the technically backward countries. The resulting losses in national income would have been predictably important. As long as raw material earnings allowed for buying technology and industrial products at relatively low prices in terms of export prices for these countries and as long as there was a theoretical perspective that investment undertaken by institutions of the non-market economy would allow diversification without such devaluation, the adoption of devaluation was improbable. This was even more the case if the choice had to be made in a phase of low export opportunities for manufactures as well due to the protectionist climate during the world economic crisis and the interwar period in general.

7.3 Bureaucratic Development Societies Under the Dominance of State Classes

Because it was difficult to appropriate rents available from mineral and agricultural exports by means of coordinating private "landlords" organized as oligarchies, the state in the Third World rose to new importance (Elsenhans 1991: 276–283, 1994a: 89–101). Strata whose members had been critical of common practice of wasting rents and of the low degree of appropriation of rents saw in the state the privileged remedy. The state rose in order to increase the volume of rent (to correct the deteriorating terms-of-trade) and to proceed to a wiser and more coherent allocation of rents with the aim of transforming the "disarticulated" productive apparatus.

The appropriation and allocation of rent require non-market structures (Elsenhans 1996b [1981]: 109–117). The state is superior to an oligarchy. Its monopoly is more comprehensive. It can provide an institutional arena where groups in control of the state can confront views of the future economy to be constructed on the basis of investment financed through rent. In a world in which the crisis of capitalism led to a largely shared belief in the necessity of state planning as a means of society's reappropriation of its material basis, the perspective of intensified state intervention into the economy appeared intellectually attractive. It corresponded to the interests of the middle strata of technically backward countries with their weak financial resources available for private accumulation. It constituted a protection for private small agricultural producers who suffered from the decline in their terms-of-trade which they attributed to foreign private monopolies. It was close to the socialist ideas of emerging working classes.

Allocation of rent for development requires its channeling into uses where the ratio between future earnings and investment is lower than in the rent-generating sector. The emergence of centralized classes which use the state for rent appropriation and allocation excludes the dominance of capitalist mechanisms of regulation. Rent in most cases was much more important than profit of the private sector as shown by the relative importance of public and private investment even in the industrial goods producing sector. So the rent-controlling class was economically prominent. Rent, in addition, could be used for satisfying some aspirations of rivalling classes, binding the leaders of such classes to the rent-appropriating class, coopting collaborators and clients and thus isolating potential opponents from their political basis and depriving the latter of their leadership. In many countries of the South, the SAC could therefore build a relatively stable political system on the basis of patronage and clientelism as well as repressive apparatuses which maintained its power. I use for theses rent-based relatively centralized classes the notion of state class (Elsenhans 1976). A state class draws its politico-economic basis from its control of the state apparatus through which it appropriates surplus as a rent. Verbal development orientation and a strengthening of the development agency, the state, provide the justification for this power. It takes the form of a convergence of the interests of the exploited and the rent-appropriating class in the superior unity of the community. Like the rent itself, such state classes are a danger and a chance for development. In distinction to an oligarchy, such state classes are at least theoretically able to realize a comparatively higher degree of centralization of rent appropriation and allocation.

The requirements for such a process of overcoming underdevelopment can be made clear by looking at the solution proposed by Keynes in the case of disempowerment of labor in the wake of economic crisis. There is no theory of the efficiency of state-guided investment in capitalist countries in Keynesianism. The reason is a simple one: Keynes expects the economy to come back to full employment on the basis of multiplier effects of income generating (and not capacity building) investment, so that the normal capitalist mechanism of empowerment through full employment would work. In the marginality-ridden economy this is not possible due to the low marginal product in agriculture as long as the state does not employ all the marginal population. In order to overcome marginality and hence in order to empower labor, a state which is not able to employ all marginals due to limited resources has not to proceed to the promotion of general growth but only to the promotion of wage goods production, especially in agriculture. This implies a reduction of the rent used for investment and subsidies to consumption as can be realized by redistribution of agricultural land, redistribution of income, employment programs and additional exports. These measures all imply a decreasing availability of resources for the rent appropriating class. The chance of their implementation depends on a strong commitment of the state classes for poverty eradication against its own privileges. In the following I discuss therefore, why the state classes were not able within the framework of their orientation to investment and satisfaction of their own needs to develop a rational strategy for promoting growth with the expected trickle-down effects. I dismiss the economic problems of such predominantly import-substituting strategies and concentrate on the political problems.

A non-market controlled process of appropriation and allocation of rents is characterized by the absence of reliable data provided by anonymous markets. All relevant data for decision-making depend on expectations about the future, which can be introduced into decision-making only when it is supported by social and political forces: Data for decision-making have a weak empirical base and reliability and become "hard" through political support. They therefore depend on the conscious behavior of important political forces. Whether an investment project is adopted as economically sound does not depend on the future demand which does not yet exist and also not on the extrapolation of actual trends as a conscious restructuring of the economy is attempted. Such an extrapolation can become reality if other participants agree, especially in their interpretation. The realization of such a projection of the future economy results from a negotiating process about any single project and all other competing projects. All economic actors are hence members of negotiating processes undertaken formally through institutions like ministries, development banks, state-owned enterprises, etc., without the profit rate being a yardstick.

There are three major tasks to be performed in such negotiation processes: The allocation of the rent, the allocation of scarce inputs for the physical linkages in the production process and the interpretation of results achieved including the fixing of changes to be adopted in order to maintain such a process.

The capitalist entrepreneur can stand on the market if his products are competitive. In this case, he earns a profit which constitutes his share in society's investment fund. The total amount to be distributed does not depend on his efficiency but on his and his class fellows' propensity to invest. The private form of property in means of production goes with its macroeconomic social function and the link between both of them is known as the weakest element of the stability of a capitalist economy.

Negotiation on particular measures with respect to economic policy (formulation, evaluation) cannot be conducted in such a structure without establishing an infrastructure for political power games. Each member of the state class tries to minimize its concessions to others by forging alliances in the negotiating processes. If it engages such coalitions only from case to case, it faces high transaction costs in relation to other members, who start their coalition building from already constituted powerful groups. State classes are therefore segmented. Segments are constituted on the basis of trust. Trust can come from ascribed criteria as common descent, ties of kinship, common regional or caste origin, etc. It can also come from achieved criteria as shared activities in a political movement with precise objectives, shared membership in a specialized institution like a ministry or a state-owned enterprise, etc. The more the segments are constituted on the basis of achieved criteria the more probable that alliances are built on divergencies with respect to priorities in economic development. The more therefore the controversies about such priorities can become the basis of new alignments between segments. Issues can become politically relevant only if they can be used by competitors for power in their contest. In order to become an issue in such power games, political forces have to be or (due to the pressing character of the issue) to become aligned according to differences with respect to such issues. In that case organizations or institutions pick such items in order to promote their power interests. The less ascribed criteria prevail in segment building, the more probable that segments will refer to the economic and social reality in their fights about the rent even if resources are still plentiful.

Due to the pursuit of the goals of influence/power and prestige, state classes are characterized by cyclical movements: The available resources are used for the enlargement of their own power bases. The share of consumption in the rent increases even if for some time the amount of rent available for investment still grows. The threat of exhaustion of rent in relation to the claims on it becomes visible. More peripheral elements of the state class accuse its center of wasteful management, corruption, inefficiency, etc. The movement of a replacement of corrupt centers through more idealistically minded subaltern officers, the "captains," is one form of the cyclical movement. A curbing of privileges of the periphery of the state class through its center which then fights so-called social ills through "epurations" is another one (Sklar 1967: 8).

The tendency to eliminate opposing segments makes segment building more and more dependent on ascribed criteria. When segments with opposing views are more and more dissolved or marginalized, only segments will prevail which share the view of the other ones. Even a unified segment, which becomes predominant in the appropriation of resources, will, however, split. The increase in its size relative to the total size of the state class and/or the size of the surplus makes incremental gains from dispossessing competing segments lower than gains from starting intra-segment rivalry. Intra-segment rivalry is unlikely to be organized according to achieved criteria. The process then turns to segment building on the basis of ascribed criteria like the link to the family of the head of state, etc., especially in case of a long-established stability of the hierarchies within the state class. Self-named socialist parties may well become structured by nepotist relations.

I deduce from this a tendency a diminishing capacity of the state class to learn about long-term deadlocks.

Segments try to increase their incomes, influence and prestige by means of increasing the resources under their control. They appropriate such resources on the basis of investment projects and budgetary funds for tasks which they are able to present as important for the maintenance of stability and economic growth. The different items are normally coordinated by a central agency as a finance ministry or a planning commission, which are close to the center of decision-making, normally the presidency. Programs are however necessarily based on proposals presented by specialized agencies as industry ministries, state-owned enterprises, development agencies, development banks, etc. In order to get proposals passed, costs and benefits are estimated systematically in an overoptimistic way so that the implied equilibria can afterward be met only in case of extremely positive conditions of realization. Consistency is further threatened by the inflow of new resources as they have to be absorbed by less and less well studied projects. The successive oil price rises for the OPEC countries in the 1970s give ample evidence (Boutaleb 1981: 23–45; Sid Ahmed 1984: 231–258).

Scarcity invariably has to occur during plan realization as the real world does not conform to the expected one in any society. Segments will have to get inputs which are inscribed in the plan but not really available. They will be forced to use black money, speed money or good relations, as there is no official market for the scarce products. For any particular segment the realization of the overall plan is less important than meeting its own targets. The result is a further decrease in consistency. Any segment realizes the absence of reliability of planned economic linkages and tries to shield itself from the consequences. It increases in-house production (rising costs due to a decreasing division of labor) and maintains close links with foreign suppliers if the rent is available in the form of foreign exchange. Hence the fight for the control over the central bank is important. These "second best" adaptations further subvert what consistency there may have been in the original plan.

The planning authority tries to compensate these encroachments on the intended rationality by applying thumb rules in drawing plans through corrected data of the decentralized units, by repression in plan execution and by adhocism: Manipulated data are replaced by conjectures, however valid they may be.

The more the committed parts of the state class try to impose results close to objectives, the more they will face resistance from the lack of precision in communication. In a capitalist society, entrepreneurs can survive as members of the SAC provided that their products are competitive. In addition, labor tends to be in demand as long as it produces a surplus and the economy is near the textbook-assumptions (and hence near full employment). Favor is replaced by profit and the capacity of contributing to it. Manipulation of information is always tried, but the real data of the market limit such undertakings.

In a rent-dependent society, communication has to be instrumentalized for achieving the goals of income, influence/power and prestige especially by maintaining assets at the power game level of the system.

In a capitalist society, strategies for manipulating communication are not sought after within enterprises, as this manipulation will soon be disclosed through the market. In a rent-dependent society, manipulation of communication absorbs more and more resources. This can be shown with respect to the face-saving strategies, which Europeans have linked with specificities of Asian culture. Face-saving strategies aim at the preservation of prestige. Prestige is the less threatened, the less there information is available. Discretion therefore is the rule, because any leaking-out real information may be used in uncontrollable combinations by others. Results of measures and policies are carefully hidden or presented in a distorted way whenever there are failures or not complete successes. The disclosure of connections between a prestigious one and other segments may enable a rivalling segment to fight against. The simultaneous hiding of the power position to all other segments and the frantic pursuit of information and rumors about such connections of others lead to endemic guessing about conspiracy and the persistent endeavor to keep information from leaking out, and this applies to all types of information from the most banal phone call to the most unexpected kinship relation. Information about relations and about factual results of policies become intertwined because also facts are not fully disclosed before being wrapped into explanations which allow the purposes of the concerned segment to be served at the power game level. The fight over interpretations becomes essential for the linking of these two levels.

Information gets unreliable and communication sticky. The political center of the state class, the various segments and the whole society as well lose contact with the material reality of society, its power structure and the economy. The result can only be political decay, which is not just a phase in the process of transition from traditional society to modernity, but the inevitable complement to rent. It can lead to actual crises as the rent-induced system of communication. Power play has to lead such systems to the verge of exhausting available surplus. The interesting element is not these tendencies themselves but, instead, the considerably higher capacities shown by many, but not all state classes of bureaucratic development societies, especially in Asia, to prevent breakdown, unlike the state classes of the tributary modes of production in ancient times.

The breakdown of these state-dependent rent-appropriating models in the 1980s debt crisis and their shift to liberalization is due less to the internal contradictions and more to their reinforcement by a series of miscalculations. They had expected the West continuing to be ready to provide increasing amounts of rent also for non-oil countries with strategically less important raw materials. But the West succeeded to "persuade" the OPEC countries not to support cartelization of non-oil commodities and also not to bail out indebted countries after the two oil price crises when the debt crisis broke out. Further, these state classes had not taken account of the Soviet Union not being able to have an economic stand in the Third World because of its lack of resources which could be used for fueling rent appropriation to the benefit of the "South." Even before, but definitively when the East-West conflict ended, the South had to lose its rent of "sovereignty," which it had exploited over several decades.

7.4 Antistatist Political Movements and Export-Oriented Industrialization: The Permanence of Rent

With the exhaustion of especially the external sources of rent, the state classes see their capacity of promoting state-subsidized employment-creating investment and production programs greatly diminished, as well as their capacity to co-opt members of the middle strata. There is a macroeconomic crisis with tendencies to impoverishment wherever the bases for capitalist growth have not been established.

The middle strata which no longer serve as a reservoir for recruitment have to save their relative economic and social positions by mobilizing their remaining resources. These resources, normally limited amounts of finance and formal education, can be employed in modern but also traditional small- and medium-scale industry, as well as in voluntary agencies and non-governmental organizations which pursue non-profit humanitarian or social objectives. In both cases the state has to be combated as a rapacious and wasteful fisc which is inefficient. From strata the middle sectors of society become class (Elsenhans 1992b: 32–36) of a new tinge, no longer oriented as Halpern's new middle classes (Halpern 1969: 97–108) to state employment and state-sponsored modernization. They can establish a link with the increasingly impoverished marginal and exploited classes on the basis of traditional values. A market prone discourse in economics would divide the poor whose positions with respect to the productive process vary widely (unskilled workers, self-employed businessmen, landless farmers, small farmers, etc.) despite shared destituteness.

Religion as based on general moral principles is not discredited like most of the other ideologies which the state class adopted together with secularism in the 1930s. Religion respects the heterogeneity of such societies with respect to primary allegiances as in most precapitalist societies. Religion protects property rights as most of today's religions rose in the axial age, when individuality appears to have been threatened by a more and more expanding state.

The more new movements are market oriented, the more they will have to opt for cohesion by means of traditional values. The more movements channel remaining rents to the poor, the more they can stay with secularism and the democratic ideal. Both types of new social movements, the non-governmental organizations and the tradition-oriented political parties will not automatically be oriented to overcoming the marginality-cum-rent blockage of underdeveloped societies. This can be shown by a comparison of the political economy of the Washington consensus of concentrating on exports even at the price of deteriorating terms-of-trade and the previously followed state-guided development strategy.

State-guided development was based on the theory of economic modernization and, within the framework of the model presented here, consisted in the mobilization of rent for investments, through which the transition to self-sustained growth was expected to be achieved. In the critique of the state class, I have shown that efficiency cannot be achieved at the microeconomic level (Elsenhans 1996b [1981]: 213–214). This results in high capital-output ratios and low rates of growth of production in relation to fixed capital. On a macroeconomic level, inefficiency is demonstrated by dependence on imported technology due to a skewed income distribution and the limited availability of foreign exchange. A higher level of mass consumption even to the detriment of rent would spur local investment goods production due to homogeneity of demand and low quality requirements for locally produced consumption goods.[7]

The main aspect of the Washington consensus consists in the recommendation to devalue the currency, i.e., to approximate an international value of local labor where it can compete on the world market despite its low productivity. In this way, the absorption of marginal labor in export production is expected. This labor will get wages with which it will buy wage goods, at low levels of real incomes predominantly food and some

[7] Elsenhans (1975: 293–313, 1979b, 1983a, b, 1992d). Cf. also Senghaas (1989: 57–67), with a more political science type of modelization.

locally available products of industry (shelter, textiles, simple household equipment). Their access to earnings enables them to buy the existing surplus of agriculture. In addition it is hoped, that this orientation of the demand will increase the surplus of agriculture as prices for food may rise, in case they are free. The previously available surplus is reduced, because shifted to the consumption of labor in physical terms, whereas in value terms the reduction manifests itself in the decreasing foreign exchange value of earnings available for the rentier class due to devaluation. This might go with an increasing wage bill due to higher levels of employment of unskilled local labor and higher wages for scarce skilled labor. Terms-of-trade improve for the countries of destination of the exports. The rent partly goes to additional workers, partly to the consumers in the trade partners.

Obviously, a country with a low agricultural surplus which is not sufficient to feed all its population cannot proceed to any level of devaluation. At least part of the subsistence of additional export workers may have to be bought from the world market. The strategy of export-led growth hence depends on agricultural surplus or low world market prices for food in relation to world market prices for industrial exports from the technically backward countries. This could take the form of rising productivity in food production in the industrial countries in relation to productivity in those industrial branches in the industrial countries, where the technically backward countries of the South have comparative advantage. The higher the increasing productivity in exportables in the backward country, the higher the increasing productivity in agriculture in industrial countries in relation to undynamic industrial sectors and the higher the agricultural surplus in underdeveloped economies, the more the Washington consensus is applicable.

Despite a decrease in surplus, the share of profit may increase as a result of increased net investment in the wake of expanding mass demand, first through the numerical increase of workers whose income can be expected to be higher than the consumption of the marginalized ones, then, after achieving full employment, also through rising real wages. Presented in this form, the mechanism proves to be basically identical to the mechanism of an egalitarian agrarian reform or the subsidies paid to the poor in the English poor laws (Elsenhans 1992a [1980], 1997). In devaluation-based export strategies previously marginal labor is given a claim to the surplus. At the old exchange rate, these workers are not able to provide for their necessities. At the lower exchange rate, they continue to be not able to buy their necessities at international prices, but due to their now higher purchasing power in local currency and constant local agricultural prices (in local currency), they are able to buy locally produced surplus. It should be added that this implies that the costs (economic and administrative costs) of exporting products are different in the manufacturing sector which is expected to produce for exports (low), and in the basic necessities (including food) sector (high), so that basic necessities are quasi non-tradables, as by quality standards, etc. they do not face an important demand in the rich countries.

There are striking similarities between the strategy of export orientation and social reformist strategies: In an egalitarian agrarian reform, the redistribution of land makes farms so small that each single farmer has not only to provide the labor which is highly productive, but also additional labor time, through which additional earnings increase only at a low rate. The additional product represents a lower share in his total earnings than this additional labor time in his total labor time. He provides this additional labor time because the product of his highly productive "first-hour" labor time is not sufficient for survival (Elsenhans 1979a: 550–562).

In the English poor laws, the poor were farmed out to capitalist entrepreneurs at wages which did not cover their subsistence. The capitalists—despite Marx's interpretation—had however to pay for this difference between wages of the poor and cost of subsistence by being taxed by the parishes, which otherwise would not have been able to pay the difference. In both cases, surplus is reduced but profit may increase on the basis of net investment and rising mass demand (Elsenhans 1992a [1980]).

Whether the basic capitalist mechanism of shifting surplus to the support of marginal labor in order to create a productivity-increasing and investment-provoking pattern of demand is achieved by additional exports depends on the rates of devaluation necessary for achieving full employment in a marginality-ridden economy. In case of low elasticity of demand on the external markets for the export products of such an economy, the rates of devaluation may have to be important. The extent to which devaluation is possible depends on the amount of agricultural surplus (and in dynamic perspective on the possibility of increasing this surplus and productivity in other wage goods industries through investment).

A country which produces a surplus of food and basic necessities large enough to maintain its whole labor force at low levels of real wages can accept any international price of its labor, even much lower than the international price of the subsistence goods for this labor. It may be forced to do so if it wants to achieve full employment and if exports are laggard despite devaluation.

A country which has a less productive agriculture can accept devaluation only to degrees where the additional export workers can be provided subsistence goods, part of which at least have to been imported and paid at the prices which prevail on the world market.

The Washington consensus is superior to state-led economic modernization despite decreasing resources for a then market-oriented investment process only if the rate of increase in wage goods production after liberalization is superior to previous rent appropriation through the state and its channeling into state-determined investment.

The greater the availability of agricultural surplus in relation to existing marginality, the greater the chances to achieve the results expected by the Washington consensus. The condition for success is nearly the same as the one for state-led strategies of overcoming underdevelopment, the difference being essentially that in state-led strategies of overcoming underdevelopment surplus increasing technical progress in agriculture has no effect for employment but only marginality reducing progress.

The successful East and Southeast Asian nations have dynamized therefore their agricultures through redistribution of land and achieved full employment through intensified specialization. Latin America[8] seems to proceed to market regulation on the basis of the middle-income strata being carefully sheltered from labor market competition of the poor. These poor have already migrated to the cities but do not constitute a political threat. Due to their previous experiences with state classes they refrain from opting for non-market economies which are out of their immediate control, as is the case of neighborhood movements. The promoters of a withdrawal of the state in Subsaharan Africa are often the previous members of the state classes. They are said to have emigrated externally or internally, and indulge in a discourse oriented to 1776 and 1789 in order to reopen the flow of external resources from the donors. They do not see any possibility of raising production and surplus on the basis of an increasing demand from the rural areas, which would imply rising productivity in their agricultures.

[8] In more detail: Elsenhans (1994d: 114–119).

Most of the countries of Northern Africa and Asia are characterized by levels of marginality which could be absorbed only at high levels of devaluation. To achieve such absorption the Western countries have to be ready to increase their mass incomes no longer only in line with their own productivity, but in addition in line with substantial improvements in their terms-of-trade. This may accelerate the process of replacement of First World workers by Third World workers.

In many countries of the Global South, the newly emerging middle classes and the NGO fit, in as much as they can have an economic role, into a pattern where devaluation is limited either because of the absence of a firm commitment to eradicate marginality through development or due to redistribution. Political movements based on traditional values, which may be called nativist movements, are not forced to press devaluation beyond the level where additional export workers cost more than additional export earnings on the world market because they do not base their legitimacy on economic performance. They will not go for devaluation if additional export earnings become negative. It is, however, on this option that the possibility of overcoming marginality through export orientation is based. The nativist movements will not achieve full employment through export orientation, as they will refrain from strategies such as massive devaluation, through which export earnings decline in relation to local costs of production, especially if this implies rates of devaluation where foreign exchange earnings of already well established exporters will decline.

The Washington Consensus pretends to aim at maximum employment through unlimited devaluation until such a level of employment is achieved. It normally assumes a maximum of foreign exchange earnings at that level of employment, possibly with the exception of earnings from traditional exports. The model proposed here with differential lags in productivity also in manufacturing in relation to the technically leading countries implies higher export earnings being possible for an economy and especially for some categories of exporters at higher than full employment exchange rates. Greater respect for private sector interests and less search for legitimacy through economic performance with respect to the interests of the poor result in the nativist movements having only limited capacity (and interest) in transforming the economy in the direction of self-sustained growth. Thus, the rent is not channeled into export promotion via reducing the international price of local labor. But as it is still available, it can be used for export promotion. The obvious result is that the entrepreneurs in societies ruled by nativist movements will seek a new relationship with the non-market economy, possibly but not necessarily a new state. Even if such a state will be less burdensome for them than were the old state classes, it still would imply rent channeling, in this case in favor of their export productions.

NGOs have a similar social basis as the previous state classes with whom they entertain ambivalent relations of simultaneous rivalry and cooperation. They are inferior to state classes in rent appropriation but especially in rent allocation. The attempt to develop an overall plan of channeling rents, the type of surplus they are based on, into overall programs of economic transformation, is limited due to the smallness of these organizations and their sectoral limits. Hence also, they do not develop the type of gate by which rents to be channeled from one sector to another can be appropriated. The projects they develop can rarely overcome the problem of low marginal productivity in agriculture. Their main impact—beside the formation of political attitudes—consists in supplying subsidies to the poor, exactly what the English poor laws did. They may, as any other increase in mass consumption, create markets which trigger off investment and hence net profit, so that they will ultimately fulfill the function of reducing (worldwide) surplus in order to launch profit.

The political future of marginality-ridden societies is therefore a rationalized decentralized system of rent appropriation which economically may not be very different from the one realized by the state classes, and which will go hand-in-hand with the continued presence of the state in the rent allocation process. As any of the different instruments, state centralization of resources, redistribution, agricultural reform, etc. as well as devaluation will face diminishing returns, the different actors will go for mixed strategies. Due to their political aspect of being controversial between different political groups, these mixes will reflect political compromises instead of rationality. It is probably this theoretically based necessity of eclecticism which has induced the followers of more straightforward or simpler theoretical approaches to give credit to the assumption of an end of the Third World and of grand designs in the theory of development.

The advice to be given in such a situation of dominance of rent is to render automatic as much as possible the allocation of rent which is used for investive purposes, and to rely on redistributive programs. The more the market for mass consumption goods expands, the greater the possibility for net investment and hence for profit to absorb surplus. The more investment programs are not subject to negotiations between rent appropriating members of state classes and oligarchies, the less the economic losses in financial resources. The less important the internal mechanisms of channeling rent into mass consumption, the higher the rates of devaluation required and the higher the contribution of foreign trade to national income.

There is room for a systematic analysis of such eclectic strategies, which, however, are not disarticulated but unified through two basic recommendations: a lean rent-managing process through increasing mass consumption and localized technology production. When South Korea was facing a low price elasticity of its textile exports, it did not proceed to taxing these exports and subsidizing other productions, as an oil country would have done, but stopped the imports of textile machinery. Prices in local currency had to rise as locally produced textile machinery had a lower performance-cost ratio. Higher local costs of textile exports could be shifted to the clients due to a low price elasticity of demand for these products. The rent was automatically channeled to the textile machine producers without any administration directly intervening, as these textile machine producers had via market structures higher prices for their products than had been possible in the case of free imports. Hence, the costs of the textile producers in inputs increased after their imports in machinery had been barred.

The more demand is concentrated on relatively simple products, the more surplus can be transformed into profit-via market-induced net investment. This reduces rent. The more technologies are locally produced, the more the market process can rely on multipliers from fiscal, monetary, exchange rate policies and even global demand management which reduce the scope of state intervention. The more egalitarian the demand, the more probable the cost-effectiveness of initially locally produced technology. There is a self-enforcing process of market and equality provided that marginality has been overcome. This goes fairly well with the observation that the initial distribution of assets before development starts has an important bearing on the dynamics of the growth process (Morris and Adelman 1983: 43–55). In addition, the proposed modelization demonstrates that the debate about whether socialist forces have to conclude coalitions with capitalists or fight immediately for the socialist transformation of the respective systems, in which so much intellectual energy had been "invested" in the 1960s and 1970s (Frank 1969: 371–375), is theoretically irrelevant. By fighting for the social, but not statist transformation of the systems, the popular masses reinforce profit against rent, as the South Korean social movement has understood very well (Irwan 1989: 410).

7.5 The Transfer of the Rent-Appropriating State to the West as Result of the Persistence of Rent in the South

The persistence of rent and new possibilities of devaluation and export drives has implications for the capitalist developed countries. This occurs at a moment where the development of productive forces has led to the possibility of qualitatively reducing alienation. Hours worked have to go down in the wake of material needs growing less rapidly in relation to other needs than before. The restriction of the sphere of scarcity, which is economy, will dilute the solidarity of labor and render political alliances in the West more complex and less determined by the capital-labor-divide. The export drive from the South enhances this tendency, as it makes an increasing share of labor in the West unable to increase its wages in line with average productivity increases even despite their own marginal product having increased in physical terms. In fact, in a capitalist economy, the increase in marginal product of any labor does not depend only on the latter's increase in physical marginal product. The economic marginal product of any labor is mediated through changes in the system of relative prices, where products of branches with below average productivity increases become relatively more expensive (and vice versa). The production of some among these same products may, however, become competitive in the marginality-ridden countries of the South—despite a lower physical productivity which is compensated by the exchange rate and hence a greater difference in physical productivity in other leading export branches of both economies. From that moment on, the workers in the capitalist countries who are employed in branches with below average productivity increases in the more productive West can no longer participate in the general increase of wages in their own societies. Their wages tend to go down to the level of international costs of labor in the marginality-ridden countries (when differences in physical productivity are taken into consideration).

Cases can be constructed where in real terms the real wage in the marginality-ridden country may be higher than in the technically more advanced country, as non-tradables in the subsistence basket of a worker's family may be more expensive in the technically more advanced one.

Two mechanisms explain why this challenge has not come much earlier but develops its disruptive consequences in a sudden way which makes adjustment very difficult within a free world economy (Elsenhans 1996a). The first mechanism is the increased scope for transforming comparative into absolute advantage through the exchange rate. The possibility of using an additional agricultural surplus for devaluation has already been mentioned. Productivity in agriculture has been increasing since the 1930s in the industrial countries more rapidly than in many industrial branches, although at a lower pace than average productivity in industry. The low productivity increase branches are by necessity characterized by comparative disadvantage in the industrialized countries and comparative advantage in the marginality-ridden countries. With productivity increasing more rapidly in agriculture than in these low-productivity industrial branches, a same amount of physical exports from these industrial branches in the underdeveloped world will buy more food on the world market than before this differential rise in productivity. At the same time, increasing productivity in the technically backward countries, for example due to government efforts in improving skills and infrastructures or technology transfers through multinational corporations, will enable more food to be bought for the same amount of working hours than before.

Once more, the wage rate in the industrial countries is irrelevant. Exchange rates for the industrial countries remain high due to their export surpluses which they achieve with their high technology sectors. They still have enough productivity advances to enable them to sell well on the world market, but these advances in productivity are concentrated in certain sectors which are no longer large enough to provide full employment in their economies. At the beginning of the process of uneven, regionally concentrated industrialization, advanced countries drew their superiority from small advances in a large variety of industries, based on immobile skills and immobile infrastructures. Now technical progress has become mobile, but not equally in all branches, so that the exchange rates remain high (due to the branches with immobile advances), but unemployment rises (due to the mobile sectors of production).

In both situations foreign trade improved the terms-of-trade of the more advanced countries. In the latter case with comparative advantages restricted to a small sector of production and growing unemployment due to devaluation. So terms-of-trade improvements are no longer a source of growth, as they had been. At the start of industrialization with full employment not being threatened in the more advanced countries through comparative advantage of the less advanced countries being transformed into absolute advantage, improving terms-of-trade provided for additional possibilities for increasing mass incomes. Productivity-oriented wage increases could exceed the increase in productivity by the improvement in the terms-of-trade. With labor being under competition due to the exchange rate, improving terms-of-trade require additional increases in mass incomes in order to make consumptive capacity match productive capacity. Under the new situation of competition from "low-wage" areas, this will lead to additional job destruction.

With the new developments, technically leading countries have comparative advantage in a small number of branches, called high technology (investment goods and some sophisticated consumption goods), where their advance in productivity is very high, but where demand depends on total world demand (investment goods) or on booming high-wage markets in the advanced countries.

There are two equally problematical ways to deal with this problem without overcoming marginality in the underdeveloped world. The first consists in taxing the export sectors and subsidizing labor. The idea of developing the social sector of employment fits into this scenario. Growing numbers of workers become dependent on the state. The autonomy of civil society will decrease as well as the solidarity of labor. The interests of individual workers become dependent on the branch and the subbranch of employment. They do not have a prospect of ready access to the high technology jobs the number of which is limited due to global demand conditions.

The second way consists in shifting the labor force into the high technology sectors by subsidizing them via the instruments described in industrial policy. The solution implies benign instruments such as an end to subsidies for doomed branches so that imports can increase which may bring the exchange rate down. The mechanism consists in giving up the aim of trade surpluses and to concentrate on increasing shares of high technology products in total exports. This aim is expected to be facilitated by cutting the international prices of one's own high technology products through wage cuts, price and exchange rate manipulations and subsidies in order to undersell other advanced capitalist countries. The mechanism obviously implies rent channeling in the form of appropriating surpluses through the non-market economy in doomed branches and channeling these surpluses into branches which are to be promoted. The aspect of rapidly decreasing unit costs and hence the necessity of early increasing shares in world markets for future "winning" products contributes to the politicization of such strategies. Whoever is best at subsidizing will be best positioned afterward to enjoy the lean state of more free trade.

There is therefore a danger of the rentier state of the South being exported to the North (Elsenhans 1992c) where the world of labor and its influence on social and political interactions decreases through the decline of alienated work, through the splitting of solidarities, through an increasing dependence on state protection or state-sponsored employment, and through the preparedness of labor to follow the advice of cutting wages in order to defend its jobs. All these tendencies curb the bargaining power of labor and facilitate underconsumptionist tendencies in addition to the ones which are triggered off by the increased rates of devaluation in the South. This, as well, brings the state into a position where adhocist interventionism will be applied.

The alternative would be to deal with marginality in the underdeveloped world. The benign cases are actually the so much feared East Asian tigers. They are the leaders of the movement, because among other complementary measures they have applied measures for widening the impact of export growth and achieving fully fledged growth by transforming their agricultures and producing an agricultural surplus. Due to these mechanisms, increasing export employment nowadays leads to scarcity of labor, the expansion of mass consumption and finally to the transfer of the capitalist mode of regulation to these societies, as has been observed in the last years. The more problematic case are those economies which are not yet seen as very performing on the world market. Their possibilities of devaluation are limited by the continuing poverty of their agricultures, although they are capable of devaluation and becoming competitive to a limited extent. Despite devaluation and productive capacity growing more rapidly than consumptive capacity, the international prices of their labor will not decrease enough for full employment and empowerment of labor, so that they will be long-term suppliers of cheap labor via (successive, always however too limited) devaluations. Low-labor cost economies with continuing marginality are the real problem for the future of a free world economy. They add only to world productive capacity but not to world consumptive capacity and hence tend to destroy more jobs than they contribute to create.

If these pockets of relatively high capacity to devalue cum persisting marginality remain important, the rest of the world has to engage in rent seeking, as the capitalist mechanism of reducing rent through rising mass consumption will not be established at a world level.

The rent problem is hence much more difficult than assumed in the North American critique of rent seeking. Rent emerges structurally in the transition to capitalism and this the more, the more the economies are latecomers in which the empowerment of labor has not preceded the introduction of market regulations. The left has contributed to the rent problem in as much as it has denied the dependency of capitalism on mass consumption and, together with mainstream economics, considered capitalism as possible only because of the increase of amounts of "value" available for accumulation. If the development state and its state classes have not succeeded in the last five decades to eradicate marginality, the forces which replace them are able to end marginality and rent only under particular conditions even if they follow strategies which make the rent problem less offensive at the internal level.

The technically advanced developed industrial countries seem to indulge in a second-best solution of taking refuge in specialization on high technology products, convinced as they are since the end of late-colonial reforms, that they cannot substantially contribute to ending poverty in the South (Elsenhans 1974: 285–293). This second-best solution enhances otherwise already emerging tendencies to a decline of labor in its relation with capital in the developed West. This may be an important element of the possible end of the bourgeois age. This end will not be replaced by the hope for an age of freedom, but an age of rent, extended also to the West, a sort of generalized feudalism at the world level (Elsenhans 1994c: 551–563). Rent as a form of political/social power-based form of surplus has been suppressed in developed capitalism on the basis of labor's ability to eliminate all other forms of surplus appropriation than that part of surplus needed for investment in order to adapt capacities of production to rising needs of labor. Whenever labor weakens, rent reemerges.

References

Abrahamian, Ervand. 1975. European Feudalism and Middle Eastern Despotisms. *Science and Society* 39 (2): 129–156.

Audretsch, David B., and Hideki Yamawaki. 1988. Research and Development Rivalry, Industrial Policy and U.S.-Japanese Trade. *Review of Economics and Statistics* 70 (3): 438–447.

Boutaleb, G. 1981. Les dangers de l'extraversion. In *Révolution africaine*, 23–45.

Chao, Kang. 1986. *Man and Land in Chinese History*. Stanford, CA: Stanford University Press.

Crafts, Nicholas F.R. 1989. Revealed Comparative Advantage in Manufacturing, 1899–1950. *Journal of European Economic History* 18 (1): 127–135.

Dollar, David, and Edward N. Wolff. 1988. Convergence of Industry Labour Productivity Among Advanced Economies 1963–1982. *Review of Economics and Statistics* 70 (4): 549–558.

Elsenhans, Hartmut. 1974. *Frankreichs Algerienkrieg 1954–1962. Entkolonialisierungsversuch einer kapitalistischen Metropole. Zum Zusammenbruch der Kolonialreiche*. Munich: Carl Hanser.

Elsenhans, Hartmut. 1975. Overcoming Underdevelopment. A Research Paradigm. *Journal of Peace Research* 12 (4): 293–313.

Elsenhans, Hartmut. 1976. Zur Rolle der Staatsklasse bei der Überwindung von Unterentwicklung. In *Strategien gegen Unterentwicklung. Zwischen Weltmarkt und Eigenständigkeit*, ed. Alfred Schmidt, 250–265. Frankfort on Main, New York: Campus.

Elsenhans, Hartmut. 1977. *Ungleichheit und Unterentwicklung. Staat – Wirtschaft – Gesellschaft in der unterentwickelten Welt: Eine kommentierte Textsammlung*. Rheinstetten: Schindele.

Elsenhans, Hartmut. 1979a. Agrarverfassung, Akkumulationsprozeß, Demokratisierung. In *Agrarreform in der Dritten Welt*, ed. Hartmut Elsenhans, 505–652. Frankfort on the Main, New York: Campus.

Elsenhans, Hartmut. 1979b. Grundlagen der Entwicklung der kapitalistischen Weltwirtschaft. In *Kapitalistische Weltökonomie. Kontroversen über ihren Ursprung und ihre Entwicklungsdynamik*, ed. Dieter Senghaas, 101–148. Frankfort on the Main: Suhrkamp.

Elsenhans, Hartmut. 1983a. Égalité et développement. L'expérience européenne et le monde sous-développé d'aujourd'hui. *Cultures et développement* 15 (2): 187–215.

Elsenhans, Hartmut. 1983b. Rising Mass Incomes as a Condition of Capitalist Growth. Implications for the World Economy. *International Organization* 37 (1): 1–38.

Elsenhans, Hartmut. 1991. The Great Depression of the 1930s and the Third World. *International Studies* 28 (3): 273–290.

Elsenhans, Hartmut. 1992a [1980]. English Poor Law and Egalitarian Agrarian Reform in the Third World. In *Equality and Development*, ed. Hartmut Elsenhans, 130–162. Dhaka: Center for Social Studies.

Elsenhans, Hartmut. 1992b. *Global Change and Implications for India*. New Delhi: Lancer Books.

Elsenhans, Hartmut. 1992c. The Logic of Profit and the Logic of Rent. *Voice of Peace and Integration* 1 (1): 4–48.

Elsenhans, Hartmut. 1992d [1982]. Overcoming Underdevelopment through Mass Production for Mass Consumption: Evolution of a New Development Concept. In *Equality and Development*, ed. Hartmut Elsenhans, 80–129. Dhaka: Center for Social Studies.

Elsenhans, Hartmut. 1994a. Decolonisation: From the Failure of the Colonial Export Economies to the Decline of Westernised State Classes. *Maghreb Review* 19 (1/2): 95–122.

Elsenhans, Hartmut. 1994b. Rent, State and the Market. The Political Economy of the Transition to Self-Sustained Capitalism. *Pakistan Development Review* 33 (4): 393–428.

Elsenhans, Hartmut. 1994c. State, Economy, Power and the Future of the International System. *Strategic Digest* 24 (4): 551–563.

Elsenhans, Hartmut. 1994d. Wirtschaftsliberalismus ohne bürgerliche Revolution: Wer stützt die liberale Weltwirtschaft im Süden. In *Umbruch in der Weltgesellschaft. Auf dem Wege zu einer „neuen Weltordnung"*, ed. Wolfgang Hein, 101–124. Hamburg: Deutsches Übersee-Institut.

Elsenhans, Hartmut. 1996a. Gegen das Gespenst der Globalisierung. In *Jahrbuch Arbeit und Technik 1996: Zukunft der Industriegesellschaft*, ed. Werner Fricke, 25–36. Bonn: Dietz.

Elsenhans, Hartmut. 1996b [1981]. *State, Class and Development*. New Delhi, London, Columbia, MO: Radiant; Sangam; South Asia Books.

Elsenhans, Hartmut. 1997. The Relevance of the Principles of Keynesian Economics for the Transition to Capitalism in Today's Underdeveloped World. In *Improving the Global Economy. Keynesianism and the Growth in Output and Employment*, Paul Davidson, and Jan A. Kregel, 283–303. Cheltenham, Lyme: Edward Elgar.

Frank, André Gunder. 1969. *Latin America: Underdevelopment or Revolution. Essays on the Development of Underdevelopment and the Immediate Enemy.* New York: Monthly Review Press.

Fremdling, Rainer. 1991. Productivity Comparison between Great Britain and Germany, 1855–1913. *Scandinavian Economic History Review* 39 (1): 28–42.

Halpern, Manfred. 1969. Egypt and the New Middle Class: Reaffirmations and New Explorations. *Comparative Studies in Society and History* 11 (1): 97–108.

Irwan, Alexander. 1989. Business Patronage, Class Struggle and the Manufacturing Sector in South Korea, Indonesia and Thailand. *Journal of Contemporary Asia* 19 (4): 398–434.

Kalecki, Michal. 1942. A Theory of Profits. *Economic Journal* 52 (205–206): 258–267.

Kregel, Jan A. 1971. *Rate of Profit, Distribution and Growth. Two Views*. London: Macmillan.

Krueger, Anne O. 1974. The Political Economy of the Rent-Seeking Society. *American Economic Review* 64 (3): 291–303.

Ladejinsky, Wolf. 1969. Green Revolution in Bihar. The Kosi Area: A Field Trip. *Economic and Political Weekly* 4 (39): A147–A159.

Lenin, Wladimir Ilyich. 1960. *The Development of Capitalism in Russia* [1899]. Lenin Collected Works (3). Moscow: Progress Publishers.

Morris Taft, Cynthia, and Irma Adelman. 1983. Institutional Influences on Poverty in the Nineteenth Century: A Quantitative Comparative Study. *Journal of Economic History* 43 (1): 43–55.

Nadiri, M.Ishaq, and M.A. Schankerman. 1981. Technical Change, Returns to Scale and the Productivity Breakdown. *American Economic Review* 71 (2): 314–319.

Okishio, Nobuo. 1961. Technical Change and the Rate of Profit. *Kobe University Economic Review* 7: 85–99.

Olson, Mancur. 1982. *The Rise and Decline of Nations: Economic Growth, Stagflation, and Social Rigidities*. New Haven, CT: Yale University Press.

Richards, Alan. 1979. The Political Economy of Gutswirtschaft: A Comparative Analysis of East Elbian Germany, Egypt and Chile. *Comparative Studies in Society and History* 21 (4): 483–518.

Robinson, Joan Violet. 1956. *The Accumulation of Capital*. London: Macmillan.

Ruby, Jürgen. 1991. Der Weg von der Drehmaschine zum Drehautomaten im deutschen Werkzeugmaschinenbau. *Technikgeschichte* 58 (4): 297–314.

Schöffer, I. 1959. The Second Serfdom in Eastern Europe as a Problem of Historical Explanation. *Historical Studies, Australia and New Zealand* 9 (33): 46–61.

Senghaas, Dieter. 1989. The Development Problematic: A Macro-Micro Perspective. *Journal of Peace Research* 26 (1): 57–67.

Sid Ahmed, Abdelkader. 1984. Petróleo y desarollo: El caso argelino. *Trimestre Económico* 51 (202): 231–258.

Sklar, Richard L. 1967. Political Science and National Integration—A Radical Approach. *Journal of Modern African Studies* 5 (1): 1–11.

von Bortkiewicz, Ladislaus. 1907. Wertrechnung und Preisrechnung im Marxschen System (3). *Archiv Für Sozialwissenschaft Und Sozialpolitik* 25 (2): 445–489.

Vries, Jan de. 1984. The Decline and Rise of the Dutch Economy, 1675–1900. *Research in Economic History* (SH 3): 149–189.

Watanabe, Susumu. 1991. The Japanese Quality Control Circle: Why it Works. *International Labour Review* 130 (1): 56–80.

Young, Allyn A. 1928. Increasing Returns and Economic Progress. *Economic Journal* 38 (152): 527–542.

CHAPTER 8

Terms-of-Trade and Underdevelopment: How to Benefit from Improving Terms-of-Trade: A Discussion of the Link Between Terms-of-Trade and the Development Blocking Internal Social and Economic Structures

Hartmut Elsenhans

At this point it might be worth noting the curious ambivalence which price relations in foreign trade play for the underdeveloped countries. Good prices for their primary commodities, specially if coupled with a rise in quantities sold, as they are in a boom, give to the underdeveloped countries

Paper submitted for a Festschrift in honor of H. M. W. Singer, to be edited by Rameshwar Tandon. The publication could not be realized.

H. Elsenhans (✉)
University of Leipzig, Leipzig, Germany
e-mail: helsen@rz.uni-leipzig.de

© The Author(s), under exclusive license to Springer Nature Switzerland AG 2021

H. Warnecke-Berger (ed.), *Development, Capitalism, and Rent*,
https://doi.org/10.1007/978-3-030-62605-1_8

> the necessary means for importing capital goods and financing their own industrial development; yet at the same time they take away the incentive to do so, and investment, both foreign and domestic, is directed into the expansion of primary commodity production, this leaving no room for the domestic investment which is the required complement for any import of capital goods. Conversely, when the prices and sales of primary commodities fall off, the desire for industrialization is suddenly sharpened. Yet, at the same time, the means for carrying it out are sharply reduced. Here again it seems that the underdeveloped countries are in danger of falling between two stools: failing to industrialize in a boom because things are as good as they are, and failing to industrialize in a slump because things are as bad as they are. (Singer 1950: 482)

Hans Wolfgang Singer earned his reputation as a founder of development theory at an early stage of the discipline with his research on the distribution of gains from foreign investment between underdeveloped and developed countries. He became one of the founding fathers of the theory of deteriorating terms-of-trade in underdeveloped countries. Singer maintained that deteriorating terms-of-trade are at once a factor that conditions underdevelopment as well as a tendency created by it. This link is the focus of the following contribution. The rents that emerge in the wake of improving terms-of-trade create the financial basis for industrial diversification, yet they have to be kept from creating political structures that block this diversification. This can only be achieved by taming rents through their embeddedness in appropriate social structures, and ultimately though the "entitlement" of the "masses."

8.1 The Precapitalist Character of the Argument that Improving Terms-of-Trade Are an Instrument for Overcoming Underdevelopment

In a pre-Keynesian world of economics it was no surprise to find an intensified discussion about terms-of-trade and the particularly burdensome effects of the world economic recession of the 1930s on the raw-material exporters of the Third World. This preoccupation reveals that the precapitalist view of growth was thought to depend on additional financial resources, somewhat in line with theories about previous accumulation (Preobrazenskij 1971: 109–122; Marx 1967 [1867]: 507–542).

During the Great Depression and its aftermath the elites of today's underdeveloped continents of the South observed that the industrialized countries did better in resisting price decline and that the cost of investing in new productive capacity to replace hitherto imported products in underdeveloped economies was extremely costly. In looking towards the West in order to find out how to catch up with the West's technical capacity, Third World elites felt it necessary to complement internally generated resources with external ones. Was it not morally justified to ask for better terms-of-trade because the prices of raw materials had declined much more than the prices for industrial products, not only during the Great Depression of the 1930s but for a much longer period of time?

The second wave of European colonialism began in the last quarter of the nineteenth century. During this period, the "periphery" came to supply the industrial West with burgeoning quantities of increasingly cheap raw materials. These initially consisted of food and beverages as well as cotton. From the early twentieth century, they also comprised mineral products, first tin and copper, then oil. Marxist authors such as Lenin (1964 [1916]: 241–242; Brown 1963: 67) merely echoed the many jingoist colonialist pressure groups active before the First World War. The natural resources and, later on, the reserves of cheap labor in Asia, Africa and Latin America could at least temporarily offset the decline in economic prosperity in the West or the decline in the rate of profit. Luxemburg (1951 [1913]: 299–325) complemented this perspective by highlighting the importance of expanding colonial markets for capitalist growth, an important aspect of the colonialist lobby. Indeed, the view that the West's wealth is based on the South's poverty echoes much older perspectives on, for example, the British plunder of India (Digby 1901: 222; Dutt 1949: 98–102), or the West's Industrial Revolution being based on the exploitation of slave labor in the West Indies and Africa (Williams 1964). The West forcefully imposed this poverty, both by use of force and, in the period analyzed by Singer, through market structures. Structural "violence" played a key role in the terms-of-trade argument long before it was highlighted by Galtung (1971).

It was the exploitation of the non-capitalist world which upheld capitalism and allowed accumulation and technical progress to take place. The exploited nations had to increase their international bargaining power, among other means by achieving political independence. Improving terms-of-trade became the central economic demand of underdeveloped countries from the start of decolonization till the world debt crisis of the

1980s and the silent end of the Integrated Programme for Commodities in the mid-1980s, better terms-of-trade being considered an instrument for diversifying the economy. The theory of deteriorating terms-of-trade was the linchpin in the creation of the Third World as a political entity made up of the proletarian nations with a right to better terms-of-trade and other transfers from the West. It found its climax in the demand for a New International Economic Order after the oil price crisis of the 1970s.

8.2 Deteriorating Terms-of-Trade as the Basis of Industrial Development in the Center

This insistence on favorable terms-of-trade for economic growth is in complete opposition to the experience of developed capitalist economies. This was the case even during the world economic depression. The colonial powers reacted with measures for stabilizing the prices of commodities in their colonies to maintain purchasing power and organize public capital transfers. Britain and the U.S. engaged in dirty-floating exchange-rate systems in order to push exports. The argument that their exports faced higher price elasticities of demand than raw materials may have been correct, but is not pertinent. Much more than the exporters of industrial products, the exporters of commodities were able to maintain quantities exported during the Great Depression. They did not, however, achieve an expansion of their local markets on which to base a local industrial production, despite the increase of imported manufactures in terms of their local currencies. Developed industrial countries, however, benefit from deteriorating terms-of-trade through higher employment even in the period of normal business activity. This is shown by prosperity in Western Europe after the decline of the euro relative to the dollar in the wake of its introduction in 2000. Britain's rise to industrial leadership in the nineteenth century was based on a massive deterioration of its terms-of-trade after lowering its costs of production for manufactured products (Imlah 1950).

Proponents of the link between good terms-of-trade and growth will raise the objection that developed economies are characterized by a high degree of economic diversification. This, such proponents claim, allows developed economies to react flexibly to declining terms-of-trade with import substitution and innovation. This is achieved on the basis of the local production of investment goods and hence on the local capacity for technical innovation. In reality, however, this flexibility is not the result of a previous accumulation based on the inflow of external resources, but of the absence of good terms-of-trade for major exports. It is because the terms-of-trade are deteriorating that the development of local technology production is possible in the first place, even for technically backward countries.

If there is no source of income inflows that allow the purchase of foreign technology even at high prices, a capitalist economy will be characterized by a mechanism that leads to the convergence of factor productivities in all branches of the economy. With tendential full employment and a change in technology (innovation) or relative prices due to changes in demand, the benefiting branch will have either lower costs of production or rising prices, so that its profit rate increases. It attracts labor wooed away from other branches by higher incomes. Non-innovative branches have to pay higher wages as labor becomes scarce and are able to do so by reducing production that renders their products more expensive. The same mechanism works in the case of a shift in demand as long as foreign suppliers cannot provide them at cheaper costs. If such suppliers exist, in case of massive imports the usual mechanism of a decline in the international value of the local currency raises the prices of these supplies and makes local supplies competitive.

If these mechanisms are to work, then a low difference in productivity among the various branches of the economy is decisive. This homogeneity of productivities is not primarily the result of technical performance but of full employment at any level of development of technical capabilities. Thus, it is in principle accessible to any economy tending to full employment.

With full employment the rise of labor costs through the demand of additional labor for employment in dynamic branches is accompanied by the expansion of production, and hence declining prices, whereas the shedding off of labor by the non-dynamic branches leads to reduced production and ultimately to an increase in prices in the non-innovative branches. Productivities measured in prices converge across branches despite high differences in the growth of physical productivity.

Sectoral productivities are homogeneous because labor is scarce, not because physical productivity is growing at the same rate in all branches of the economy. However, this process might contribute to the spread of technical innovation into less innovative branches, with the latter experiencing significant cost pressures. But if increasing productivity is impossible or too costly, this might not occur. This is amply demonstrated by the equal productivity of hairdressers irrespective of where they are in the world, or by the underdeveloped world's increasing dependency on imports (especially in investment goods) during the period of imperialism.

Where the convergence of productivities works, it leads to a convergence of wages and profit rates with three important consequences. First, any innovation in a particular branch and any change of the demand mix will lead to adjustments in the distribution of labor among branches even at very low rates of change in earnings (and very low exchange rates for their earnings). The economy easily adapts to shocks. State intervention is limited and the lean state of a capitalist economy which does not interfere in daily investment decisions about investment comes into view.

Second, labor becomes a homogeneous "factor of production" independently of its branch-wise employment. The political process is reduced to a struggle between two camps, one of which defends profits for capital accumulation and the other consumption. As capital accumulation on the basis of local equipment production requires spending before additional capacities of production can go onstream, accumulation—at least initially—reinforces labor in the wage bargain. The organizational strength labor acquires in this process makes wages sticky, so that rising real wages are the result of higher price competition on product markets during slumps.[1] But labor can never consume the financial resources necessary for equipment. At full employment, any profitable innovation can be financed out of credit and injects additional labor incomes into the economy. These labour incomes then compete for the amount of consumption goods the economy can produce at the existing levels of productive capacity for consumption goods.

The overarching conflict between labor and capital makes both forces interested in the reduction of rents used for non-productive purposes, inducing them to impose the lean state. Thus—the third consequence—because of their relative well-being, both classes of a capitalist economy can finance the activities of a lively, state-free civil society. Social connections are not necessary in order to improve one's economic lot because competition precludes any partner from paying above-average rates and the full employment of all factors of production makes preferential payments unnecessary for the ones that perform.

[1] Habakkuk (1972: 273), Tucker (1936), Montgomery (1938: 52), and Richardson (1939).

Suppose a decline in the terms-of-trade of such an economy. Export sectors become less profitable and imports more expensive. Labor and capital in the export sector are attracted to inward-looking branches. Lewis has proposed an explanation for the possibility of deteriorating terms-of-trade based on agricultural productivity:

> The market price gave the Nigerian for his peanuts a 700 lb of grain per acre level of living, and the Australian a 1,600 lb level of living not because of differences in competence nor because of marginal utilities of productivities in peanuts or wool, but because these were the respective amounts of food their cousins could produce on the family farms. (Lewis 1978: 12)

This is an extreme example of the argument outlined above that a high level of productivity in inward-looking branches precludes serious declines in terms-of-trade. The observation of Prebisch concerning differences in monopoly power addresses the same fact. He argues as follows:

> The greater ability of the masses in the cyclical centres to obtain rises in wages during the upswing and to maintain the higher level during the downswing and the ability of these centres, by virtue of the role they play in production, to divert cyclical pressure to the periphery (causing a greater reduction of income of the latter than in that of the centres) explain why income at the centres persistently tends to rise more than in the countries of the periphery, as happened in the case of Latin America.
>
> That is the clue to the phenomenon whereby the great industrial centres not only keep for themselves the benefit of the use of new technologies in their own economy, but are in a favourable position to obtain a share of that deriving from the technical progress of the periphery. (Prebisch 1962: 6)

In the long term, workers in the developed capitalist economy can defend their high wages only if business activity recovers. Unemployment in inward-looking branches will allow export businesses to cut wages. If, however, wages in inward-looking branches remain high due to low differences in productivity between export and inward-looking branches and high levels of employment, wages in export sectors remain high even in a slump or with worsening export conditions. Developed capitalist economies may experience declines in their terms-of-trade, but do not suffer from it. They are characterized by rising mass incomes in the wake of high levels of employment. High labor incomes are no obstacle to international competitiveness, as the homogeneity of productivity implies that too high international costs of local labor simply lead to devaluation and the competitiveness of new exports and new import-competing industries. The development of local technology production is the consequence of, and not the reason for, these high levels of employment. Scarcity of labor leads to decentralized innovation-promoting activities in all areas of the economy, even if these activities are supported by state subsidies.

The terms-of-trade controversy arises when economies do not react to worsening import capacity by launching new plants and equipment. Apparently, the inability to do so derives from a lack of flexibility due to the absence of local technology production.

If the terms-of-trade problem is so closely linked to the cost of adjustment for only one category of economy, i.e., the technically dependent economy, it would be worthwhile to examine more closely the characteristic structural deformation of such rent-based economies.

This absence corresponds to technical backwardness, but results from an absence of the capitalist growth mechanism: rising mass incomes creating incentives for innovation and markets for the increased production of standard products manufactured with increasingly sophisticated machinery.

The terms-of-trade problem is therefore the result—and not the cause—of the mechanism of capitalist growth being absent locally. It arises because not-yet capitalist economies can become sectorally competitive in certain products without being transformed into capitalist economies. They gain comparative advantage by virtue of the differences in productivity increases in developed capitalist countries. In the branches benefiting from this comparative advantage they earn better incomes than in their other activities, without necessarily increasing productivity, neither in this branch nor in their other activities. Typically, the branches where lags in productivity in relation to the capitalist industrialized countries are lowest have been raw-material branches. Here the exhaustion of rich deposits in the capitalist developed countries has counteracted the productivity-enhancing effects of technical innovation since the late nineteenth century. Moreover, productivity lags are highest in technology production because of the specific characteristics of technical progress under capitalist conditions (cf. paragraph 8, below).

The terms-of-trade problem results from the differences in structure between developed and underdeveloped economies. Underdeveloped economies are not characterized by full employment, hence the homogenization of productivities does not take place there. Flexibility in adjustment is not achieved. Surplus is not reduced to the requirements of investment but exists as rent. Rent precludes a simplification of the social structure into two contending camps which, by means of a ping-pong effect, would reinforce each other, providing greater markets and strong incentives to innovate. If rent predominates as the form of surplus appropriated by the powerful, the strategies followed by the poor will only reinforce this pattern of rent-seeking in the form of access of the poor to small amounts of the rent the powerful rentiers leave to them. What is more, strategies aimed at overcoming these blockages in underdeveloped economies will devolve into further rent-seeking, because they imply the removal of competition and because they require heroic efforts if the easy solution of simply "buying" development is to be avoided.

8.3 The Marginality-*Cum*-Rent Syndrome as the Key Characteristic of Underdevelopment

Full employment is impossible if a substantial share of the able-bodied population produces less than it must consume even at very low levels of mass consumption. If there is a substantial surplus of labor, productivity increases will not lead to higher wages. The neoclassical mechanism of matching productive and consumptive capacity is blocked along with the emergence of mass demand and cost pressure. Both are important mechanisms for triggering off technical innovation in the manufacturing of mass consumption goods and its components, especially technology.

The typical underdeveloped country is characterized by the fact that there is surplus labor which neither starves from poverty nor disappears in the wake of technical progress. The existence of a surplus of labor whose marginal product is lower than its costs of reproduction is a basic assumption of nearly all comprehensive approaches to development theory (Fei and Ranis 1964: 13–17; Lewis 1954). It is this assumption which distinguishes development theory as an independent discipline from mainstream neoclassical economics.

The economic conditions for the emergence of a surplus of labor can be briefly summarized (Elsenhans 1994, 1995, Chapter 5 in this volume). At a low level of mass consumption the share of food in household spending is high, about 50–60%. The share of food production in total employment is also high, even somewhat higher due to lower productivity. Fertile land is scarce, so marginal product of labor decreases. At a certain level of employment, marginal product becomes lower than the costs of subsistence of a laborer and his nuclear family. This additional labor may be called marginal.

Labor whose marginal product is lower than its costs of reproduction would have to disappear in neoclassical economics, either because it starves or because it is kept from reproducing itself. The decrease in marginal product does not automatically abolish the surplus produced by more productive labor on more fertile land, however. There is therefore a surplus of food as well, which is available for political redistribution. This surplus does not disappear through competition between landlords or through the competing claims of the laboring classes as it does in capitalism. The landlord can revert to a closed-estate economy whenever he is unable to sell his surplus on the market and can transform the labor he feeds from this surplus into political power, i.e., a private army. Laborers do not become scarce as long as surplus labor is maintained, which means that they cannot increase their incomes in their individual wage bargains.

There therefore have to be non-economic reasons why surplus labor does not disappear. These are to be found in the behavioral pattern of the two constituent classes of a marginality-ridden economy: the surplus-appropriating one and the poor. Both classes follow strategies aimed at maintaining a surplus of labor. In doing so, they undermine their political solidarity and follow strategies for individually increasing their share of rents. There is no class-consciousness and a dense network of personal ties. The limits to the formation of classes as political actors are especially detrimental to the political clout exercised by the poor.

The surplus-appropriating class (feudal landowners, warlords, members of patrimonial state apparatuses) operates in an economy where labor costs and mass incomes do not rise, as there is a labor surplus. Without mass-market expansion any innovation in new products merely involves luxuries for the rich. The demand for these luxuries can be maintained because the rich do not face perfect competition on the markets for their incomes. The rich can collect incomes from scarce land, from "power," i.e., any non-economic asset created by force, and from the ownership of any not easily reproducible assets used in the production of commodities. The access to scarce land and to power depends on the position of these privileged in the political hierarchy and, in the extreme case of a complete breakdown of law and order, on the capacity to command instruments of force. Assets which would allow earning additional incomes are limited by a low demand for mass-produced goods, as the great majority of the population is poor and there is most likely no large middle class.

Models can be constructed in which consumption of the rich spawns the emergence of a large commercial sector producing luxuries and military goods (Sombart 1913a, b). The capitalist entrepreneurs emerging in the wake of such consumption will, however, be unable to disestablish the precapitalist class as long as the impact of this Prussian way to capitalism does not create a large working class on which a political struggle against the political rights to surplus appropriation of the precapitalist class can be based.

Even if these emerging capitalist businessmen were able to demolish the barriers to income appropriation erected by precapitalist lords, they would only destroy the purchasing power on which their investment spending and the income flows earned from their investment are based. A non-capitalist order can therefore be expected to be politically stable as long as it does not create large working classes. Invariably, in seventeenth-century England, in eighteenth-century France and in contemporary South Korea or Taiwan the bourgeois revolution against monopoly, state enterprises or chaebols, has been based on coalitions between the part of business denied privileges and large working classes.

The marginality-*cum*-rent configuration cannot be overcome by technical progress alone. A higher productivity in luxury production will increase the quantity or improve the quality of luxury consumption. An increase in productivity in the manufacturing of industrial mass-consumption goods will lower the threshold of marginality, i.e., the income necessary for survival, so that the number of laborers still producing at least as much as their costs of reproduction increases. If the share of food in the costs of reproduction is still considerable, the potential effect is low. An increase in productivity in agriculture may, in turn, be characterized by capital intensity: product per worker increases, but marginal product does not. To the difference labor-intensive technical progress leads to a rise in the marginal product of labor. Only this type of technical progress automatically contributes to a reduction in the level of marginality. Lewis's insistence on the importance of agricultural progress acquires a quite different meaning in this context: An increasing marginal product of labor in agriculture leads to scarcity of labor, orienting industry toward the production of mass-consumption goods with increasing levels of employment.

The non-capitalist order is stabilized by the spending patterns of the lords. The lords can appropriate rent if they are powerful, regardless of their economic efficiency. A more efficient lord cannot disestablish an economically inefficient lord if the latter is powerful enough to maintain his share in the overall amount of rents appropriated within the respective territory. Lords will therefore not invest primarily in economic efficiency and will even restrain their luxury consumption as described in the theories of dynastic cycle,[2] but will instead "invest" in influence and respect/prestige. Thus, they will spend on support groups that allow them to increase their means of power, whether in the form of professional armies or political support groups among the peasantry. As competition on markets cannot become securely established, the share of each lord in the total surplus depends on his position in the political hierarchy. Allocation of the surplus can be extremely centralized and proceed in the form of rule by fiat. It can also be more decentralized, with inheritance rights and virtually irremovable feudal property relations (Abrahamian 1975). In both cases upholding one's position ultimately depends on the capacity to mobilize political support by means of force, prestige and financial resources.

Let us suppose that the "productivity" of support labor, i.e., average people engaged in providing political or military support on a full-time or part-time basis, is a function of the number of laborers employed for that purpose, regardless of the time they devote to this job. In this case, marginal labor in agriculture producing less than its cost of reproduction can be employed for support at a relatively low price because it needs only to complement its low production in agriculture. The lord therefore has no interest in maximizing the surplus from agriculture. His interest is best served by letting the population grow, at least to a certain degree. Many precapitalist arrangements in agriculture are characterized by a combination of transfers from the lord or the centralized structure to the deficitary subsistence production of marginal laborers and low production of the marginal ones.

Lords therefore have a tendency to waste rent on political power struggles and to maintain a surplus of labor producing less than it consumes

[2] Reischauer and Fairbank (1960: 117), Ibn Khaldûn (1967), Usher (1989: 1044), and Skinner (1971: 273).

by establishing redistributionist systems. The poor are interested in the continued existence of the given power structure as long as the "good" emperors and lords do not exaggerate their exploitative practices. The lords will be successful in promoting a worldview justifying the existing hierarchy.

8.4 The Lack of Solidarity of the Marginalized and the Exploited in a Marginality-*Cum*-Rent Situation

Rent appropriation and demographic growth are supported by the strategies which the poor perceive as being available to them.

The poor have an interest in being members of large primordial groups based on strong communal ties such as kinship or caste. There is no economic criterion allowing them to claim access to the group of highly productive workers. Productive workers can be immediately replaced by marginal ones. Thus, the labor market is organized in a lottery-type system. No peasant can be sure whom the lord will expel from his land. A large number of children will increase a family's chances on the labor market, the less so the more other solidarity groups exist. With their interest in support groups, the lords will use some of the surplus for employing labor with a low marginal product that would otherwise be shed off. The lord can pay more for some labor, since average product per worker is higher than marginal product. There will be a large variety of work contracts, varying in terms of security and compensation as described in the literature about clientelism (Mishra 1994; Scott 1972).

In order to survive under conditions of restricted but nonetheless existent competition, laborers will create associations in order to spread the risk. Without enforceable rights in redistribution, groups will necessarily remain small, and have to be governed by a ban on exiting. In geographically restricted areas, objective criteria such as family or caste are one means of enforcing this. They will try to maximize the chances of their primordial group by their reproductive behavior; the more children they have, the greater the chances that some of them will have access to highly remunerative employment or to another source of additional income. The lottery-type character of the labor market and the importance of a group having some access to sources of income that are higher than the marginal product of labor lead to internal mechanisms of discipline, with the group itself imposing discipline on each member.

Within such groups those earning less from outside employment, casual or privileged, will try to improve their position within the group, whereas those who are better off with their earnings from outside employment will try to restrict redistribution. In an analysis of the behavior of peasants in Zimbabwe, it was shown that only the expectation of permanent higher incomes through the market diminishes the acceptance of redistribution within the extended family (Bogedain 1994: 238–239). Permanent high incomes create the hope of never again having to rely on the solidarity of the extended family. Because of diverging interests in the amount of redistribution and the parallel interest in limiting one's own contribution to redistribution, these small solidarity groups are characterized by an essentially political struggle. Prestige comes to occupy a central position here, because blatant force and the use of financial clout are unusual instruments of coalition-building in small groups characterized by the economy of affection (Hyden 1980: 18).

Most members of the group will try to improve the group's overall position in the struggle for above-average work contracts by presenting the group as respectable and favorable to the values of the overarching community, represented by the lords. Keeping conflicts within the group from seeping out becomes an important element of face-saving. Moreover, certain members of primordial communities are able to create the belief within the community that they are contributing most to the respectability of the group in the outside world. These group members are best placed to benefit from redistributionist measures within the group. Economic efficiency is only one such criterion for achieving this reputation. Some, highly important members of the group (such as the father or the mother, as well as the elderly) will never be exposed to the necessity of finding work contracts outside, but will be judged by their capacity to maintain the group's cohesion and their own moral authority, often called wisdom.

In-group fighting is therefore based on the struggle for prestige, resources and influence, possibly by relying on outside alliances. The in-groups are segmented and pursue an overarching aim of maintaining solidarity, which is inevitably hierarchized, as religious norms of behavior are not clear-cut. The struggles will be more intensive the less there is a decalogue imposed from outside. Dissenting members can refer to the latter in opposing compromises based on "positive" thinking, which attempts to make mandatory the results of in-group power struggles and the compromises they yield to. The cultural pattern is determined by the rules applicable to in-group fighting over rents. It does not challenge the pattern of decision-making at the higher levels, where higher amounts of rents are centralized, but, through isomorphism, enhances the legitimacy of the struggle over rent at the higher levels.

The lords and the lower strata of society permanently create the conditions for labor surplus and block the emergence of large, class-based solidarities which could serve as the basis for expanding mass incomes, creating the conditions for capitalist accumulation. They permanently create cultural norms and patterns of behavior which condone the wasteful use of rents for non-development-oriented purposes.

The lower strata do so because they need the mechanisms of redistribution, since a large part of average-skilled labor cannot become proletarians of the Marxist type, which, economically, have the option of exit. The marginal product of proletarians is higher than their costs of reproduction enabling them to earn enough to accept or reject employment contracts without complementary favors, either from the group or from the lord (Elsenhans 1999a: 23–28).

It is not only the capacity of family farms in Australia to produce a higher quantity of food than in Nigeria, but, irrespective of property rights, the capacity of marginal laborers in Australia to produce a higher marginal product than in Nigeria. A high average of productivity in agriculture is not the decisive variable, but the empowerment of labor through a high marginal productivity in agriculture. As a short-term increase in marginal productivity in agriculture is most likely very difficult to achieve, the transition to capitalism requires a social and political restructuring of society. As a result the exploited and the marginalized seize power, appropriate the rent, and invest it in productivity-increasing new plant and equipment as well as social institutions which block the operation of the marginality principle, at least for the time span required to increase the marginal product of marginal labor to beyond the costs of reproduction. This links the terms-of-trade argument via the marginality-*cum*-rent model to a basically politically determined strategy of overcoming underdevelopment.

8.5 Overcoming the Marginality Trap Through a Redistribution of Rent and the Empowerment of Labor

In a marginality-ridden society, overcoming marginality is primarily a supply-side problem. The worker at the center of Prebisch's quote occupies a more powerful position because the scarcity of labor has homogenized productivities across branches, whereas scarcity itself results from a high marginal product of labor. Emmanuel's idea of redistributing rents to labor, developed after the oil-price rises in the 1970s (Emmanuel 1977: 27), neglects that it is impossible to pay such wages to all laborers if the local wage-goods production does not react flexibly to this new mass demand.

The marginality-cum-rent model showed that such homogenization was inevitably absent. This was described in the literature about structural heterogeneity in a variety of forms, such as the simultaneous existence of various modes of production, e.g., capitalism, feudalism, petty commodity production, etc. As heterogeneity of this sort has also been found in the most developed economies, structural heterogeneity has ultimately come to be defined as the simultaneity of sectors with various levels of productivity (Nohlen and Sturm 1982).

In contrast to structural heterogeneities in developed economies, marginality-ridden economies are characterized by very high productivities in their export sectors in comparison with the rest of their economies. Currency depreciations do not lead to increases in employment, because they are not sufficiently drastic to render local producers competitive in substituting hitherto imported goods, especially equipment.

These export sectors could experience relatively high performance because conditions were favorable for the integration of marginality-ridden economies. So they were easily integrated into the world market. The prices Western customers were ready to pay for tropical beverages had nothing to do with the productivities of the respective economies in producing these goods, but with new demands due to already higher mass incomes and the high prices for substitutes. They represent a ground rent, as did the high prices paid for mineral products from rich, virtually untapped deposits in Africa, Asia and Latin America. Thus, the growth of colonial export economies in the late nineteenth century was characterized by improving terms-of-trade until the end of the First World War

(Bairoch 1986: 206; Sen 1976; Palacios 1983: 49–53). Better terms-of-trade in the wake of scarcity of these goods stimulated raw material production in the South. The subsequent decline in terms-of-trade after 1919 indicates that neither business nor labor was able to maintain this scarcity by introducing market imperfections in the form of export regulations.

The demand for improving terms-of-trade implies a demand calling for rents not necessarily to be invested in the highly profitable export sectors, but to feed consumption, especially of the land-owning and shipping interests. With declining demand for the export products of marginality-ridden economies, these interests can be defended only if the rich shift to locally produced luxuries. This implies that there is no drive to invest in mass consumption goods industries for the needs of the poor. In case of distribution of rents to the poor, these incomes can be defended only if the local production of mass-consumption goods has, through this redistribution, been triggered before the outbreak of depression. Given that marginality-ridden economies manufacture these products at much lower rates of productivity than developed capitalist countries, such economies would have been flooded with imported mass consumption goods in case of rising mass incomes. Only very drastic declines in the earnings of the export sector would have launched export-competing local substitutes. The case of Uruguay can be quoted here as negative examples (Barran and Nahum 1984: 663).

If the rents were invested in enlarging export sectors, prices would have to decline. Because of saturation of markets this would have by necessity driven down terms-of-trade to levels where earnings in the export sector equal the earnings in the internal-market-oriented sector. Factor earnings would have been equal at this level, and in the case of backward countries low.

The theoretical foundations of the demand for better terms-of-trade changed once these inflexibilities were realized. The appropriation of rents was justified with the argument that rents constituted the financial means for financing investment in economic diversification, as mentioned in the opening quote of H. W. Singer.

Three problems are relevant to the failure to overcome the politico-economic and cultural foundations of marginality-ridden economies' dependency on terms-of-trade: the political implications of any rent-based process of industrialization, the neglect of internal demand to the benefit of investment and the systematic reliance on imported technology. These three mechanisms were interdependent and blocked the emergence of a competition-oriented business class, which would have opposed market distortions introduced by the state, and a vigorous working class, which, through rising consumption, would have allowed the emergence of a local equipment-producing sector.

8.6 The Reinforcement of Rent-Based Political Structures Through Rent-Financed Industrialization

If a new investment process aims at diversifying the economy by establishing new industries for which the necessary skills and infrastructure are nonexistent, then this initiative cannot be geared to the profit rate. This is because the profit rate is higher in all the "wrong" old sectors, especially if the country has successfully defended high incomes in the rent-generating export sectors, i.e., if the country has enjoyed favorable terms-of-trade. Such an investment process has to involve instead administratively channeling rent from a rent-generating, normally—but not necessarily—export-oriented, sector to a new sector.

In order to define a new sector, and more so to create it, the agent must be able to appropriate resources through an extra-market mechanism. Unlike a capitalist profit, resources appropriated in a highly productive sector and channeled into a not yet profitable sector of the economy will, by definition, not immediately generate surpluses in this new area of production. They may not even do so in the medium term, because the improvements in infrastructure, labor skills, institutional arrangements, etc. may not be captured by the agents that invested in them. Channeling a rent from an export sector into economic diversification requires that a political decision be made by some institution beyond the sphere of market control.

Decisions of this sort are possible without exposing the respective agent to economic losses because the agent is no longer institutionally bound to price competition. In view of achieving economic diversification, this may be the intended aim. But the pursuit of this aim also implies that the discipline normally imposed on capitalists by the market is removed. Baran's (1952: 67) argument about the possible desirability of destroying feudal patterns of behavior by means of full-fledged capitalist competition should be highlighted here:

> A complete substitution of capitalist market rationality for the rigidities of feudal or semi-feudal servitude would have represented, in spite of all the pains of transition, an important step in the direction of progress. Yet all that happened was that the age-old exploitation of the population of underdeveloped countries by their domestic overlords was freed of mitigating constraints inherited from the feudal tradition. This superimposition of business mores over ancient oppression by landed gentries resulted in compounded exploitation, more outrageous corruption, and more glaring injustice.

It is not the historical legacy of a precapitalist pattern of behavior that causes those in control of rent to be wasteful. Instead, it is a principal-agent problem rendered acute by the fact that, in societies where such rents become the predominant form of surplus, those in control of these rents evade not only economic control but also political control. They can become successful only if they centralize available rents by replacing decentralized oligarchies with a hierarchically organized apparatus. This apparatus appears as a state commanding over administrations. They are held together by alliances based on segments I have described as state classes.[3] The latter were expected to channel resources according to master plans, which were best formulated in Leontief's (1953) input-output analyses, and later in social-accounting matrices. This type of representation of the interlinkages of an economy can accommodate the rise in productivity only through analogies based on coefficients drawn from elsewhere. The distribution of investment between branches depends on rises in productivity, at least in a dynamic perspective. Rises in productivity are, however, only based on assumptions, e.g., analogies drawn from other countries but never imposed on entrepreneurs by actual competition.

Essential elements of such matrices are decisively dependent on choices. If technical progress was not simply the direct result of capital accumulation, then at least the "disembodied" elements of technical progress were expected to be produced automatically by capital accumulation. The choice of parameters, such as time horizons in final demand (in the Mahalanobis model 1953: 307–312), and the modeling constraints

[3] On this notion cf. Elsenhans (1996 [1981] : 173–222), Graf (1988: 226–233), and Sturm (1984: 532–533).

of existing backwardness (hence the choice of the implied costs of transforming the economic environment of investments) had a determining influence on the predictions of the model. All agents of execution faced enormous problems in "transforming" their economic environments, inducing them to insist on soft plans even at the level of plan implementation (Elsenhans 2001a: 147). Parameters were inevitably chosen on the basis of negotiations, hence voluntaristic proceedings. The choices were made within hierarchically organized agencies, and resulted from a process of political conflict between different groups struggling for access to political decision-making by mobilizing power/influence, financial resources and prestige.

In the process of screening projects, promoters tried to cut costs in relation to expected benefits, making the parameters in the projected input-output matrix unrealistic. Information was negotiated. Like marginal laborers and the old lords, the new lords also fight for prestige, power and resources in a culture where the fight for respect becomes indispensable in order to prevail in decision-making (Elsenhans 1987: 78–87). They do their best to keep the flow of information sticky. Rent produces at the top what marginal labor produces at the bottom. Whatever the level of sophistication achieved in the mathematical presentation of projects and the models built upon them, all of these projects and models are inevitably biased for political reasons.

Unforeseen losses will be presented on the basis of soft data as an indication of general or specific deficiencies due to the underdeveloped state of the economy. This type of argument encourages wasteful spending even more, for instance in the case of Algeria at the end of the Boumediene period, where the whole of planned investment spending was realized and the capacities of production, however, were less than 50% of the original projections.

Inconsistencies occurred at the level of plan formulation and were exacerbated during the execution phase. Integration was achieved as far as possible, with those who were powerful having access to the rent and therefore being able to achieve their goals at the level of production, to the detriment of others, i.e., to the detriment of those who failed to provide the necessary complementary production projected in the plans.

Inefficiencies invariably gave priority to making rents accessible to "investors," and not to consumers, scarcities being the most visible result of the inconsistencies this gave rise to.

8.7 The Priority of Investment as an Ideological Heritage

The politics of diversification were the result of macroeconomic models which privileged investment and considered consumption to be a result of investment. Bankers and Marxists have a quite similar view on this link, to the point that Rostow's model of take-off into self-sustained growth could satisfy the banks and at the same time be criticized as a Stalinist model (Carré and Dumont 1985: 11). The Marxist and capitalist justification of the priority of investment contributed to a consistently uncritical view of this strategy for many years.[4]

Inefficient investment can be considered exploitation by inefficiency. Marx's reproduction schemes (Marx 1956 [1885]: 298–318) contributed to this acceptance of exploitation by wasteful investment in a rather ironic manner. Marx's petite bourgeois extremism in rejecting the possibilities of "reformist" perspectives for overcoming the contradictions of capitalism, such as real wage increases in order to limit accumulation, induced him to represent the capitalist growth process ("enlarged reproduction") in terms of a disproportionate growth of investment goods production ("division I") so that the growth rate of capital stock was inevitably higher than the growth rate of production. This obviously leads to a fall in the profit rate, a situation diagnosed by neoclassical economics as well, endogenous growth theory being the economic mainstream theoretical solution to the Keynesian observation of the absence of this phenomenon.

In the Eastern European Marxist discussion there were some timid attempts, at least in Eastern Germany, to reject the thesis that the capital stock had to grow more rapidly than national income.[5] These East German Marxists were particularly exposed to what at that time had been called the competition of systems, in which Keynesian authors had opposed neoclassical ones on the issue of a rise in the capital-output ratio. Keynesian authors observed that the capital-output ratio did not rise in long-term capitalist development.[6] This allowed taking an increase of mass income into consideration.

[4] The exception is Peter T. Bauer, cf. Bauer (1957). Later on: Bauer (1984).

[5] Bartl and Luck (1961: 1500), Reichenberg (1967: 1786), Barthel and Karbstein (1967: 221).

[6] Kendrick (1961: 166), Helmstädter (1969: 48–91), Domar (1961: 101–114).

A capitalist economy is characterized by limited capital accumulation. The accumulation of physical capital is accompanied by the creation of skills and knowledge (Fine 2000: 246). These elements are difficult to define. They emerge because capitalists have to make their investment decisions under the conditions of competition. If, according to the Bortkiewicz/Okishio criterion (von Bortkiewicz 1907: 451–460; Okishio 1961: 85–90) for profitable investment, any new investment had to increase productivity to a degree at least sufficient to offset any additional capital costs, rising consumption and, with competitive labor markets, rising mass consumption had now become a condition for capitalist growth (Elsenhans 1983a, b). Any increase in the rate of accumulation beyond technical progress implies non-profitable investment which does not create subsequent resource flows. Rising mass incomes impose competition, hence greater efficiency, and create markets on which more, and also new, products can be sold profitably.

New endogenous growth theory has integrated into the neoclassical model the Keynesian observation of a rather constant ICOR (Incremental Capital-Output Ratio, $\delta C/\delta Y$) in developed capitalist economies with rising mass incomes, referring to it as unidentified technical progress (Romer 1996: 202–206). Technical progress is not a linear function of the accumulation of physical capital. The rate of growth of physical capital may outpace the rate of growth of technical progress. Hence in the case of stagnant consumption capital accumulation may not be limited enough to not outgrow the rate of technical progress. The restrictions on the growth of investment which keep the emerging competitive capitalist sector from overaccumulation may either be absent or maintained only by the expansion of luxury consumption, which, in turn, is possible only if competition is removed. A rent-financed industrialization process could lead to a developed capitalist economy only if its ruling class has a very firm commitment to favor not only investment but also mass consumption, despite the poor having low levels of entitlement to consumption according to their economic position (i.e., their marginal product).

The large class alliances in typical marginality-ridden economies and the interest of their state classes in self-privileging was a less favorable social-power configuration than the Soviet-type centrally planned economies with their high commitment to the value of social equality and an omnipotent party imposing this commitment. Even these economies, however, failed to launch development by curbing the privileges of those in control of the economic surplus through competition on the market.

This was even less so in marginality-ridden economies, with their new, privileged state classes, their allies, and their entrenched and propertied rentier interests.

Capitalism escapes the tendential fall in the rate of profit through "disembodied" technical progress, i.e., technical progress not included in the costs of machinery. Real socialism was attractive during the underconsumptionist situation of the 1930s and lost out to capitalism when the challenge it presented compelled capitalists to accept government responsibility for state intervention to achieve full employment along Keynesian lines. Real socialism was able to maintain similar rates of growth only by continuously keeping the rate of capital accumulation above the rate of growth of national income. The capital-output ratio invariably increased and the share of consumption in total income decreased, along with the rate of profit (Elsenhans 2000). The capacity of capitalism to check the tendential fall in the rate of profit by continuously generating disembodied technical progress is, however, both the source of continued technical dependency, and the reason why marginality-ridden economies have to pursue declining terms-of-trade in order to overcome underdevelopment.

8.8 The Necessity of Accepting Deteriorating Terms-of-Trade as an Instrument of Catching up

Suppose that there are decreasing returns on investment, as assumed by standard neoclassical growth theory. Despite the birth pangs associated with a delayed transition to capitalism, the "globalization" of capitalism and worldwide full employment would be inevitable. Increasing marginal costs of capital in relation to increases in productive capacity in the leading countries would have led to the relocation of production to the less developed world. On the basis of still lower labor costs and limited amounts of capital employed, the Third World would have experienced a rapid growth of production and employment. This is the common vision of Marxists such as Lenin (1964 [1916]: 242–246) and Bill Warren (1980: 14), as well as standard neoclassical convergence theories of the Heckscher, Ohlin and Samuelson type.[7]

[7] Heckscher (1949), Samuelson (1948), and Ohlin (1927).

If there are no decreasing returns on investment because of disembodied technical progress, catch-up economies are systematically induced to rely on imported technology (Singer 1975: 376–382). A producer of machinery will be able to introduce a new model if it reduces the unit costs of production of its user. Otherwise nobody will buy the new model. The innovator will try to increase or maintain market shares by lowering prices and spending on further innovation. The relation between the performance of new machinery measured in physical terms and its costs increases. This relation can be considered the measure of productivity in machinery production.

No technology-producing enterprise can remain on the market without spending on innovation. As any enterprise not engaging in such spending will disappear, all enterprises that do will ultimately be able to recover their costs due to the scarcity of surviving suppliers of new machinery. The knowledge and skills acquired in the search for innovation probably constitutes the bulk of the residual factor so greatly emphasized by modern growth theory. But these elements of technical progress are only created in the company that takes part in this search process.[8]

Many users of new machinery can operate at the same level of efficiency, although they have not acquired the skills and knowledge of the innovating economy. Empirical studies have shown that differences in productivity between developed and underdeveloped economies are relatively low in industries employing high amounts of physical capital.[9]

There are two possibilities to lessen the lock-in effect of this pattern of specialization. The backward economy can increase its productivity in investment-goods production or decrease its "productivity" (as measured in earnings) in non-investment-goods production. The first option resembles the strategies applied in import-substituting industrialization, although few of the countries following these strategies have been able to launch investment-goods industries capable of withstanding competition on their own internal markets later on without protection. The second option is similar to export-led manufacturing, although the theory of export-led industrialization normally warns against the goal of greater

[8] Posner (1961), Vernon (1966), Perroux (1968), Krugman (1991).

[9] Boatler (1974: 838, 1978: 61), Clague (1967: 492, 1970: 201, 1991: 526), Díaz-Alejandro (1965: 209), and Siggel (1984).

technical independence. In the first option, good terms-of-trade are advocated in order to finance diversification from incomes out of rent. The second option involves the acceptance of deteriorating terms-of-trade. The economy specializes in technology-dependent branches. It increases production and has to accept declining prices on the world market, normally through devaluation of its currency. The more the currency devaluates, the more expensive imported investment goods become in relation to export products. Relative productivity as measured in earnings in the technology-using export branches decreases. Relative productivity in investment goods production increases.

8.9 Export-Led Manufacturing: Productively Dissipating a Rent Through Declining Terms-of-Trade

Export-led industrialization, the pet subject of neoclassical economics and free marketers, is not characterized by a race to lower real wages in catch-up economies. Real wages are not significant for international competitiveness; international labor costs are. Real wages obviously have an influence on international labor costs, but this impact is largely mediated by the exchange rate, in the case of paper money, or the general price level, in a gold-standard system (Yotopoulos 1996: 7–10). Managers who have to evaluate labor costs in low-wage areas of the South usually do not know the level of real wages, but rather the dollar costs of labor (Kenney and Florida 1994: 31).

The difference between the per capita product at the exchange rate and in-purchasing parities is about 1:4 for most underdeveloped countries.[10] A Chinese household can buy about ten times as much in Beijing as it could in Canada if its income were converted into Canadian dollars at the official exchange rate (Chen et al. 1994). The real poor are living in sub-Saharan Africa and South Asia—both of which have not been particularly successful in export-led manufacturing—and not in East and Southeast Asia, which have been successful in export-led manufacturing. Low labor costs may be compatible with high real wages, provided that the goods consumed by wage earners are produced locally and not exported.

[10] Cf. Guillaumont-Jeanneney and Hua (1996: 851–860) and Lafay (1996).

Most underdeveloped economies are assumed—in agreement with empirical reality—to be able to produce a surplus of food as long as there are appropriate price incentives. These economies nevertheless have labor in agriculture that produces less than its costs of reproduction. Like a peasant household that maximizes food production in order not to have to buy anything from the market, and which offers its surplus labor in rural bi-employment in a sort of vent-of-surplus strategy (Myint 1971: 130–131), the devaluation-driven export-oriented industrializing economy supplies most wage goods to its labor from internal production and offers industrial products at the lowest possible prices.[11] The surpluses of the local food-producing sector and of the local "informal" industrial sector are the resources used to supply previously unemployed labor with basic goods.

No one can survive with 1/50th or 1/70th of the salary of an American or West European worker if he has to pay American or West European prices. Additional workers can be employed in the successful export-led economies because the local wage-goods-producing sectors there supply goods at lower prices than the goods available from the world market. These additional workers earn local money from commodities sold on the world market at prices where the products necessary to satisfy even the most basic needs of these workers cannot be bought on the world market. Subsistence goods for the additional export workers have to be supplied through the local production of wage goods. The locally produced rent, especially in agriculture, which under import-substituting industrialization was supposed to be mobilized for investment, is bought up by the additional export workers with their salaries paid in local currency. In order that these workers do not have to compete with external buyers for the surplus of food and low-quality industrial products produced by the informal sector, it is sufficient that transport costs for food are high and that the demand from high-income countries for this food is low (because of protectionist measures). The rent is taken away from the privileged, and consumed in its physical form by the additional export-sector workers and the workers employed to meet the rising demand for basic goods resulting from this new employment. The value of this rent goes partly to the local workers and partly to consumers in the countries receiving the additional exports of manufactures. These

[11] The theory of the peasant "subsidizing" market production is, indeed, quite old, cf. Chayanov (1966: 41) and Vergopoulos (1974: 195).

consumers enjoy the benefits of rising terms-of-trade. The terms-of-trade of the devaluation-driven export-oriented countries, on the other hand, fall.[12]

If real incomes of labor are low, the share of food in household consumption is high, whereas the import propensity of consumption of industrial goods may also be low due to low quality requirements, etc. An economy at such an early stage of development in terms of consumption and which produces a surplus of basic goods, especially food, can in principle accept any rate of devaluation. If it pursues the aim of transforming its labor market in order to transform its internal power configuration, it could even accept a fall in the foreign exchange value of its total exports, or a level of export earnings where the share of labor in export earnings tends to zero.

It is obviously a costly strategy to promote industrialization simply by devaluation, as it implies sacrificing foreign exchange in order to create employment, especially if price elasticities of demand for exports are low. A government might conclude that taxing certain products with low price elasticity of demand can provide resources, for example, for state subsidized investment in infrastructure or even in the improvement of the conditions for profitability in the export sector. This explains why export orientation is often accompanied by state intervention in the investment process, as seen in Taiwan, South Korea and even Singapore (Holtgrave 1987; Mytelka 1986: 258; Shih 1968: 121–123), and now openly claimed by East Asian economists (Khan 2000). Only the more ideologically biased literature of the Washington institutions did not take the fundamentally rent-based character of the East Asian miracle into account until about the early 1990s (Page 1993: 157–159), although East Asian economists had, prior to this, clearly described the power games between business and government (Baer et al. 1999: 1743), and even modeled the turning point on the labor market where the transition to capitalism had succeeded (Bai 1982; Minami 1992: 26; Irwan 1989: 410).

Devaluation is limited if the share of local factors of production (especially labor) in value creation decreases. Labor constitutes an important share of value creation only in labor-intensive products. Most labor-intensive products are also skill-intensive, as demonstrated already by Leontief (1954, 1956). Devaluation enables reducing the costs of factors

[12] Falling terms-of-trade for manufactured exports are reported: Köhler (2001), Sarkar and Singer (1991: 333–340), and Briguglio (1993: 269–276).

reproduced locally, local natural resources such as land, and local labor, provided that there is a surplus of food production and a reasonably dynamic informal sector. Devaluation does not allow reducing the costs of investment goods and imported intermediate products. The higher the share of imported products in the costs of production, the lower the effect of devaluation on total costs. Further devaluation has a diminished impact on prices, especially if diversification is pursued by engaging in the export-led manufacture of new products, where technology and imported intermediate products are more costly in relation to local labor and have to be imported (Elsenhans 1999b: 41–45, 2001b: 257–266). The successful "tiger" nations, with the exception of Hong Kong, have all engaged in the "preemptive" creation of upstream plants for new exports and skills. This has been referred to as "upgrading" (Jomo 1998: 12).

The presence of a rent-collecting state which subsidizes investment is not an anomaly in an otherwise laissez-faire economy that grows through a process of integration into the world market. It is a central feature of the catch-up process via integration into the capitalist world system.

Singer's analysis has not lost any of its relevance. There may be an optimal level for terms-of-trade where the political structures that emerge out of rent are not yet wasteful enough to suffocate any attempt to mobilize rent for investment in diversification.

8.10 Pragmatism, State, Market and Overcoming Underdevelopment

Although rents can be used for investment, they tend rather to bolster the non-capitalist traits of "elites," i.e., the non-capitalist character of the surplus-appropriating class. This owes to the fact that there are no automatisms that politically impose the investment of rent, and there are blockages on the road to full employment. Even if rents are spent on investment, the channeling of rent into productive investment and economic diversification requires using part of the rent either for non-capitalist investment, which is not profit-bearing, or for consumption in order to launch capitalist investment.

The debate over better terms-of-trade indicates that catch-up economies may have greater access to surplus from their exports than forerunner economies had, because these catch-up economies are cohabiting with richer societies. The latter can pay higher prices for the export products of economies that are lagging behind. The backward economies are thus facing the challenge of higher rents, because there are richer economies able to pay for them. At the same time, in comparison with the European transition to capitalism, the precapitalist social structures in the part of the world nowadays that is trying to catch up with the West economically, are more firmly entrenched, because available rents provide financial support for non-capitalist social classes.

There seem to be combinations of reduced rents and increased market mechanisms with participation which depend on a variety of factors, such as the pattern of specialization and the social structure.

The great advantage of the East and Southeast Asian tigers in relation to other underdeveloped countries rests in the fact that rent was produced as food and not as foreign exchange, as, for example, in the case of oil. Local labor became competitive and earned income in national currency through a reduction in the exchange rate. By way of contrast, rent earned from oil exports has to be transformed into foreign exchange and then into imports (hopefully of technology) to be combined with local investment spending by government administrations. The labor force created by a rent in labor-intensive food production is quite large, and increases if the purchasing power of additional export workers increases. Labor power in an oil sector is limited, though often highly qualified and therefore capable of imposing wages considerably above average.

Differences in technological requirements according to the rent-generating sectors involved have an impact on the possibilities of creating local investment-goods industries. Minerals and fossil fuels have since the late nineteenth century normally been high-technology industries, and therefore rarely give rise to local investment-goods production, as textiles and clothing have done increasingly (Sid Ahmed 1990: 60–61). The less numerous and the more privileged the labor force linked to a rent, the more threatening the impact of rent on the goal of investment for mass needs, and vice versa.

The battle over the establishment and the maintenance of the mechanisms appropriate to tame rent is waged at a variety of levels. Rent is an economic resource appropriated on the basis of political power and spent by agents who are isolated from price competition, and who spend part of the rent on strengthening their positions of political power. There are, however, some rules of thumb.

In the economic realm employment is the major instrument for entitlement. Low exchange rates that raise employment are preferable to high exchange rates that raise incomes.

According to cultural norms, luxury production may be characterized by low import intensity, and even promote employment and a limited degree of growth in local technological capacities. But rising mass incomes at low exchange rates invariably favor local investment goods production, and are an error-proof solution, as they do not create privileges and hence monopolies.

More general mechanisms of redistribution which automatically channel resources into the budgets of poor households are better suited than finely targeted programs, even if such programs are administered by morally high-standing benevolent agents. The initial enthusiasm concerning NGOs has been greatly dampened, not unlike the once positive appreciation of the benevolent, idealistically minded administrators and military officers the theory of political modernization had relied on (Sklar 1967: 8).

Automatic redistribution in the form of an agrarian reform allows directly appropriating a land rent for consumption and maximizing production, but does not increase investible surplus (Janvry 1981: 384–392; Elsenhans 1979: 559–561). The English poor laws represented a general program of subsidies which reduced surplus and increased mass consumption and profit, but were susceptible to administrative corruption (Elsenhans 1992 [1980]). The West alone, yet more so the West together with the countries receiving mineral rents, commands the resources for the creation of an artificial industry at a global level which would be capable of creating full employment. I have outlined such a program elsewhere (Elsenhans 1991: 283–286). It would involve dropping easily identifiable objects into remote areas, which would then be gathered by the poor in those areas and exchanged at rates where a gatherer could earn his daily subsistence. By creating purchasing power for imports, too (the easily identifiable objects can be exported for foreign exchange), there is no danger of inflation, but instead an expanding market which slightly better-off farmers and businessmen in the small and medium-scale informal sector would be happy to supply. With one billion poor and the necessity of supplying foreign exchange of $100/year per poor, the cost of a program amounting to $100 billion per year could be easily financed out of a Tobin tax-like mechanism levied on the $1–2 trillion financial turnover per day in the world economy.

Wherever rents require more targeted intervention for their appropriation, especially in the case of raw material rents, it is not decentralization, but Jacobinism which is preferable for its execution. This could be accompanied by the allocation of resources through local bodies, although there is the danger of a lack of accountability. This has little to do with the statist character of these bodies. Despite the opposite conviction in more recent literature, political parties, even in rent-dominated sections of the Third World, may in fact be more accountable to mass demands than NGOs (Kuhn 1998: 265).

The demand for democratically accountable bodies often overlooks the inevitable birth pangs involved in establishing the basis for such bodies. They do not automatically emerge with economic growth and liberalization. Development is uneven between the various levels of the sociopolitical and economic structures of underdeveloped countries. In South Korea full employment led to a combative working class that was rapidly able to engage in alliances with middle strata, and even with the non-monopolistic business sector. But political parties have continued to depend on regionalism, patronage, corruption, etc. They do not assemble large alliances of social "classes," the guarantee for downplaying particularistic interests against larger collective interests that Olson had hoped for (1982: 31).

In India, long-standing traditions of patronage, clientelism and the importance of casteism are critical for the mobilization of votes. Nonetheless, the political consciousness of the Indian poor and their determination to stick to the defense of narrow economic interests have forced both major political parties, the Congress and the BJP, to develop large, 'transclass' coalitions. Within these coalitions, patronage ultimately matters less than one might expect, given the cultural variables involved (Malik and Singh 1994).

The main problem highlighted by Singer involves the efficient use of better trade terms for economic diversification, and the overcoming of underdevelopment. This touches on the behavior of elites in regions in which the poor tend to be marginal and thus powerless, at least insofar as the poor are not able to organize politically and in advance of their low economic status. The West has an influence on the terms-of-trade, together with elites in the South. The West has little contact with the marginalized poor in the South. Even powerful Western NGOs communicate with the poor of the South via non-Western (Southern) NGOs.

The West can make use of the strategy of an artificial industry in the South. They can do so irrespective of the power of elites, their potential repressiveness, their nationalistic discourse, and the other unsavory instruments and strategies they may employ in order to prevent the marginalized poor from asserting their interests. The elites of the South would be swept away politically if they opposed an employment-generating program based on an artificial industry financed by the West. Such an artificial industry would reduce the sharp divide between the rapidly growing productive capacities for exports in the South and lower rates of increase in consumption capacity in the West and the South. The strategy would combine export-led growth with internal market expansion and relatively automatic transfers. This would provide the South with incentives from demand, and promote its transition to capitalism.

There are options to compensate the poor's lack of entitlement in the South. In line with the objective possibilities of raising prices, in particular for raw materials from the South, the strategy could also be financed from export duties on raw materials, which to date have been imposed quite successfully on oil. The theoretical underpinning and subsequent feasibility of such a strategy is just as realistic as the undeniable waste of billions of dollars by the oil monarchies of the Arab peninsula.

But any such alternative can be achieved only if one condition is met. The ideological hegemony of the neoclassical paradigm has to be broken. It is a nice model, but far from reality with its insistence that full employment is possible everywhere as long as wages are sufficiently low because those who receive the profit are always dynamic enough to invest all available resources. Singer's work, in contrast, is based on the assumption that these equilibria are often nonexistent and at best irrelevant. The link between the demand for improving terms-of-trade and a conscious building-up of backward economies was a powerful message to that effect. The contemporary proliferation of rent despite globalization and the increasingly power-shaped pattern of rivalries between transnational enterprises show that renouncing the embeddedness of rent in more or less accountable political structures does not make rent disappear. It merely makes rent subservient to the powerful. The message of political and economic modernization theory, so often criticized for its statism, is indeed much closer to a true liberalism in the sense of Eucken than that of orthodox free marketers.[13]

[13]The embeddedness of liberalism in a social structure that keeps the liberals from taking over political structures has been nicely analyzed by a grandson of Eucken, who has edited the latter's unpublished papers: Eucken (2001).

References

Abrahamian, Ervand. 1975. European Feudalism and Middle Eastern Despotisms. *Science and Society* 39 (2): 129–156.

Baer, Werner, William R. Miles, and B. Moran. 1999. The End of the Asian Myth: Why Were the Experts Fooled. *World Development* 27 (10): 1735–1747.

Bai, Moo-Ki. 1982. The Turning Point in the Korean Economy. *Developing Economies* 20 (2): 117–140.

Bairoch, Paul. 1986. Historical Roots of Economic Underdevelopment: Myths and Realities. In *Imperialism and After. Continuities and Discontinuities*, ed. Wolfgang Mommsen and Jürgen Osterhammel, 191–216. London: Allen & Unwin.

Baran, Paul A. 1952. On the Political Economy of Backwardness. *Manchester School of Economic and Social Studies* 20 (1): 66–84.

Barran, José Pedro, and Benjamin Nahum. 1984. Uruguayan Rural History. *Hispanic American Historical Review* 64 (4): 655–673.

Barthel, Wilfried, and Werner Karbstein. 1967. Zur Diskussion über einige neue Aspekte in der Beurteilung der Wachstumsrelationen zwischen gesellschaftlichem Gesamtprodukt und Nationaleinkommen sowie zwischen Abteilungen I und II. *Wirtschaftswissenschaft* 15 (2): 198–222.

Bartl, Wilhelm, and Herbert Luck. 1961. Zu den Beziehungen zwischen den Investitionen und dem Wachstum des gesellschaftlichen Gesamtprodukts sowie des Nationaleinkommens. *Wirtschaftswissenschaft* 9 (6): 1477–1501.

Bauer, Peter Tamás. 1957. *Economic Analysis and Policy in Underdeveloped Countries*. Durham, NC: Duke University Press.

Bauer, Peter Tamás. 1984. *Reality and Rhetoric. Studies in the Economics of Development*. London: Weidenfeld and Nicolson.

Boatler, Robert W. 1974. Las predicciones de la teoría del comercio internacional y el crecimiento de las exportaciones manufacturadas de México. *Trimestre Económico* 41 (164): 811–857.

Boatler, Robert W. 1978. Comparative Advantage; A Division among Developing Countries. *Interamerican Economic Affairs* 32 (2): 59–66.

Bogedain, Christine. 1994. *Entwicklung durch Privatisierung? Bauern zwischen Subsistenzproduktion und Marktorientierung in Zimbabwe*. Hamburg: Institut für Afrika-Kunde.

Briguglio, Lino Pascal. 1993. The Terms of Trade and the Direction of Trade in the Maltese Economy. *World Development* 21 (2): 269–276.

Broadberry, Stephen N., Rainer Fremdling, and Peter Solar. 2008. European Industry 1700–1870. *Jahrbuch für Wirtschaftsgeschichte* 2: 141–171.

Brown, Michael Barrett. 1963. *After Imperialism*. London: Heinemann.

Carré, Olivier, and Dumont Paul (eds.). 1985. *Radicalismes islamiques. Tome (1): Iran, Liban, Turquie*. Paris: Harmattan.

Chayanov, Alexander V. 1966. *The Theory of Peasant Economy*. Homewood, IL: Richard D. Irwin.

Chen, Haichun, M.J. Gordon, and Yan Zhiming. 1994. The Real Income and Consumption of an Urban Chinese Family. *Journal of Development Studies* 31 (1): 201–213.

Clague, Christopher K. 1967. An International Comparison of Industrial Efficiency. Peru and the United States. *Review of Economics and Statistics* 49 (4): 487–493.

Clague, Christopher K. 1970. The Determinants of Efficiency in Manufacturing in an Underdeveloped Country. *Economic Development and Cultural Change* 18 (2): 188–205.

Clague, Christopher. 1991. Relative Efficiency, Self-Containment and Comparative Costs of Less Developed Countries. *Economic Development and Cultural Change* 39 (2): 506–530.

Diaz-Alejandro, Carlos F. 1965. Industrialization and Labour Productivity Differentials. *Review of Economics and Statistics* 47 (2): 207–213.

Digby, William. 1901. *'Prosperous' British India. A Revelation from Official Records*. London: T. Fisher Unwin.

Domar, Evsey D. 1961. The Capital-Output Ratio in the United States: Its Variation and Stability. In *The Theory of Capital: Proceedings of a Conference Held by the International Economic Association*, ed. F.A. Lutz, D.C. Hague, 95–117. New York and London: Macmillan and St. Martins Press.

Dutt, Palme Rajani. 1949. *India Today*. Mumbai: People's Publishing House, quoted from Dutt, Palme Rajani. 1970. *India Today*. Calcutta: Manisha.

Elsenhans, Hartmut. 1979. Agrarverfassung, Akkumulationsprozeß, Demokratisierung. In *Agrarreform in der Dritten Welt*, ed. Hartmut Elsenhans, 505–652. Frankfort on the Main, New York: Campus.

Elsenhans, Hartmut. 1983a. Égalité et développement. L'expérience européenne et le monde sous-développé d'aujourd'hui. *Cultures et développement* 15 (2): 187–215.

Elsenhans, Hartmut. 1983b. Rising Mass Incomes as a Condition of Capitalist Growth. Implications for the World Economy. *International Organization* 37 (1): 1–38.

Elsenhans, Hartmut. 1987. Dependencia, Underdevelopment and the Third World State. *Law and State* 36: 65–94.

Elsenhans, Hartmut. 1991. Problems Central to Economic Policy Deregulation in Bangladesh. *Internationales Asienforum* 22 (3/4): 259–286.

Elsenhans, Hartmut. 1992 [1980]. English Poor Law and Egalitarian Agrarian Reform in the Third World. In *Equality and Development*, ed. Hartmut Elsenhans, 130–162. Dhaka: Center for Social Studies.

Elsenhans, Hartmut. 1994. Rent, State and the Market. The Political Economy of the Transition to Self-Sustained Capitalism. *Pakistan Development Review* 33 (4): 393–428.

Elsenhans, Hartmut. 1995. Überwindung von Marginalität als Gegenstand der Armutsbekämpfung. In *Bevölkerungsdynamik und Grundbedürfnisse in Entwicklungsländern*, ed. Hans Bernd Schäfer, 193–221. Schriften des Vereins für Socialpolitik 246. Berlin: Duncker und Humblot. Chapter 5 in this volume.

Elsenhans, Hartmut. 1996 [1981]. *State, Class and Development*. New Delhi, London, Columbia, MO: Radiant; Sangam; South Asia Books.

Elsenhans, Hartmut. 1999a. Autonomy of Civil Society, Empowerment of Labour, and the Transition to Capitalism. In *Bureaucracy—Citizen Interface: Conflict and Consensus*, ed. Randhir B. Jain and Renu Khator, 15–60. Delhi: B.R. Publishing Corporation.

Elsenhans, Hartmut. 1999b. Rent and Technology Distortion: The Two Cul-de-Sac of State Correction and Market Orientation in IAC and IBC. *Journal of the Third World Spectrum* 6 (1) (Autumn): 33–56.

Elsenhans, Hartmut. 2000. The Rise and Fall of Really Existing Socialism. Journal of Social Studies 87: 1–16.

Elsenhans, Hartmut. 2001a. *Das Internationale System zwischen Zivilgesellschaft und Rente*. Münster: Lit.

Elsenhans, Hartmut. 2001b. Renten in der exportorientierten Industrialisierung: Zur notwendigen und widerspruchsvollen Rolle des Staats. In *Staatlichkeit im Epochenbruch? Antworten aus der Perspektive des Südens und Ostens*, ed. Peter Gärtner, 251–296. Hamburg: Hamburgisches Welt-Wirtschafts-Archiv.

Emmanuel, Arghiri. 1977. A Socialist Project in an Disintegrated Capitalist World. *Socialism in the World* 2: 21–38.

Eucken, Walter. 2001. *Wirtschaftsmacht und Wirtschaftsordnung. Londoner Vorträge zur Wirtschaftspolitik und zwei Beiträge zur Antimonopolpolitik*. Münster: Lit.

Fei, John C.H., and Gustav Ranis. 1964. *Development of a Labor Surplus Economy. Theory and Policy*. Homewood, IL: Irwin.

Fine, Ben. 2000. Endogenous Growth Theory: A Critical Assessment. *Cambridge Journal of Economics* 24 (2): 245–265.

Galtung, Johan. 1971. A Structural Theory of Imperialism. *Journal of Peace Research* 8 (1): 81–117.

Graf, William D. 1988. *The Nigerian State. Political Economy, State Class and Political System in the Post-Colonial Era*. London: James Currey.

Guillaumont-Jeanneney, Sylviane, and Ping Hua. 1996. Politique du change et développement des exportations manufacturées en Chine. *Revue économique* 47 (3): 851–860.

Habakkuk, Hrothgar J. 1972. Fluctuations and Growth in the 19th Century. In *Studies in Economics and Economic History*, ed. H.M. Robertson and M. Kooy, 259–279. London: Macmillan.

Heckscher, Eli F. 1949. The Effect of Foreign Trade on the Distribution of Income. In *Readings in the Theory of International Trade*, ed. Howard S. Ellis, 272–300. London: Allen & Unwin.

Helmstädter, Ernst. 1969. *Der Kapitalkoeffizient. Eine kapitaltheoretische Untersuchung*. Stuttgart: Gustav Fischer.

Holtgrave, Wilfried (ed.). 1987. *Industrialisierung in Singapur. Chancen und Risiken industrieorientierter Spezialisierung*. Frankfort on the Main, New York: Campus.

Hyden, Goran. 1980. *Beyond Ujamaa in Tanzania. Underdevelopment and an Uncaptured Peasantry*. London: Heinemann.

Ibn Khaldûn, Abd-al-Rahman. 1967. *Discours sur l'Histoire universelle. Al-Muqaddima. Traduction nouvelle, préface et notes par Vincent Monteil*. Paris: Sindbad.

Imlah, Albert H. 1950. The Terms of Trade of the United Kingdom 1798–1913. *Journal of Economic History* 10 (2): 170–194.

Irwan, Alexander. 1989. Business Patronage, Class Struggle and the Manufacturing Sector in South Korea, Indonesia and Thailand. *Journal of Contemporary Asia* 19 (4): 398–434.

de Janvry, Alain. 1981. The Role of Land Reform in Economic Development: Policies and Politics. *American Journal of Agricultural Economics* 63 (2): 384–392.

Jomo, Kwame Sundaram. 1998. Malaysia Props up Crony Capitalists. *Asian Wall Street Journal* 21: 10.

Kendrick, John W. 1961. *Productivity Trends in the United States. A Study by the National Bureau of Economic Research*. Princeton, NJ: Princeton University Press.

Kenney, Martin, and Richard Florida. 1994. Japanese Maquiladoras. Production Organization and Global Commodity Chains. *World Development* 22 (1): 27–44.

Khan, Mushtaq H. 2000. Rents, Efficiency and Growth. In *Rents, Rent-Seeking and Economic Development. Theory and Evidence in Asia*, ed. Mushtaq H. Khan and Kwame Sundaram Jomo, 21–69. Cambridge et al.: Cambridge University Press.

Köhler, Gernot. 2001. A New Look at Unequal Exchange. *Asien – Afrika – Lateinamerika* 29 (4): 332–346.

Krugman, Paul R. 1991. Increasing Returns and Economic Geography. *Journal of Political Economy* 99 (3): 483–499.

Kuhn, Berthold (ed.). 1998. *Participatory Development and Local Self-Government Reform in Rural India*. New Delhi: Radiant.

Lafay, Gérard. 1996. Les origines internationales du chômage européen. *Revue d'économie politique* 106 (6): 943–963.

Lenin, Vladimir Ilyich. 1964. *Imperialism, the Highest Stage of Capitalism. A Popular Outline* [1916]. Lenin Collected Works (22). Moscow: Progress Publishers.

Leontief, Wassily W. (ed.). 1953. *The Structure of American Economy, 1919–1939. An Empirical Application of Equilibrium Analysis*. New York: Oxford University Press.

Leontief, Wassily. 1954. Domestic Production and Foreign Trade: The American Capital Position Re-examined. *Economia Internazionale* 7 (1): 9–38.

Leontief, Wassily. 1956. Factor Proportions and the Structure of American Trade: Further Theoretical and Empirical Analysis. *Review of Economics and Statistics* 38 (4): 386–407.

Lewis, William Arthur (1954): Economic Development with Unlimited Supply of Labour. In *Manchester School of Economic and Social Studies* 22, 4 (May), pp. 139–191.

Lewis, William Arthur. 1978. *The Evolution of the International Economic Order*. Princeton, NJ: Princeton University Press.

Luxemburg, Rosa. 1951 [1913]. *The Accumulation of Capital*. London: Routledge & Kegan Paul.

Mahalanobis, P.C. 1953. Some Observations on the Process of Growth of National Income. *Sankhya* 12 (4): 307–312.

Malik, Yogendra K. and V.B. Singh. 1994. *Hindu Nationalists in India. The Rise of the Bharatiya Janata Party*. Boulder, CO: Westview.

Marx, Karl. 1967. *Capital (1): The Process of Production of Capital* [1867]. Moscow: Progress Publishers.

Marx, Karl. 1956 [1885]. *Capital (2): The Process of Circulation of Capital* [1885]. Moscow: Progress Publishers.

Minami, Ryoshin. 1992. Economic Development of Japan: Factors, Consequences, Implications. *Journal of Economic Development* 17 (2): 7–35.

Mishra, Ajit. 1994. Clientelization and Fragmentation in Backward Agriculture: Forward Induction and Entry Deferrence. *Journal of Development Economics* 45 (2): 271–284.

Montgomery, Arthur. 1938. *How Sweden Overcame the Depression*. Stockholm: Alb. Bonniers Boktryckeri.

Myint, Hla. 1971. *Economic Theory and the Underdeveloped Countries*. London: Oxford University Press.

Mytelka, Lynn Krieger. 1986. The Transfer of Technology. Myth or Reality? In *The European Community's Development Policy: The Strategies Ahead*, ed. Carol Cosgrove and J. Jamar, 243–281. Conference organised at the College of Europe, Bruges, 4–6 July 1985. Brugge: De Tempel.

Nohlen, Dieter, and Roland Sturm. 1982. Über das Konzept der strukturellen Heterogenität. In *Handbuch der Dritten Welt (1). Unterentwicklung und Entwicklung – Theorien, Strategien, Indikatoren*, ed. Dieter Nohlen and Franz Nuscheler, 92–116. Hamburg: Hoffmann & Campe.

Ohlin, Bertil. 1927. Ist eine Modernisierung der Außenhandelstheorie erforderlich? *Weltwirtschaftliches Archiv* 26 (1): 97–115.

Okishio, Nobuo. 1961. Technical Change and the Rate of Profit. *Kobe University Economic Review* 7: 85–99.

Olson, Mancur. 1982. *The Rise and Decline of Nations: Economic Growth, Stagflation, and Social Rigidities*. New Haven, CT: Yale University Press.

Page, John (ed.). 1993. *The East Asian Miracle. Economic Growth and Public Policy*. Washington: World Bank.

Palacios, Marco. 1983. *El café en Colombia 1850–1970. Una historia económica, social y politica*. Mexico, Bogotá: Colegio de México; Áncora.

Perroux, François. 1968. L'intégration et l'échec de la théorie traditionnelle des échanges extérieurs. *Economie Appliquée* 21 (2): 379–396.

Posner, M.V. 1961. International Trade and Technical Change. *Oxford Economic Papers* 13 (3): 323–341.

Prebisch, Raúl. 1962. The Economic Development of Latin America and Its Principal Problems. *Economic Bulletin for Latin America* 7 (1): 1–22.

Preobrazenskij, Evgenij. 1971. *Die neue Ökonomik: Übersetzung der zweiten erweiterten Ausgabe*. Berlin: Verlag Neuer Kurs.

Reichenberg, Rudolf. 1967. Zur Diskussion über das Gesetz der vorrangigen Entwicklung der Produktionsmittelproduktion im Sozialismus. *Wirtschaftswissenschaft* 15 (11): 1775–1786.

Reischauer, Edwin O., and John K. Fairbank. 1960. *East Asia. The Great Tradition*. Boston, MA: Houghton Mifflin.

Richardson, Henry. 1939. Real Wage Movements. *Economic Journal* 49 (195): 425–441.

Romer, Paul M. 1996. Why Indeed in America? Theory, History, and the Origins of Modern Economic Growth. *American Economic Review* 86 (2): 202–206.

Samuelson, Paul A. 1948. International Trade and the Equalization of Factor Prices. *Economic Journal* 58 (230): 163–184.

Sarkar, Parbirjit, and Hans Wolfgang Singer. 1991. Manufactured Exports of Developing Countries and their Terms of Trade Since 1965. *World Development* 19 (4): 333–340.

Scott, James. 1972. The Erosion of Patron-Client Bonds and Social Change in Rural Southeast Asia. *Journal of Asian Studies* 32 (1): 5–37.

Sen, Nabendu. 1976. India's Terms of Trade 1871–72 to 1892–93. *Economic and Political Weekly* 11 (46): 1795–1803.

Shih, Chien-Sheng. 1968. Economic Development in Taiwan After the Second World War. *Weltwirtschaftliches Archiv* 100 (1): 112–134.

Sid Ahmed, Abdelkader. 1990. *Development and Resource-Based Industry. The Case of the Petroleum Economies. A Brief Survey of Recent Studies*. Vienna: OPEC Fund for International Development.

Siggel, Eckhard. 1984. On the Nature of Technology Shelves Facing Less Developed Countries. Some Hypotheses and Case Studies. *Journal of Developing Areas* 18 (2): 227–246.

Singer, Hans Wolfgang. 1950. U.S. Foreign Investment in Underdeveloped Areas. The Distribution of Gains between Investing and Borrowing Countries. *American Economic Review* 40 (2): 473–485.

Singer, Hans Wolfgang. 1975. The Distribution of Gains from Trade and Investment Revisited. *Journal of Development Studies* 11 (4): 376–382.

Skinner, G.William. 1971. Chinese Peasants and the Closed Community: An Open and Shut Case. *Comparative Studies in Society and History* 13 (3): 270–281.

Sklar, Richard L. 1967. Political Science and National Integration—A Radical Approach. *Journal of Modern African Studies* 5 (1): 1–11.

Sombart, Werner. 1913a. Krieg und Kapitalismus. Munich, Berlin: Duncker und Humblot.

Sombart, Werner. 1913b. Luxus und Kapitalismus. Munich, Berlin: Duncker und Humblot.

Sturm, Roland. 1984. Staatsklasse. In *Lexikon Dritte Welt. Länder, Organisationen, Theorien, Begriffe, Ressourcen*, ed. Dieter Nohlen, 532–533. Reinbek b. Hamburg: Rowohlt.

Tucker, Rufus S. 1936. Real Wages of Artisans in London, 1729–1935. *Journal of the American Statistical Association* 31 (1): 73–84.

Usher, Dan. 1989. The Dynastic Cycle and the Stationary State. *American Economic Review* 79 (4): 1031–1044.

Vergopoulos, Kostas. 1974. Capitalisme difforme (Le cas de l'agriculture dans le capitalisme). In *La question paysanne et le capitalisme*, ed. Samir Amin and Kostas Vergopoulos, 61–284. Paris: Anthropos.

Vernon, Raymond. 1966. International Investment and International Trade in the Product Cycle. *Quarterly Journal of Economics* 80 (2): 190–207.

von Bortkiewicz, Ladislaus. 1907. Wertrechnung und Preisrechnung im Marxschen System (3). *Archiv Für Sozialwissenschaft Und Sozialpolitik* 25 (2): 445–489.

Warren, Bill. 1980. *Imperialism: Pioneer of Capitalism*. London: NLB.

Williams, Eric. 1964. *Capitalism and Slavery*. London: André Deutsch.

Yotopoulos, Pan A. 1996. *Exchange Rate Parity for Trade and Development: Theory, Tests, and Case Studies*. Cambridge: Cambridge University Press.

PART IV

Postscript

CHAPTER 9

Postscript by Hartmut Elsenhans

Hartmut Elsenhans

9.1 At Odds with Neoliberalism and Marxism

The contributions assembled in this volume are based on a politico-economic approach which is, in essence, Keynesian. However, these contributions also aim to integrate major elements of a neoliberal theory of microeconomics, as well as elements of the Marxist approach concerning the social embeddedness of capitalist economies. The articles which comprise this volume do not share the basic conviction of mainstream neoclassical economics—that market economies possess an impressive capacity to self-regulate, provided that non-market actors are excluded. On the contrary, market economies can maintain their basic structures only under conditions of labor empowerment. Thus the contributions in this volume share the Marxist belief in the social and political embeddedness of any economic system. However, they also reject the Marxist critique of capitalism as a system which is determined by a structurally inevitable law governing the behavior of capital; that is, that capitalists are compelled to accumulate as much as possible. This is not to deny that capitalists do indeed behave in this manner. However, it must

H. Elsenhans (✉)
University of Leipzig, Leipzig, Germany
e-mail: helsen@rz.uni-leipzig.de

© The Author(s), under exclusive license to Springer Nature Switzerland AG 2021

H. Warnecke-Berger (ed.), *Development, Capitalism, and Rent*,
https://doi.org/10.1007/978-3-030-62605-1_9

be recognized that, if capitalists prevail in this respect over the interests of the many (i.e., of labor), then they inevitably undermine and destroy the capitalist system itself.

Capitalism, then, must be saved from the capitalists. Yet the Marxist critique of capitalism is an obstacle to accomplishing this. The Marxist critique unnecessarily limits the political alliances capable of imposing such a subordination of capital under the conditions of a functioning capitalism. It replaces the realistic hope of efficiently managing capitalism in the interests of the masses with a nebulous utopia. In this utopia, according to Marx's earliest writings, humankind has been liberated from the oppression and alienation of labor.

My own approach is basically at odds with much of mainstream economics, including Marxist economics.[1] This is probably not because my writings are inherently exotic. In fact, it most likely owes to the very limited familiarity of "critical" political economists with economic models developed after the Marxist classics prior to the first decades of the twentieth century (Robinson W. I. 2014; MacDonough 2014). To be sure, I have not been met with universal rejection, especially not among mainstream liberal thinkers. And yet, this body of opinion seems to accept my contributions as constituting an analysis of dysfunctional capitalism under conditions where it was not possible to establish market dominance.[2] This is not actually my argument, however.

Because of this limited acceptance and limited understanding, I will restate my central argument here: Rent is the normal form of surplus appropriation. Capitalism and profit are the exception. Capitalism and profit emerge due to unique social configurations of classes in specific regions of the world. Because of its very unstable social and economic conditions, the perpetuation of capitalism throughout history is by no means guaranteed through the spontaneous tendencies of the capitalist economic, social, and the corresponding political systems. Despite the expansionary character of the emerging capitalist systems, it did and does

[1] I had the honor of being rejected by a well-known Anglo-Saxon journal which probably considers itself Marxist with the argument that nobody was found capable of evaluating my theory, this article being afterward published by very respectable journals in India (Elsenhans 2019c), Mexico (Elsenhans 2019a), Algeria (Elsenhans 2019b), Russia Elsenhans (2019d), while an article close to the argument proposed here was published in the most renowned journal of Keynesian economics (Elsenhans 2019e).

[2] Elsenhans (1989, 1991, 1995) (in this volume Chapter 5), (1999, 2004).

not lead to the inevitable transfer of capitalist structures to non-capitalist economies and societies (the Global South) *unless* these societies have empowered their labor. Because of this lack of transformative impact, penetrating capitalism destroys the very elements in these regions which could be favorable for the emergence of capitalism.

Ultimately, I argue that this destruction, which I call the *globalization of rent*, impacts on those capitalist systems in particular regions which are generally referred to as "centers" as opposed to underdeveloped "peripheries." Indeed, this process ultimately pushes the capitalist economies themselves into new rent-dominated structures.

9.2 On the Limits of Mainstream Rent Theory

The approach presented here takes account of competing approaches to the question of rent, especially the phenomena on which they base their theoretical arguments. However, it does not follow these existing approaches in their central tenets. It does to some extent share the (predominantly) Anglo-Saxon critique of rent seeking. This critique holds that rents are appropriated on the basis of naturally or politically created market imperfections. Differential rents and consumer rents in raw material production appear here as the basis for state intervention in rent appropriation. Because of an alternative theory of the origin of profit from neoliberalism and from Marxism, I consider this type of rent only as a special case of the otherwise ubiquitous presence of rent.

Conversely, I follow many of the principles articulated in the literature on the Dutch disease. This points to high incomes from the export of products with limited transformative capacity and limited trickling down on productivity-increasing technical innovation in the regional setups where rent is generated. Rent discourages diversification of production, especially to the detriment of local innovation outside the raw materials sector. I also share certain assumptions with sociological and political theories about rent's influence on the centralization of political power; for example, that rents exert a negative impact on the horizontal organization of society, which is characteristic of capitalism.

I am, however, skeptical with respect to any solution which sees salvation in marketization without addressing the basic aspect of rent; the disempowerment of average skilled, "normal" labor. This even applies under the stewardship of a benevolent ruling class, such as the state classes. These—initially idealistic—classes commit themselves to using available rents as financial resources for investment in the productivity of average labor (i.e., in development policies).

9.3 Profit Depends on Rising Mass Incomes

The precariousness of profit in relation to rent is amply illustrated in Kalecki's theory of profit (Kalecki 1942). Profit depends on net investment spending. It is not some kind of leftover; it comprises the amount earned by capitalists on the basis of consumption demand which exceeds the direct and indirect spending of consumption goods entrepreneurs on labor, essentially wages. This enables the producers of the consumption goods industries to generate a positive profit rate. They are compelled to accept prices for investment goods which correspond to a similar profit rate in investment goods industries. Otherwise, the entrepreneurs of this economic sector would shift to consumption goods production on the basis of their own investment goods.

Investments have to be microeconomically profitable. Technical innovation which does not entail an expansion of consumption reduces overall demand and ultimately also net investment. More of the same products, with the same number of factors of production, new products, and products produced with highly increasing capital intensity because of rising labor costs—all of these require rising mass incomes.

Ultimately, then, profit itself depends on rising mass incomes, whatever the microeconomic convictions of capitalists. Rising mass incomes are no threat to profit because wage earners can only consume until full capacity utilization of the consumption goods sector. Further wage increases would merely peter out into inflation. Capitalism is not threatened by the apparent contradiction that it needs both rising mass incomes *and* limited mass incomes in order to preserve profit. Labor can only impose inflation—to its own detriment. But it cannot expand consumption demand beyond full capacity utilization. However, labor may force those who call themselves capitalists to abandon the rent incomes they draw from the monopolistic control of production facilities (which capitalists are prone to do, especially in periods of crisis, when profit disappears).

9.4 On the Emergence of Raw Material Rents and the Transfer of the System of Relative Prices from the Center to the Periphery

The "Dutch disease" consists in a specialization in export productions with limited growth possibilities because of high rent incomes. In fact, this is merely a special case of the more general problem of the transfer of the system of relative prices of the most developed economies to the world market. Consequently, this process also entails the transfer of this system to the periphery which has not undergone capitalist productivity development (Amin 1976: 216–228). In capitalism, branch-specific productivities converge despite very different rates of growth of productivity. In production lines with high productivity growth, capital and labor are attracted with high remunerations. The best opportunity for capitalists to invest their capital lies in their own high profit rate production lines. This increases production and triggers saturation. Prices decline, and so do wages and profit rates. In case of high levels of employment, production lines which did not enjoy productivity increases will face declining employment. If their services are still in demand, waiting lines appear. In order to retain their labor force, entrepreneurs in such production lines will increase prices and use price increases for increasing wages. Wages and profits in production lines with high productivity growth and wages and profits in low productivity growth production lines will converge. This leads to a concomitant convergence in the measure of productivity—that is, the net product per "factors of production" (capital, labor) engaged. Relative prices reflect productivities made equal by the system of relative prices despite different growth rates in productivity.

Just as only one price can exist on the world market, these are also the same prices which accommodate the conditions of technically backward countries. If we measure at these prices then, in some of the backward countries' production branches, costs are very much higher than the prices at which the products are available on the world market. In other branches, the disparity may be significantly less glaring. Given the international price of local labor, such cases may even be characterized by competitiveness.

Parallel to rising mass incomes in the already industrialized world, the quality of mineral deposits decreases, because mining initially concentrates on the rich deposits near industrial centers. The attempt to halt a decline in productivity because of deteriorating natural conditions of production leads to technical innovation in the industrial centers which can be applied on a global basis. With the aid of newly developed technology, untapped deposits in the Global South allow for much lower costs than in the more developed world. Mining thus becomes delocalized, at first in the case of metals with high prices in relation to weight (and low transport costs in relation to their values).

Moreover, rising mass incomes give rise to new tastes. Many agricultural raw materials from the Global South find customers in the industrialized world. Both types of raw materials face a price-and income-inelastic demand: Capitalism constantly saves on raw material input per unit of production as one form of productivity increase. The demand for food items—after an initial hike—increases more slowly than household incomes in the industrialized world.

The argument about deterioration of terms-of-trade reflects these elasticities. If we turn the argument on its head: Artificial reduction in supply allows for increasing earnings, despite slightly decreasing quantities sold. In the case of mineral raw materials, price increases are also facilitated if marginal reproducers are maintained as suppliers. This owes either to the amount of demand or to considerations of security of supply.

In both cases, an income above average remuneration of the factors of production which are engaged becomes available. This is called rent. In the case of agricultural products without competing production of the more developed countries, these are consumer rents; in the case of much lower costs of production in the Global South than in the marginal plants in the West, they are differential rents.

The appropriation of these rents was the major demand of the countries of the Global South during the process of decolonization. They were considered sources of finance for economic diversification and especially for the creation of industries.

9.5 On the Failure of Using Rent for Overcoming Rent, or the Contradictions of Rent-Based State Classes

The appropriation of such rents—and even more so, their utilization for projects which have not clearly demonstrated profitability on the market—requires a centralization of surplus appropriation and surplus allocation. If there is perfect competition, most rents cannot be appropriated. Furthermore, if rents are given to entrepreneurs who compete on markets, then the entrepreneurs will reinvest these rents in their already profitable activities, not in a diversification of the economy. Using rents for overcoming rents by investing in economic diversification is connected to a centralization of rents, and therefore to the emergence of *owners* of these rents.

However, these owners are not administrations in the classical, bourgeois-political sense. They are not under the jurisdiction of a particular social class; in fact, they are largely independent in this respect (Elsenhans 1996 [1981]). Their access to surplus depends on their access to state power. I therefore call them state classes. The different segments of such classes will try to attract as much as possible of these rents in order to increase their clout within the state class. An increasing share of the rents will inevitably be diverted toward such power-preserving activities. These will include the satisfaction of the material interests of other segments of the state class in order to build alliances.

There will still be an emerging bourgeoisie and an emerging working class, because a degree of industrialization is occurring. However, the state classes will prevent these "classical" social classes from creating independent organizations. This will be accomplished partly through the co-option of some elements of the competing classes. Self-organization will be further blocked through the creation of clientelistic and dependent organizations, so that truly oppositional elements can be marginalized. To be sure, the fact that the state classes do not levy taxes against the local population does not exempt from the necessity of gaining popular support. The consumptive utilization of rent will increase. Conflict with the broader mass of the population will take the form of radical outbursts of protest, unruly crowds, and violence, depending on the historical memory of the population. Conflict with the bourgeoisie will be replaced with clientelization.

The predominance of the state will remain, and it will block any evolution to large popular participation. If the state classes can be held accountable because they are perceived as prominent and politically responsible, then decentralization of the rent-appropriating class in the form of oligarchies will further weaken popular resistance. After all, it is very difficult to hold these oligarchies accountable.

9.6 The Shift to Export-Oriented Manufacturing and the Threats to Developed Industrial Countries

The inefficiencies of state classes and most oligarchies in promoting technical innovations have resulted in overspending and financial crisis. It soon became apparent that societies which were not blessed with abundant raw materials were actually performing better. But not even these export-based manufacturing societies refrain from rent seeking.

Initially, at least, these societies specialized in products with low price and low-income elasticities—what we might call labor-intensive low-skill products. Textiles are a good example. Here, and in similar product lines, price and income elasticity on the world market are low. The reaction of the exporting countries consisted in burdening exports with additional charges in order to promote diversification. Local content rules are an example: Companies were required to buy local inputs despite their greater expense or inferior quality. The classic example is Singapore, a very "pro-capitalist" country which indexed products produced with low-skilled labor in order to finance programs of skill promotion for its labor force. Once again, state responsibility for promoting the catch-up process is of central importance. This is evident from examples such as South Korea, Taiwan and even the People's Republic of China.

When this process of state-guided industrialization fails to result in an empowerment of labor, manufactured products exporters are able to limit rises of internal consumption in order to compete with the industrialized world. The essential mechanism is the exchange rate and the change of comparative advantage. With increasing science-based technical progress, the possibilities of learning from books or the internet are enhanced. In such an environment, on the spot training, and thus the accumulated skills of industrial workers, decline in importance.

A leading economy may have comparative advantage in very modern already established industries. By contrast, a catching up economy has no training on the spot in these industries. A new technology may emerge which can at least partly be mastered on the basis of knowledge drawn from books and the internet. The catching up economy may be backward in these new technologies, but its backwardness is greater in the older industries where only the leading economy has learning by doing. In the new emerging technology, however, neither the advanced nor the catching up economy have an established tradition of learning by doing.

Already being a technical leader will certainly facilitate learning new technologies, but the advance in a new technology will not be as large as in the old technologies. Moreover, according to comparative advantage, the leading country will almost certainly specialize in the old production lines in which it already enjoys a tradition of success—unless it opts for a government-subsidized entry into the new technologies. This could assume various forms, from government procurement to government subsidies to technical innovation systems.

Provided that the catching up economy has reserves of unemployed labor, it is economically feasible to hold down the international price of labor. As increasing exports do not lead to labor scarcity and imported inflation, employing additional workers in the export sector who earn less on the world market than they consume in international prices is possible if the local economy produces a surplus of wage goods. All export-oriented East Asian economies had undervalued exchange rates and rapidly growing agricultures. By blocking agricultural exports, they derived rents from these sources which would otherwise have been earned on the world market.

9.7 On the Export of Rent Structures to the West

Advanced industrial countries consider this to be a form of wage dumping. They react by trying to protect their own labor market. If they keep their markets open, they will complement such protection not only through industrial policy, but also through subsidies to labor. In this way, labor is rendered increasingly dependent on government funding.

Such processes are supported by other developments in capitalism which will surely threaten the mechanism of mass demand creating profit. Higher income households tend toward post-materialist behavior—and in particular, toward saving. Saving rates go up so that incomes paid to households do not return as demand to consumption goods industries. Provided that barriers to entry do not allow oligopolistic pricing, profit triggered by net investment spending comes under threat.

The rent structure of the South is thus exported to the West. This also occurs because the growing maturity of western capitalism weakens the basic capitalist mechanism there. And this weakening of the capitalist mechanism on a global scale is only exacerbated by the fact that the bargaining power supplied by the market mechanism to both classes, labor and business, also weakens. Business has the option of shifting to oligopolistic competition, creating new market imperfections. Labor does not have this option because, in the long term, its political model depends on its bargaining power on the labor market. In this way, the globalization of rent intensifies.

This does not mean that the transition to new rent-based structures is inevitable. However, it does mean that, in order to avoid such an outcome, we must save capitalism from the capitalists. In the high-income countries of the West, this also means that future risks for households are socialized in order to hold down savings rates. In the relationship between Global North and South, this implies keeping open the markets of the high-income countries in exchange for policies in favor of rising mass incomes applied by the exporters of manufactured products from the South. This will maximize local multiplier effects.

9.8 Rising Mass Incomes, Greener Growth and the Philosophy of History

Attempts to preserve the world from climate change represent no obstacle to increasing consumption. Degrowth implies productivity degrowth because of an exclusion of "cheap" polluting technologies in favor of technologies whose cost in relation to output increases, and by compensating measures which constitute additional consumption. For the overall balance between capital accumulation and consumption, the alternative between private and public consumption is of little importance.

This approach has implications far beyond the issue of a correct description of how capitalism operates, or what policies can be used for maintaining capitalism's progressive functions against the dominance of rent and elite political power. This approach implies a break with the conception of history so characteristic of European philosophy since Hegel (1952 [1807]), Comte (1963 [1842]), and Marx (1972 [1844])—that history is a process of improvement, an ongoing shift to higher forms of social organization and civilization.

Capitalism is not a stage of evolution which automatically results from productive forces and the emergence of new social classes. In fact, capitalism emerges as a possibility when the human claim to equal dignity can be imposed because labor is empowered as a result of its being scarce, and because labor can translate this scarcity into large coalitions. Indeed, such coalitions may be composed of groups which, beyond the economic realm, hold variegated cultural preferences. But only with the formation of such coalitions can social classes based on limited economic interests, and society as the sphere of exchange (Tönnies 1935 [1887]), function without the political and social stabilization mechanisms characteristic of a community.

9.9 On the Danger of Turning Back to Rent-Based Structures

The privileged have always tried to impose inequality. They have done so since the dissolution of primitive communities. They have repeated these attempts whenever periodically hierarchical structures collapse. Ibn Khaldûn (1967) has aptly described the decay of dynasties. Karl Jaspers' axial revolution (1949) postulated ritual equality of all humans in a struggle against the pretensions of the powerful. For thousands of years, the mindset in favor of equality remained romantic and inconsequential. It could come to exercise a decisive influence on the historical process only when labor won bargaining power because of its own scarcity. The idea was always present, but it became powerful only when economic structures allowed for its realization. This was difficult, as attested by the Marxist argument about the limits of the bourgeois revolution. But Marx's (1972 [1844]) analysis of the causes of these limits is misleading, because it identifies them in market regulation.

The nineteenth century marked the rise of labor due to stable scarcity. This allowed for the organization of labor and reinforced this scarcity. The experiment of capitalism was sheltered at the time, because the capitalist world enjoyed comparative advantage in the job-creating lines of production. Consequently, there occurred no transfer of capitalist structures to the world where labor was not scarce. This was despite the penetration of capitalist forms of interaction in economic and partly in social relations.

Over the last 50 years, this configuration of comparative advantage has changed. More competitive production sites in the labor rich regions of the Global South have arisen. It is, however, not probable that this push of employment will create scarcity of labor in the Global South, given the new characteristics of technical progress in the information age. There will either be a return to the kind of rent-based structures described above or a concerted effort in both the Global North and South for empowering labor by rendering labor scarce.

Because of the dominance of the neoliberal identification of low wages with high employment, one essential element of any attempt to save capitalism from a return to rent structures resides in renovating political economy and showing the interdependence of rising mass incomes and profit against rent.

References

Amin, Samir. 1976. Unequal Development. *An Essay on the Social Formation of Peripherial Capitalism*. New York: Monthly Review Press.

Comte, Auguste. (ed.). 1963. Discours sur l'esprit positif [1842]. Paris: Union Générale d'Editions.

Elsenhans, Hartmut. 1989. Zur Theorie und Praxis bürokratischer Entwicklungsgesellschaften. In *Zur Analyse von Institutionen im Entwicklungsprozess und in der internationalen Zusammenarbeit*, ed. Heiko Körner, 101–141. Schriften des Vereins für Socialpolitik 186. Berlin: Duncker und Humblot.

Elsenhans, Hartmut. 1991. Reforming the Economic System of Bangladesh. Main Fields of Action. In *Wirtschaftspolitische Reformen in Entwicklungsländern*, ed. Hermann Sautter, 109–133. Schriften des Vereins für Socialpolitik 209. Berlin: Duncker und Humblot.

Elsenhans, Hartmut. 1995. Überwindung von Marginalität als Gegenstand der Armutsbekämpfung. In *Bevölkerungsdynamik und Grundbedürfnisse in Entwicklungsländern*, ed. Hans Bernd Schäfer, 193–221. Schriften des Vereins für Socialpolitik 246. Berlin: Duncker und Humblot. Chapter 5 in this volume.

Elsenhans, Hartmut. 1996 [1981]. *State, Class and Development*. New Delhi, London, Columbia, MO: Radiant; Sangam; South Asia Books.

Elsenhans, Hartmut. 1999. Wirtschaftswachstum und institutionelle Entwicklung. Korreferat zum Beitrag von Rainer Klump. In *Neue Wachstums- und Außenhandelstheorie – Implikationen für die Entwicklungstheorie und –politik*, ed. Renate Schubert, 115–128. Schriften des Vereins für Socialpolitik, Band 269. Berlin: Duncker und Humblot.

Elsenhans, Hartmut. 2004. Globalisierung von Profit oder Globalisierung von Rente. *Jahrbuch Für Wirtschaftswissenschaften* 55 (3): 263–289.

Elsenhans, Hartmut. 2019a. La amenaza inminente de la globalización de las rentas. *Convergencia – Revista cd Ciencia Sociales* 81: 1–25.

Elsenhans, Hartmut. 2019b. Le danger imminent d'une globalisation par la rente et la défense du capitalisme par les travailleurs. In *Hartmut Elsenhans: Guerre de libération nationale et voie algérienne de développement. Naqd - Revue d'études et de critique sociale*, ed. Daho Djerbal and Rachid Ouaissa, 245–278. Hors série. Algiers: NAQD.

Elsenhans, Hartmut. 2019c. The Impending Threat of Globalisation of Rent and the Defence of Capitalism by Labour. *International Studies* 56 (2): 109–128.

Elsenhans, Hartmut. 2019d. Nadvigayascayacya ugroza globalizatsii renty i zascita kapitalisma trudom. *Etnosotsiyum I Mezdunarodnaya Kultura* 127 (1): 123–142.

Elsenhans, Hartmut. 2019e. Rising Mass Incomes as a Condition of Capitalist Growth. Preserving Capitalism through the Empowerment of Labor in the Past and the Present. *Journal of Post Keynesian Economics* 36 (2): 1–36.

Hegel, Georg Wilhelm Friedrich. 1952. *Phänomenologie des Geistes* [1807]. Hamburg: Felix Meiner.

Ibn Khaldûn, Abd-al-Rahman. 1967. *Discours sur l'Histoire universelle. Al-Muqaddima. Traduction nouvelle, préface et notes par Vincent Monteil*. Paris: Sindbad.

Jaspers, Karl. 1949. *Vom Ursprung und Ziel der Geschichte*. Frankfort on Main: Fischer.

Kalecki, Michal. 1942. A Theory of Profits. *Economic Journal* 52 (205–206): 258–267.

MacDonough, Terrence. 2014. Stages in Capitalist History. A Marxian Response to Hartmut Elsenhans. *Erwägen – Wissen – Ethik* 15 (4): 577–579.

Marx, Karl. 1972. Zur Kritik der Hegelschen Rechtsphilosophie. Einleitung [1844]. In *Marx Engels Werke*, vol. 1, ed. Karl Marx and Friedrich Engels, 378–391. Berlin: Dietz.

Robinson, William I. 2014. Clarity, Theoretical, Conceptual and Normative Commitment in the Critique of Global Capitalism. *Erwägen – Wissen – Ethik* 24 (4): 599–601.

Tönnies, Ferdinand. 1935. *Gemeinschaft und Gesellschaft* [1887]. Grundbegriffe der reinen Soziologie. Berlin: Curtius.

Index

© The Editor(s) (if applicable) and The Author(s), under exclusive license to Springer Nature Switzerland AG 2021
H. Warnecke-Berger (ed.), *Development, Capitalism, and Rent*,
https://doi.org/10.1007/978-3-030-62605-1